A PORTRAIT OF THE SURREY HILLS

Jane Garrett has been a journalist for over thirty years and was news editor of the *Surrey Advertiser.* A specialist in the rural economy, she has worked for the Surrey Hills Area of Outstanding Natural Beauty Partnership and has written extensively about the area for local magazines. She has lived in the Surrey Hills since she was a child and has explored the area extensively both on horseback and on foot.

A PORTRAIT OF THE SURREY HILLS

JANE GARRETT

FOREWORD BY
VIRGINIA McKENNA

Robert Hale • London

First published in Great Britain 2010

ISBN 978-0-7090-8561-4

Robert Hale Limited
Clerkenwell House
Clerkenwell Green
London EC1R 0HT

www.halebooks.com

A catalogue record for this book is available from the British Library

10 9 8 7 6 5 4 3 2 1

Typeset by Dave Jones
Printed in China

Contents

List of Illustrations

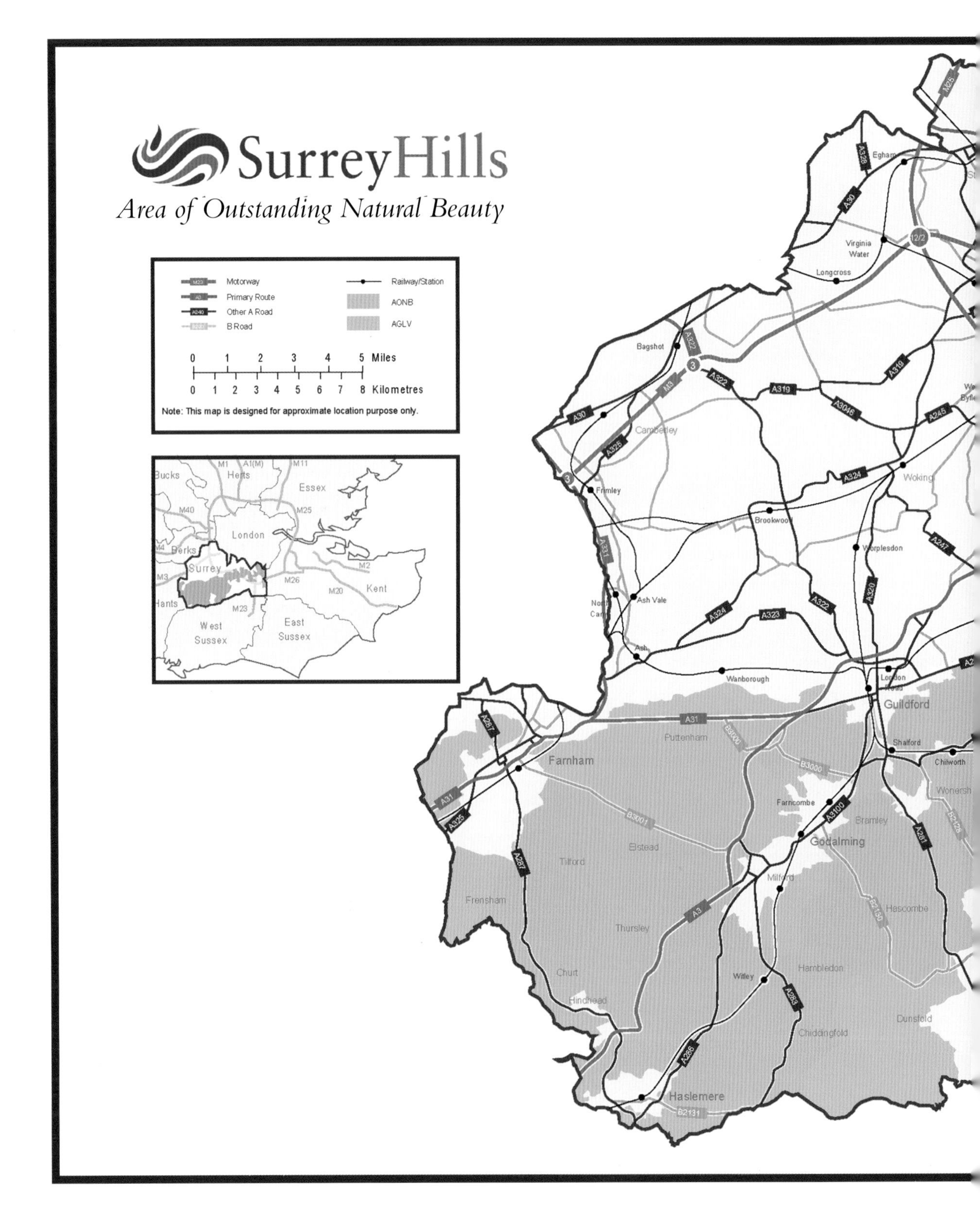

SurreyHills
Area of Outstanding Natural Beauty
Motorway
Primary Route
Other A Road
B Road
Railway/Station
AONB
AGLV
0 1 2 3 4 5 Miles
0 1 2 3 4 5 6 7 8 Kilometres
Note: This map is designed for approximate location purpose only.
Bucks
Herts
Essex
London
Berks
Surrey
Hants
West Sussex
East Sussex
Kent
Egham
Virginia Water
Longcross
Bagshot
Camberley
Frimley
Woking
Brookwood
Worplesdon
Ash Vale
Ash
Wanborough
Guildford
Puttenham
Farnham
Shalford
Chilworth
Wonersh
Farncombe
Bramley
Godalming
Elstead
Tilford
Milford
Frensham
Hascombe
Thursley
Hambledon
Churt
Witley
Hindhead
Dunsfold
Chiddingfold
Haslemere

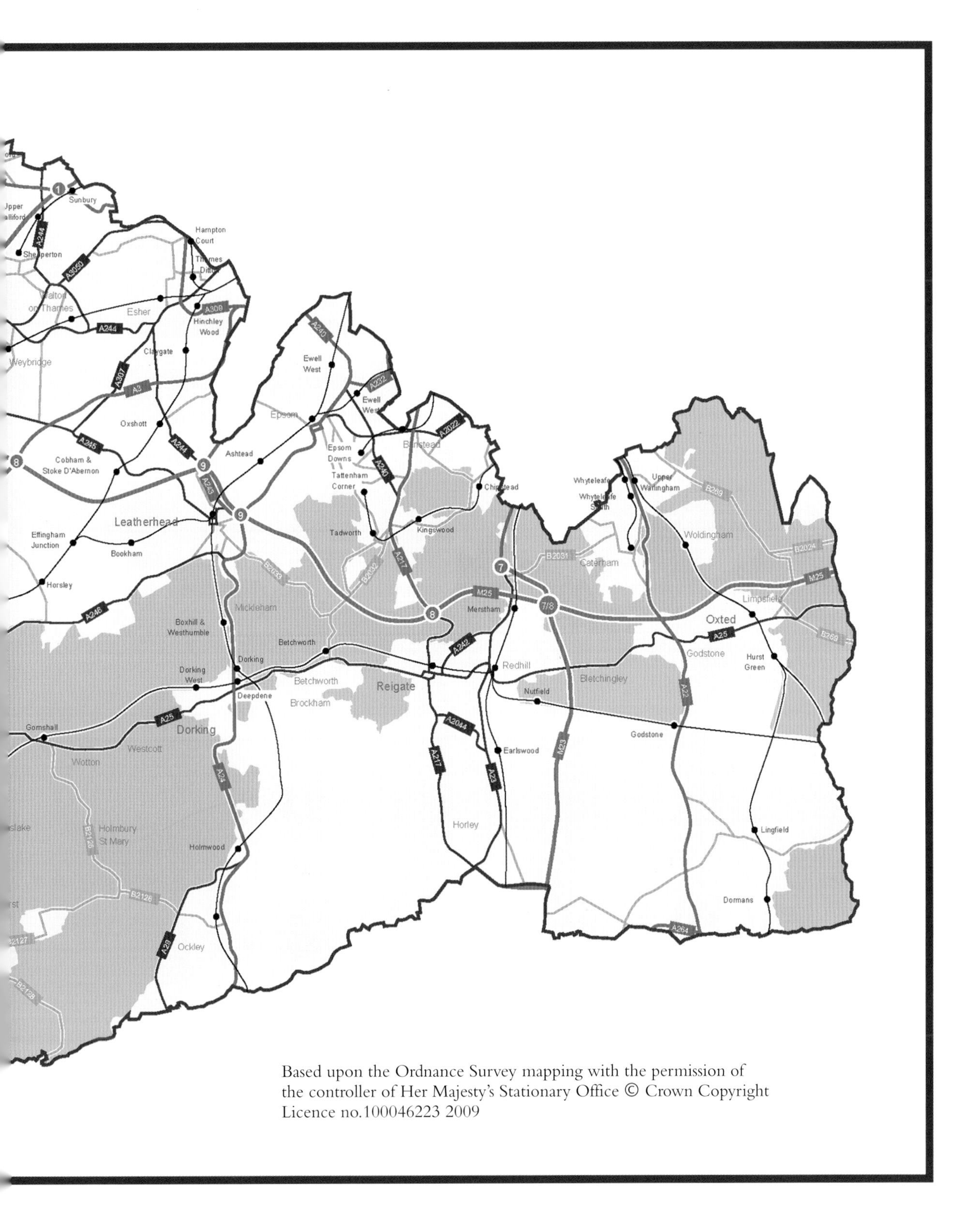
Sunbury
Shepperton
A244
A3050
Hampton Court
Thames Ditton
Walton on Thames
Esher
A309
Hinchley Wood
A244
Claygate
Weybridge
A307
A3
Ewell West
A240
A232
Ewell West
Epsom
Oxshott
A245
A244
Ashtead
Cobham & Stoke D'Abernon
Epsom Downs
Tattenham Corner
Banstead
A2022
A240
Chipstead
Whyteleafe
Upper Warlingham
Whyteleafe South
B269
Leatherhead
A243
Tadworth
Kingswood
Effingham Junction
Bookham
Woldingham
B2031
Caterham
B2024
B2033
B2032
A217
Horsley
Mickleham
M25
Merstham
M25
Limpsfield
A246
Boxhill & Westhumble
Oxted
A25
B269
Betchworth
A242
Godstone
Hurst Green
Dorking
Redhill
Dorking West
Betchworth
Reigate
Bletchingley
Deepdene
Brockham
Nutfield
A22
Gomshall
A25
Dorking
A2044
Godstone
Westcott
Earlswood
Wotton
A217
A23
M23
A24
Horley
Holmbury St Mary
B2126
Holmwood
Lingfield
B2126
Dormans
A264
A29
Ockley
B2128

Acknowledgements

My thanks to everyone who has helped in the painting of this portrait of the Surrey Hills. During my research I have felt humbled by the encyclopaedic knowledge and authoritative writing of dozens of local historians passionate about their particular village, hamlet or manor house. Help has been generous and Surrey History Centre has been a great resource. Thanks to the Surrey Hills Area of Outstanding Natural Beauty Partnership for its support for the book, and to John Miller, Malcolm Pendrill, the Wealden Cave and Mine Society, Surrey Wildlife Trust, Butterfly Conservation and Peter Haynes, for permission to reproduce their wonderful photographs.

Foreword

When I sit out in front of my house and look, in the far distance, to the North Downs, I am looking at a landscape I have loved for over twenty-five years. Surrey is a fascinating and extraordinarily diverse county – which I thought I knew quite well. Until I read this book!

I now realise how little I know and I am eternally grateful to Jane Garrett for her deep and intriguing insight into the county's history, its geological formation millions of years ago, its people, industry, farming, environment and its wildlife.

The timing of this book is particularly pertinent. Through her descriptions of the changing face of farming and therefore land use, we realise how increasingly precious are the 'areas of outstanding natural beauty' that the various wildlife trusts and groups try to protect so fiercely. Urbanisation and the threat of 'natural resource' exploration are never far from our doorsteps, and this excellent and well-researched book provides many compelling reasons why the unique Surrey Hills should be cherished and conserved.

For me what makes the book different from a more conventional history of Surrey is that it is written in a very personal way, by someone who has lived in the area since her childhood. Her memories thread through the fields and byways and over the hills as she walks or rides her horse through a land she loves.

I will now look at the view, travel the lanes, hear the birdsong and look at the forests and hills with ever deeper appreciation. And I am sure all who read this book will feel the same.

Virginia McKenna

Introduction

From the top of the North Downs, the horizon to the north is marked by the spiky silhouette of Canary Wharf's skyscrapers. You can even see the arc of Wembley Stadium. By night it is a vast orange glow studded with millions of lights. Then turn your back on London and look south. By day the panorama is breathtaking. The eye is drawn across wooded hills and patchwork farmland, through the Shoreham Gap in the far South Downs to a glitter of sea beyond. At night, it is dark and you can see the stars.

Barely an hour south of London, the change in the landscape is so extreme it could almost be a different country. Leave the solid grey suburban sprawl behind, head through odd pockets of green, past more houses and you come to the North Downs. To the east, the eight, hectic, traffic-packed lanes of the M25 cut across this otherwise fine natural boundary but, despite the motorway, the spine of the Downs still manages to act as a defining border between rural and suburban Surrey.

The fact that urban development has been contained, and that the Downs and the glorious countryside south towards the Weald have not been consumed by housing, is one of post-war planning's most fantastic success stories.

The Green Belt, which celebrated its fiftieth anniversary in 2005, covers 73 per cent of Surrey and is still a robust planning tool to contain sprawl and village coalescence. The public understands it and broadly supports its aims and achievements. The shape of the Green Belt is understandable, a wide sweep of countryside in a rough circle around the capital, wrapping tight around market towns and corridors of existing development. It was, and still remains, a pragmatic approach to land use: a green lung, a guarded open space.

By contrast, the Surrey Hills Area of Outstanding Natural Beauty (AONB), which celebrated its fiftieth anniversary in 2008, and covers 27 per cent of Surrey, is

▼ The view north from the spine of the North Downs takes in Thames landmarks such as the towers of Canary Wharf

an expression of aesthetic judgement, a section of landscape singled out for its quality. It is an extraordinary disconnected shape: east of Dorking a narrow, jagged-edged finger of land following the top of the Downs; to the west, a broad span spreading south to Haslemere, Chiddingfold and the edge of Ockley. It stretches from Oxted in the east to Farnham in the west, and south to the Hampshire/Sussex borders.

This official government recognition means that the Surrey Hills have the same conservation status as a National Park, a protected area, overlapping and reinforcing the Metropolitan Green Belt and Area of Great Landscape Value, which has helped preserve one of the most sought after places in England. It was one of the first of the thirty-seven tracts of UK countryside to be given AONB status – a prescient move because without it, Surrey's countryside could so easily have been swallowed in an orgy of asphalt, mock Georgian executive homes, pony paddocks and golf courses.

AONB status has not just been another big defensive gun in the planning armoury, however. It has meant that the landscape, and the economy of the countryside that sustains it, have been positively valued in their own right. This was underlined in 1998, when the Surrey Hills Partnership (now a board) was formed to provide strategic management, because the Government recognized that AONBs were not being actively cared for: the partnership was set up to take the landscape seriously.

Gritty questions of economic sustainability, tourism and leisure activities such as off-road driving and mountain biking take priority – issues more obviously associated with National Parks. The Surrey Hills AONB is already absorbing the associated area designated as of Great Landscape Value to provide more uniform protection, and it certainly needs to raise its profile as a wonderful landscape to be treasured.

A casual glance in any estate agent's window reveals the astronomical cost of housing in rural Surrey, the tip of a gargantuan iceberg of unseen housing pressure that has its roots in the arrival of the railways in the nineteenth century. Commuting is easy, good schools abound and the countryside is stunning – no wonder the desire to live in rural Surrey pushes prices up. Sir Arthur Conan Doyle and Ralph Vaughan Williams are just two of the famous people who have been drawn to its hills. It is hard to untangle demand from need, particularly local need, and it is a testament to the robustness of conservation guidelines that villages have not merged; that the view from the top of Guildford High Street is still of green grass.

But it is hard to deal strategically with something that has such a bizarre shape that few people living inside its

▼ The view to the south stretches to the South Downs

boundaries know where and what it is. The South Downs, the New Forest, the Cotswolds, the Peaks and the Lakes have a particular identity, a homogeneity that is instantly recognizable. People would say perfectly naturally that they come from the Lake District. No one would spontaneously say they came from the Surrey Hills. That is not to say that the beauty and significance of Surrey has been unappreciated. Jane Austen set the famous picnic in her novel *Emma* on Box Hill. Landowner Richard Hull built Leith Hill Tower in 1765.

John Miller

What characterizes the Surrey Hills AONB? Hills, obviously, but not all of Surrey's hills are included. It has high viewpoints, ancient lookouts, refuges and beauty spots offering spectacular panoramas and dense woodland, but these features also extend beyond its boundaries. The North Downs across the border in Kent is also an AONB and south of Haslemere the Surrey Hills share a border with the Sussex Downs AONB. And there are acres of superbly beautiful Surrey countryside that are excluded.

Broadly, the Surrey Hills AONB traces an outline round the Surrey section of the North Downs and the Greensand Hills, a succession of promontories looking south and east towards the ridge of the South Downs. Understandably, one of the first moves of the new Surrey Hills Partnership was to try and stamp a brand on this idiosyncratic area. People might never find out what an AONB means but they might learn to appreciate that they are entering special territory.

Twelve massive oak sculptures carved by international artist Walter Bailey were erected at strategic points around the area, backed up by hundreds of smaller oak way-markers. Wielding his chainsaw with a combination of spiritual vision and lumberjack confidence, Bailey somehow managed to bring subtlety and finesse to the great tree-trunk sculptures, carving filigree fretwork in swirling seed-pod designs. The idea of a seed was meant to symbolize new beginnings and the design also incorporates a figure of eight that represents infinity - light years away from dry planning guidelines.

'People drive through the Surrey Hills very quickly and do not realize what an asset they have in the landscape. I want people to feel curiosity and surprise when they see the boundary markers. They are all carved as lattice work so people can see the landscape through the

◀ The Hog's Back sculpture – one of the twelve great chainsaw sculptures by Walter Bailey designed to create a sense of identity for the Surrey Hills AONB

▶ One of Walter Bailey's chainsaw sculptures on Leith Hill

sculptures. I hope that by drawing people's eye they will look at what is around them a bit more,' said Bailey, when I visited him in his open-air sculpture studio deep in the forest, surrounded by what looked like giant totem poles.

What people see is a landscape that was one of the first in the UK to be settled by humans. The hills rising out of the dense Wealden forests afforded perfect sites for Iron Age forts, followed by Roman villas and medieval manors in a continuum of agricultural and industrial activity. Thanks to an accessibility unparalleled anywhere in the UK, people do not just see it from a distance; they can immerse themselves in it.

What is clear, though, when one considers those historical activities, is that, geology apart, the Surrey Hills landscape is entirely man-made, the result of thousands of years of human interference. The current 'outstandingly naturally beautiful' landscape is just the face of these hills *now.* Conserving landscape is a curious concept when it is essentially an artificial creation. Which period is one aiming for? When the hills were blanketed by forest? Or when they were grazed to short turf by the sheep that made towns like Guildford, Godalming and Farnham so rich? When they reverberated to the sound of quarrying, blacksmithing, smelting and timber felling? Or when they were silent and peaceful because it was no longer economical to harvest the trees or employ legions of farmworkers?

Driving landscape conservation now are other issues too, such as biodiversity, habitat and wildlife protection. The flora and fauna and the environments that support them are threatened not so much by building development but by agricultural practice and changes in the rural economy. Gathering together these strands and working out a strategy for land management in partnership with all the private landowners is one of the strengths of the AONB, and the launch in 2008 of the Surrey Hills Society, a membership organization that will act as everything from lobby and campaign group to conservation volunteer force and project fundraiser, was a sensible move.

Largely privately owned, the countryside of the Surrey Hills has always had to pay its way. More than just agricultural land, much more than just part of London's green lung, its role for tourism, leisure and sport, and the issue of tranquillity flagged up by the Campaign to Protect Rural England (CPRE), are all important aspects. Balancing needs and pressures, wants and wish lists, will always be precarious. So close to the throbbing capital, the Surrey Hills are a fragile resource that will always require vigilant protection.

John Miller

Geography, Geology and Archaeology

French Connection

When the earth across southern England buckled some 60 million years ago and the magnificently named Wealden Dome rose up from the sea bed, the landscape would have been vast and dramatic. Until then, most of the South-east had been a marshy plain, disappearing gradually beneath the sea and accumulating around a kilometre of sedimentary rock. The Dome stretched from the Bas Boulonnais in northern France right across the Channel through Kent, Sussex and Surrey to the Hampshire Downs. But sedimentary rock is vulnerable to erosion, and over some 20 million years, most of the Dome simply washed away.

Today we are just left with hints as to what happened – the two chalk outcrops of the North and South Downs and between them, splaying out towards the sea, the Weald. Perhaps they should be called 'ups' rather than 'downs' because nobody now makes the etymological connection between 'downs' and 'dunes'. The erosion was on a colossal scale, exposing a succession of rock layers beneath, and as sea levels rose, they disappeared beneath the waves altogether. Imagine slicing through the side of an onion; you would see concentric rings. The outer band in this geological 'onion' is the chalk. Inside are bands of first Upper Greensand and Gault, then Lower Greensand. Inside them are Weald Clay and finally Hastings Group sands and clays that have not been fully eroded and form the central core of the onion. The Kent and East Sussex coastline cuts right across the bands to the south-east (they continue again on the French side of the Channel) but to the west, the North and South Downs head towards each other and the Greensand forms a continuous swathe of beautiful wooded hills from Farnham south to Haslemere and round into West Sussex.

This geological/morphological anticline of chalk and sandstone, also known as the Wealden Uplift, was created during the Tertiary Period, which lasted for 63 million years, ending 1.8 million years ago. It is almost impossible to grapple with such a time-frame but it was in this period too that the Alps were scrunched up into a mountain range made of more robust rock than Surrey's chalk and sandstone, and mammals began to evolve and multiply. The climate started off very warm and moist compared with today and much of the earth was tropical or sub-tropical; traces of palm trees have been found as far north as Greenland. Forests were dense and grasslands lush. Gradually the climate changed, however, growing progressively colder until the land was locked in an ice age. Snow and glacier melt caused even more change to the landscape.

The North Downs cannot compete with the Alps but the ridge does increase steadily in height and breadth as it heads east towards Dover, and reaches 900ft on the Surrey/Kent border. The Greensand Hills are even taller. Leith Hill, near Dorking, is 965ft high, and if you look east from its summit the next highest point is the Ural Mountains. They are called Greensand because the stone contains glauconite, which is green when fresh but oxidizes to yellow or red-brown limonite. The great

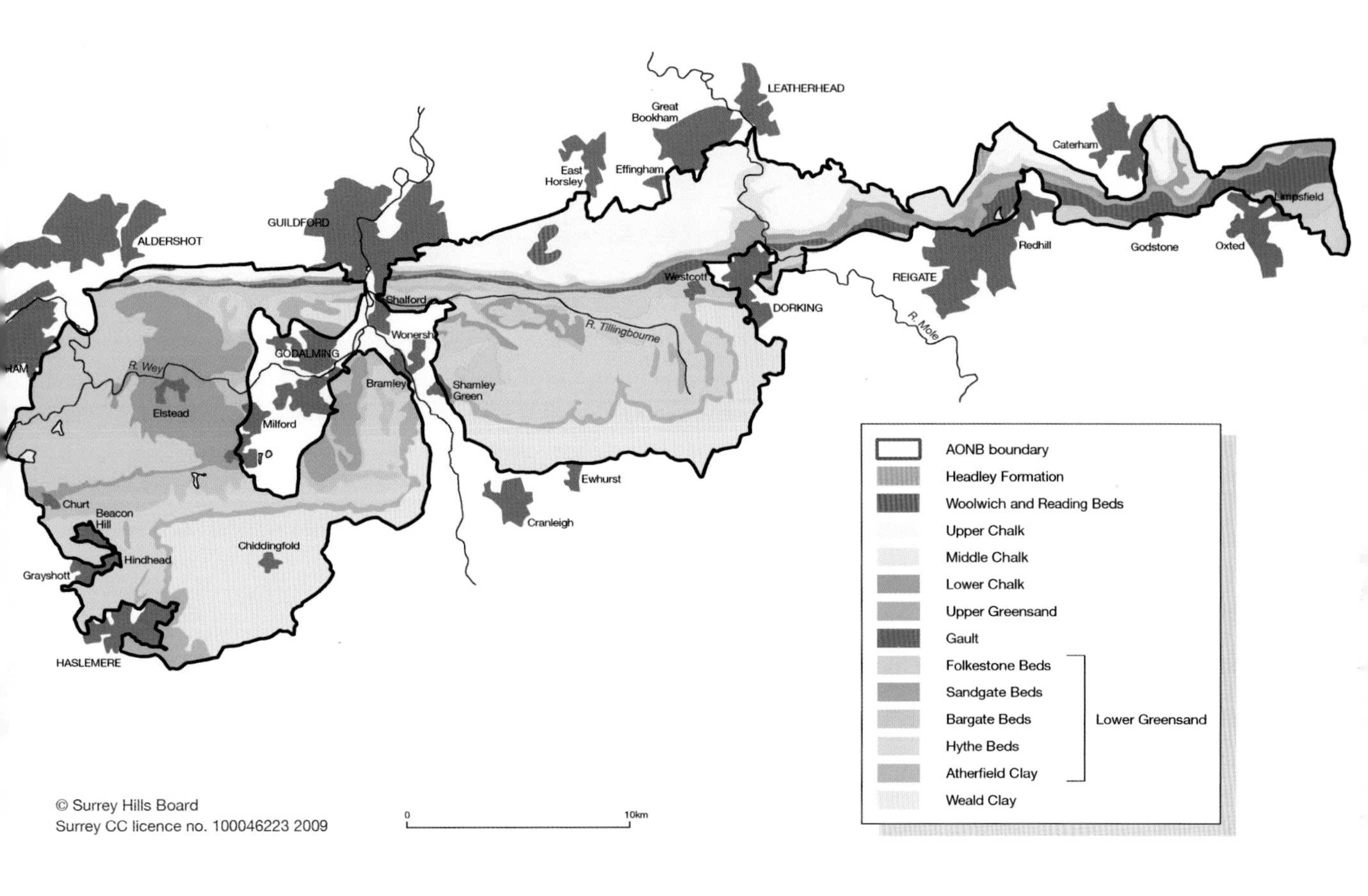

▲ Geology of the Surrey Hills

escarpments at Hindhead, Hascombe and Leith Hills have survived thanks to a hard and relatively weather-resistant siliceous substance in the sandstone known as Chert.

The Folkestone and Sandgate Beds in the Lower Greensand that occur south of Farnham and in the Tillingbourne Valley give rise to poor-quality, light and sandy soils, unproductive for agriculture but stunning as heathland habitat and open space for leisure activities. Outcrops of Carstone, a tougher sandstone, have enabled the survival of well defined conical hills like St Martha's, just south of Newlands Corner. The most fertile land for agriculture is the narrow strip of Gault Clay just south of the chalk. This rich soil is the Vale of Holmesdale, running from the foot of the downs at Guildford in an arc around the edge of the Weald to the south of Ashford in Kent. The Weald Clay forms a wide tract of low-lying land consisting of green, grey, blue, brown or red clays and mudstones, interspersed with thin beds of sandstones, shelly limestones and clay ironstones. Near Guildford it is around 1,300 ft thick.

The Gaps

Carving their way through the chalk towards the Thames are the Rivers Wey and Mole, both of which have created substantial gaps, though with completely different characters. The county town, Guildford, sits right in the middle of the Guildford Gap, its major urban development fanning out to the north of the downs, leaving the south-western side of the gap remarkably unspoilt. The dramatic nature of this river gap can be immediately appreciated from the top of the High Street, whose famous granite setts are on a steep slope leading straight down to the old Town Bridge and the incredibly steep hillside of the Mount beyond. When the main Winchester road ran straight up the Mount, coachmen had to stop off at the Wheatsheaf Inn by the river to harness extra horses to their carriages to get them up onto the ridge of the Hog's Back. It is superb that the green fields and wooded top of the Mount have survived as a completely rural view from the centre of a major town.

The Mole Gap, by contrast, is still a completely rural landscape. The Mole is a feisty river. Peaceful and placid one moment, she can catch you by surprise with an unexpected flash of temper, according to Paul Bryant of Cobham Mill Preservation Trust. He has witnessed that explosive change of mood many times over the years, when the still waters have suddenly seethed into a raging torrent, breaking their banks to deluge farmland and housing estates indiscriminately. And the river has always defied moves to make it navigable.

The Mole rises in the flat clay plain around Gatwick Airport, fed by lots of little streams. The speed with which the water level rises is due to run off from the clay soil and concrete development at Gatwick Airport, where the river passes beneath the main runway, and the urban sprawl around Crawley and Horley. Rain in Sussex takes less than 24 hours to create a river surge in Cobham. 'Ninety-nine times out of 100 it comes up in the night and very quickly. It's horrible,' according to Nick Owen of the Lower Mole Countryside Trust.

By the time it gets near Reigate it has gathered into a substantial flow which meanders north-west through Dorking, Leatherhead and Cobham before making a sharp turn towards the Thames at Molesey, joining it just upstream from Hampton Court.

A lot of flood prevention work has been done over the years on the lower reaches of the river. But with more development planned for the Gatwick area, creating greater surface water problems, the Mole is likely to live up to her flashy reputation for a long time to come.

The Mickleham or Mole Gap at Box Hill bears witness to the irresistible power of water. A sheer cliff rises

▼ The Mole at Betchworth Bridge looks tranquil enough here, but it is a feisty river that rises swiftly

hundreds of feet above the river, which curls at its foot through watermeadows rich in wildflowers. It might look innocent, but it is here that the Mole has won fame for another dramatic characteristic – its ability to disappear suddenly deep underground. Did this trick of burrowing under the chalk and popping up further downstream give it the name 'Mole'? There are several possible derivations. The name might refer to a Saxon called Mul, as Molesey was known as Muleseg or 'Mul's island' in 675, and Molesham in the Domesday Book of 1086. Another contender is the Saxon word *Emlyn,* which survives in the name Elmbridge. The word could also come from *mol*, the Latin for mill, with Molesey simply meaning 'mill island'. St George's Hill nearby was originally a Roman camp, so Latin place names are feasible. It might even have once been called the Dork, from *dorce* meaning bright river, hence Dorking. It goes without saying, however, that the mole as an underground burrower has by far the greatest appeal.

The river performs its vanishing trick in the Norbury Park to Burford Bridge stretch. As if the plug of an enormous bath has been pulled out, it disappears down swallow holes that can actually be seen when the river is low. Water has dissolved the chalk to form underground caverns, and when the roofs of these chambers collapse, they reveal dramatic holes up to 30ft deep. These can take an enormous amount of water, which then re-emerges in powerful springs in the riverbed near Leatherhead.

The river's capricious nature and tendency to flood might account for the positioning of Dorking safely to one side. Daniel Defoe wrote about the swallow hole phenomenon in his *Tour Through the Whole Island of Great Britain 1724–6.*

> The current of the river being much obstructed by the interposition of those hills, called Box Hill ... it forces the waters as it were to find their way through as well as they can; and in order to do this, beginning, I say, where the river comes close to the foot of the precipice of Box Hill, called the Stomacher, the waters sink insensibly away, and in some places are to be seen (and I have seen them) little channels which go out on the sides of the river, where the water in a stream is not so big as would fill a pipe of a quarter of an inch in diameter, trills away out of the river, and sinks insensibly into the ground. In this manner it goes away, lessening the stream for above a mile, near two, and these they call the Swallows.

The Mole has the most diverse range of fish of any river in the UK, according to a 2004 survey, and the Fetcham Splash to Thorncroft stretch has been designated a local nature reserve. Further east, at Reigate, is the Merstham Gap, where the River Wandle once flowed but is reduced now to a few springs across the Downs.

Nature as Raw Material

Man regards the earth at his feet, with no little arrogance, as something to manipulate and plunder for survival and profit, and Surrey has provided a wealth of raw material that over the centuries made the county as much an industrial zone as a pastoral landscape. In 1579, Queen Elizabeth I granted George Evelyn a monopoly for the making of gunpowder and he chose the Tillingbourne valley because it had water for power and transport and huge supplies of wood for fuel. Not as unpredictable as the Mole, but just as feisty, the Tillingbourne rises in springs on the slopes of Leith Hill and flows through the Greensand valley to join the River Wey at Shalford. This river may not have had to carve out a channel for itself through solid chalk, but it has worked extremely hard, powering a large number of mills for its size. At one time, a total of thirty-one mills were recorded along an 11 mile stretch, driving industries such as the manufacture of wire, nails, mousetraps and other metal products, leather tanning, paper making, flax retting, iron smelting and brewing, as well as flour and grain milling and gunpowder production.

The geology itself meant that mining was a major industry too. The valuable mineral deposits ranged from yellow and white sand to firestone and hearthstone,

Bargate and Hurtwood stone, coal, gypsum, fuller's earth, even oil and gas. Moreover, this is not just a historical industry: it is still going on. Yellow sand is still shipped by the lorryload from the hollowed-out sandhill on the A25 at Albury, just opposite the Silent Pool, and the massive cavity there being backfilled with rubbish, is one of the biggest landfill sites in the region. Sandstone is still quarried too and there are battles raging now over quarry plans at Eashing near Godalming and hugely controversial gas extraction and storage plans, right in the centre of the AONB on Albury Heath. A nodding donkey hidden in the woods on the Duke of Northumberland's estate has been discreetly tapping pockets of fossil fuel for many years, but in 2006 extensive exploration resulted in the discovery of a huge natural gas deposit beneath the Greensand, believed to contain around 850 million cubic metres. This might be an Area of Outstanding Natural Beauty, but it could also be seen as an 'area of outstanding national energy importance.' There is another oilfield at Betchworth.

At Nutfield, east of Redhill, the Sandgate Formation contains the largest deposits of fuller's earth in the UK, while dazzling white sands in the Folkestone Formation are found in the area between Betchworth and Reigate and Reigate and Oxted. These sands are amongst the purest in the country, with very low levels of iron oxide and alumina.

A hard type of sandstone, called firestone, was once worked extensively in underground quarries between Reigate and Godstone as a building stone or as a refractory material for lining furnaces. The softer hearthstone was used for whitening hearths and domestic scouring purposes. Both were extensively quarried until the last mine closed in the 1960s.

Living with What Nature Provided

Apart from the Vale of Holmesdale, the Surrey Hills soils are not particularly fertile for cereal crops but they provide excellent conditions for trees and, where the woods are cleared, for livestock pasture. The thickly wooded, heavy clays of the Weald, the impenetrable Forest of Anderida, were the last to be inhabited and cleared. I can remember the clear-felling of Wealden woods between Cranleigh and Rudgwick in the 1960s to make way for pasture. But from Neolithic times, around 4300–1400 BC, the woods had been extensively used for pigs to root around in, searching out acorns and beech mast. Settlers who had begun to farm the North Downs would drive their pigs south into the woods in late summer or early autumn each year to fatten them, a practice called pannage. Good old porkers. They created one of Surrey's best-loved physical features. These annual pig migrations made well-trodden north-south drove roads through the Greensand Hills seen today as beautiful, deeply sunken lanes – green tunnels with a cathedral arch of gnarled tree roots, roofed with a canopy of leaves and dappled sunlight.

Archaeology

No indigenous tribes were centred in Surrey, so its archaeology is scattered. Guildford Museum holds a selection of finds, such as axes dating from the Bronze Age, *c*.2100–750 BC, found in Guildford, Shalford, and on St Catherine's Hill, along with a bronze disc and a cast bronze ornament. Two late Bronze Age spears have also been found, but the Guildford Gap had no strategic importance at this time. The Iron Age is more exciting because the farmers built what appear to be defensive fortifications on the Greensand escarpments overlooking the Weald, whose earthworks – double ditches and banks – are still clearly visible. Holmbury Hill, Anstiebury and Hascombe Hill would have looked magnificent with their towering earthworks, though it is impossible to say whether they were built to protect communities from rape and pillage or to keep livestock safe.

Holmbury Hill Fort is a scheduled ancient monument, but encroaching trees and scrub until recently completely obliterated its contours so that it was impossible to see and interpret. Tree roots were also seriously damaging the remains, but luckily in 2004 the Hurtwood Control, which manages the site, was successful in its application for a grant from the Heritage Lottery Fund to restore the fort. Woodland and scrub were cleared, enabling the restoration of heathland habitats. The site is now a superb open hilltop with wonderful panoramas, and it is possible to see the extent and shape of the earthworks. Public access has also been improved.

Anstiebury Camp Triple-Vallate Hill Fort, 700ft up at Coldharbour, near Dorking, is also a scheduled monument. Built some time between the second and first centuries BC, it does not seem to have been extensively used, nor were its defences properly finished. Surrey archaeologist F. H. Thompson, who excavated the site in 1972–3, suggests it might have been deliberately abandoned and dismantled as a result of the Roman invasion in 55 and 54 BC.

The 644ft Hascombe Hill has a first century BC fort and its strategic significance continued to be recognized in the early nineteenth century, when it became an important naval telegraph station, using a mechanical form of semaphore to communicate with Netley Heath, on the North Downs at Shere, on one side and Blackdown, near Haslemere, on the other. A chain of these telegraph stations linked London with Portsmouth. The general strategic significance of the protective barrier of high ground, pierced by navigable gaps, was not lost on modern generations either. Because of the threat of a Nazi invasion in the Second World War, it was felt necessary to defend London from an army heading up from the south coast. The 'pillbox' gun emplacements strung across the downs and the hills, the dragon's teeth anti-tank defences and the remains of huge anti-tank barriers bear witness to the importance of the landscape in shaping national defence.

Evidence of Roman occupation in Surrey is terribly disappointing. Roman tiles crop up in the foundations of various churches, and there are hints of industry such as hammer ponds, as well as the remains of villas at Cocks Farm, Abinger, Rapsley in Ewhurst, Ashtead, Bletchingley, Walton Heath, Walton-on-the-Hill, Chatley Heath, Broad Street, Compton, Chiddingfold and Titsey Park. They were most likely to be farming estates, as there were no notable Roman towns in Surrey. There may have been small settlements at Ashtead and Dorking but the major Roman town was to the west of Surrey at Staines, where the road to Silchester crossed the Thames.

The most exciting excavations were the Romano-Celtic temple sites at Farley Heath and Wanborough, which yielded rich finds of coin and ritual headdresses. A third temple was discovered at Titsey. Stane Street through Ockley is the 'stone road' built by the Romans to link London with the Sussex tribal centre at Chichester.

Surrey began to emerge as a geographical entity after the Romans left and the Saxons filled the void in the fifth century AD, but the pattern of many rural settlements goes back beyond the Saxons and the Romans and reflects instead the north–south seasonal livestock migrations and the peculiar geology of the county. Parish boundaries on either side of the North Downs are characteristically long and thin. This meant each village had access to a range of soils, from chalk downland to fertile gault clay, sandy pasture and forest and clay woodland, as well as to a spring-fed water supply.

A map showing parish boundaries in west Surrey reveals this linear pattern very clearly. Great Bookham, Little Bookham, Effingham, East and West Horsley, and East and West Clandon are narrow strips of land cheek by jowl. Albury, Shere, Abinger and Wotton are also linear, their relatively larger size perhaps indicative of the poorer soil conditions south of the downs.

Climate and Change

Were the floods of 1968 and the storm of 1987 – so dramatic that they have inspired whole books – an early sign of climate change or just blips in a slow pendulum swing of the earth's temperature? The floods changed Surrey in that there was obviously a need for major investment in protective measures on the rivers. For gap towns like Guildford, whose commercial life crowds the banks of the Wey, flooding is a serious economic hazard. The Yvonne Arnaud Theatre, Debenhams and other shops and offices – even Bedford Road car park – are very vulnerable to rising river levels. I remember being unable to get to school in Bramley because of the 1968 flood. Driving down from Wonersh we met a bubbling sea of water over the bridge. Fantastic! A day off! But despite the investment, flooding has been a regular problem, and in 2000 a turbulent River Mole spilled into homes in Leatherhead, Brockham, Capel, Mickleham and Fetcham, in the wettest autumn for 200 years. Records showed that two-thirds of the annual rainfall fell in a matter of weeks.

Floods are violent, but once the waters have subsided, the landscape carries on much the same as before. Storms however, can change a scene overnight. The outrageous twisting winds of October 1987 wrought havoc on the heavily forested hillsides. Those magnificent stands of ancient beeches, their roots spreading over the surface of the chalk to counterbalance their canopies, did not have a chance. The scene next morning was of a random cemetery of great round white tombstones across the downs – the chalky underside of the root plates marking where the trees had come down.

The beech was the second species to be hard hit in Surrey; Dutch elm disease had taken out the elms. Now sudden oak death and horse chestnut bleeding canker are threatening more much loved broad-leaf trees. These diseases are likely to kill trees that are weakened by drought – another issue linked to global warming. A pattern is being established now of a generally more violent climate, with heavier rain, hotter droughts, more savage winds and vicious storms. But then sceptics will point to the writings of John Evelyn, who wrote in November 1703, that more than 200 trees had been blown down in a hurricane 'and that the place was no more Wotton [Wood-town] stripped and naked and almost ashamed to own its own nature.' This storm was widely used for comparison with the 1987 storm and the Met Office stated that, south-east of a line from Southampton through London to Great Yarmouth, gust speeds and mean wind speeds during the 1987 storm were as they would expect for a once in 200 years event. It took out a staggering 15 million trees across southern England. At least thirteen people died, there were hundreds of stories of damage done and of trees miraculously missing houses, cars and people. Typical is the Dorking woman who woke up to find her monkey puzzle tree in her bed.

At the time 'seen from the air' the devastation was unbelievable, but viewed twenty years on, the storm did not have a totally detrimental effect on the landscape. It got rid of many trees that had reached their natural span. It opened up views and forced landowners to reconsider forestry and land management. The immediate response was to get out the chainsaw and remove everything – trunks, branches and roots. This was obviously vital anywhere near roads and paths, but the ecological wisdom of this wholesale clean-up was quite quickly challenged because branches and debris left behind on the forest floor were recognized as providing valuable habitats for a wide variety of flora and fauna. Where swathes of woodland, and in particular those unloved, densely packed pine plantations, were destroyed by the storm, new planting of native broad-leaved trees have become possible. There was indeed a silver lining for the Surrey Hills, even though some of Capability Brown's mature specimens paid a heavy price.

The Rise of the Vine

Are we being overdramatic about climate change? Philip Underwood, retired veterinary surgeon and founder of the successful small Greyfriar's Vineyard on the Hog's Back at Puttenham, has a long-term perspective based on the temperamental vine as a climate indicator. Whatever its cause, human abuse of carbon fuel or natural cycle, he has witnessed global warming having a clear effect on viticulture. 'The change in climate has altered our vineyard dramatically,' he says. 'In 1988, when we first started planting vines, we were advised that we could not grow Chardonnay or Pinot Noir in this country but we thought we could and now we get an average of seventeen bunches of grapes per plant to the French average of four to six.'

Greyfriar's is on 24ft of pure chalk, in a hot spot very similar to the best vineyards in the Rheims champagne area. Like the much larger Denbies Wine Estate at Dorking, it has the same geology and now the North Downs have a better climate than France, as it probably did during the first millennium AD, when there was a medieval warm period before a little European ice age set in. Scientists are sceptical that these earlier climate shifts were global and now see them as localized phenomena. The warmth enabled the Romans to create vineyards in England as far north as Leeds, and the North Downs were ideal. There was a Roman vineyard at Bagden Farm, a few hundred yards from Denbies, in the first century. Wine was not made on a grand commercial scale: it was produced for home consumption, and once Christianity was established, for and by the Church. Monasteries had their own vineyards but by the sixteenth century wine-making all but disappeared. A combination of foreign trade, the dissolution of the monasteries, the Black Death and a colder climate killed it off. The perceived wisdom was that the only vine tolerant of the English climate was the German Muller Thergau, but now three Surrey vineyards grow Pinot Noir and Chardonnay with great success. 'We get twice the yield per hectare that they get in Rheims,' says Underwood. 'We can grow any variety that we want to as the land is ideal. The French vineyard owners are starting to come over here as France is getting too dry.'

The Hon. Charles Hamilton tried a vineyard at Painshill Park in the eighteenth century, producing a champagne-type wine that fooled the French Ambassador of the day, and it was planted again with Chardonnay and Pinot Noir in the 1990s. The resulting sparkling wine wins prizes.

The biggest piece of Surrey evidence for climate change has to be Denbies, however. Anyone driving along the A24 from Dorking towards Mickleham could be forgiven for thinking they had strayed into France. The hills are covered in vines, 265 acres of them, making Denbies the largest single-owned vineyard in England – around 300,000 vines producing some half a million bottles a year. It was not that long ago that English wines were being airily dismissed as inferior, but a glance at the awards won by Denbies wines shows how the situation has changed – and presumably Surrey vintages will continue improving as the temperature goes on rising.

▼ Harvesting grapes at Greyfriars Vineyard on the Hog's Back. This is one crop that will enjoy the benefits of global warming

The Landscape

Inspirational Views

You do not need to be a romantic, or even necessarily human, to enjoy a good view – my horse Clarence likes nothing better than to stop and gaze intently at each new panorama encountered on rides through the Surrey Hills. The peaks may not be on the same scale as a Matterhorn or an Everest but they give one an incentive to climb, and whether it is flying kites on Newlands Corner, picnicking in the Punch Bowl or getting fit on the Box Hill Zigzag, the views are what draw people to the summits. They are simply inspirational – the 1970s hit *Here Comes the Sun* was written by George Harrison on the top of Pitch Hill.

The great panoramas that define the Surrey Hills are dramatic because the ground literally falls away beneath your feet on both the scarp slope of the North Downs and the sandstone promontories overlooking the Weald. The steepness accentuates the contrast, and you are seldom very far away from a hill or a view. Caterham,

▲ View to the Church of St Martha on the Hill from Peaslake

Gatton, Colley, Box, Leith, Holmbury, Pitch, Hascombe and Gibbet Hills as well as Newlands Corner, St Martha's, Chinthurst Hill and others are strung like pearls on a chain right across the AONB. Standing on Holmbury Hill one can see Leith Hill to the left and Pitch, Hascombe and Gibbet Hills to the right. Their peaks are asking to be collected, like a mini version of the Scottish Munros.

A couple of years ago, I climbed the wooden ladder inside the little squat tower of St Martha's on the Hill and looked out over the Tillingbourne valley and the Guildford Gap from the parapet. It was fantastic because from ground level you could barely see a thing as the tree cover was so tall and thick. At Christmas, when the church was floodlit, all one could see, looking up from Chilworth in the valley below, was a fuzzy orange glow. It took an eagle eye to make out a fragment of the roofline. This was a far cry from the 1930s; people who remember it then say the whole hillside was bare of trees. Surrey is certainly the most densely wooded county in England now, but even I recall that when I rode over Blackheath and Farley Heath as a child in the 1960s, most of the heath was open heather. Bun, my pony, and I created our own paths across the wilderness in that lost world of unregulated freedom. Some of those paths still exist, now carefully marked 'footpath only'. I often wonder if the powers that be have any idea that they came into existence solely through the anarchic and adventurous spirit of a tall, thin child on a short, fat Highland pony. Of course in those days there were far fewer horses to threaten environmental damage.

During the 1970s, Surrey County Council, which has a public access agreement for St Martha's with the landowner, the Albury Estate, cut back some of the trees to expose the church. It was a gesture that was quickly overtaken by self-sown trees and when Michael Baxter became estate manager he was keen to clear the viewpoint properly. With the support of the Surrey Wildlife Trust, which by then had taken over the management

◀ St James's Church, Shere, with the North Downs in the distance

of Surrey County Council's countryside portfolio, and financial help from the Surrey Hills AONB Partnership's Inspiring Views Project, Mr Baxter set about exposing the landmark hilltop church to view from both east and west. Surrey Wildlife Trust is now responsible for keeping scrubby regrowth at bay.

His foresters tackled the Scots pines at the western end of the hill in January 2006 and got rid of the scrubby oak and birch at the eastern end in January 2007, an ambitious programme of tree felling that incurred passionate opposition from a few people, who only just stopped short of tying themselves to trees in protest. Christmases now reveal the complete outline of the little church bathed in its orange glow and daytime visitors have an uninterrupted view from the churchyard – no need to battle vertigo with the tower ladder these days to appreciate the landscape. It has made a tremendous difference.

▼ Magical atmosphere deep in the heart of the Surrey Hills at Friday Street, a hamlet on the lower slopes of Leith Hill. Almost impossible to think London is just a forty-five-minute drive away

The Inspiring Views Project, which started in 2003, is a good example of positive partnership effort. 'Partnership' has been a buzzword in recent years but it has achieved some real success in the Surrey Hills, where any project is likely to require co-operation between a number of different owners and managers. The Inspiring Views Project, led by the Surrey Hills AONB Partnership, involved the National Trust and other landowners such as the Royal Alexandra and Albert School in Gatton Park. Its focus was on access improvements, viewpoint clearance, the restoration of historic landscape features and their interpretation along the North Downs Way National Trail and the Greensand Way. Most of the work took place at five National Trust properties – Leith Hill, Box Hill, Reigate Hill, Gatton Park (part-owned by the school) and Limpsfield Common.

The project was not just about tree clearance; it had a strong public educational element too. Yes, wonderful hidden views were brought to light, transforming both the look and the outlook of these high points, but the project also included creative workshops to raise public awareness of the beauty spots on their doorstep. It is

another way of stamping an identity on the landscape. Children from local schools visited the sites to learn about their importance and historical significance. The experience of being inspired by the views was then given artistic expression through music, pottery, sculpture, poetry and painting.

Financial support for the project has come from the Countryside Agency, the National Trust, Surrey County Council, Surrey County Arts, the North Downs Way National Trail, Reigate and Banstead, Tandridge and Mole Valley District Councils, Limpsfield and Hambledon Parish Councils, the Friends of Box Hill and Pfizer Ltd – a successful mix of quango, local government and big business. Public projects like this are important to help people to identify with the Surrey Hills, even just to notice them and recognize that the landscape is there. And of course improving access is vital if people are to be encouraged to get out of their cars. The importance of the Surrey Hills for tourism, leisure, sport and recreation is a powerful motivator for local government support.

It is not surprising that Box Hill was top of the list for inspiration. It is one of the best-known landmarks in the south of England and there is plenty of documentary evidence to show that it has been a magnet for sightseers for hundreds of years. The seventeenth century diarist John Evelyn, wrote: 'I went … to Box Hill to see those rare natural bowers, cabinets and shady walks in the box coppses … there are such godly walkes and hills shaded with yew and box as render the place extreamely agreeable, it seeming to be summer all the winter for many miles prospect.' He was not alone. Celia Fiennes wrote in 1694: 'The hill is full of box which is cut out in several walks, shady and pleasant to walk in.' And Dr John Burton, writing around 1750, also described the scene:

> On the western slopes of this mountain is an object of curiosity .... It is a considerable space of ground covered thickly with box trees, unusually fine and tall. They do not grow confusedly nor scattered about in a natural wood, but are set in ranks in an orderly fashion and disposed as in a park. From each side are paths and entries provided for the gratification of people of taste.

Landscape came into its own for popular tourism in the eighteenth century. Wealthy young men would complete their education with the 'Grand Tour' of Europe, which fuelled an interest in dramatic landscape and architecture, and when the Romantic Movement was born in the late 1700s, the Surrey Hills provided a local source of romantic landscape. The social nature of sightseeing and holidaymaking, often involving courting, goes way back in history. Daniel Defoe wrote in *A Tour through the Whole Island of Great Britain 1724–6*:

> Here every Sunday, during the summer season, there used to be a rendezvous of coaches and horsemen, with an abundance of gentlemen and ladies from Epsome to take the air, and walk in the box woods; and in a word, divert, or debauch, or perhaps both, as they thought fit, and the game encreas'd so much that it began almost on a sudden to make a great noise in the country.

Human nature was ever the same.

And while Wordsworth immortalized the Lake District in poetry, Jane Austen, writing in the early 1800s, reflected the burgeoning popularity of landscape and stately home tourism in the famous picnic scene at Box Hill in *Emma*, Colonel Brandon's fated strawberry picnic in *Sense and Sensibility* and Elizabeth's tour of d'Arcy's country seat in *Pride and Prejudice*. If she were alive today she would be an avid supporter of the National Trust.

The Surrey Hills did not just inspire prose. Anna Barbauld wrote in 1796:

> From the smoke and the din, and the hurry of town
> Let the care wearied cit to this spot hasten down.
> Here may Industry, Peace, Contentment reign still
> While the Mole softly creeps at the foot of the hill.

John Keats finished his epic poem *Endymion* while

staying for a fortnight in 1817 at the Burford Bridge Hotel, having been inspired to write by a moonlit walk up the hill, and the nineteenth century poet George Meredith, who lived at Flint Cottage on the ZigZag, also admitted its inspirational effect, writing: 'I am every morning at the top of Box Hill – as its flower, its bird, its prophet. I drop down the moon on one side, I draw up the sun on t'other. I breathe fine air. I shout ha ha to the gates of the world. Then I descend and know myself a donkey for doing it.'

Appreciating Box Hill is certainly not just the preserve of the gentry or literati, however. In recent decades it has been a magnet for motorbike enthusiasts who traditionally hold rallies in the car park at its foot. The bikers have claimed www.boxhill.co.uk for their website domain name – a clear indication of their sense of ownership. In their view, Box Hill and Ryka's café and car park are among the best biking destinations in England and 'the place to be seen on your bike'.

Thanks to the InspiringViews Project, Box Hill is also accessible to people with mobility problems as the footpath from the visitor centre to the viewpoint has been upgraded to allow wheelchairs and pushchairs to reach the viewpoint from Saloman's Memorial.

The Mark of the Master

Further east along the North Downs ridge is Gatton Park, a perfect example of the eighteenth century interest in landscape. Its sweeping vistas, rolling hills, lakes and clumps of stately trees are surely the hallmark of a timeless natural English landscape? Perhaps not. They are more the hallmark of the legendary landscape designer, Lancelot 'Capability' Brown.

This great master of deception created an idealized landscape style that is not natural at all; it reflected his vision of harmony. And he certainly needed vision, because his projects took decades to mature and reveal their full glory. His clients needed to share his vision too, because it was often succeeding generations that reaped the benefits of his designs.

▼ The Stepping Stones over the River Mole at Dorking

▲ The renovated landscape at Gatton Park looks fantastic with its reopened vistas and new tree clumps

Two centuries of weather, not to mention the lifecycles of trees, passing fashion and changing land management ideas had all but destroyed his overarching scheme for Gatton when the Inspiring Views Project helped bring about its renaissance. Were 'Capability' Brown alive today, he would get a strong sense of *déjà vu*. Visitors can now see his landscape vision essentially through his eyes: cleanly sculpted lakes, saplings in strategic clumps, cleared scrub and breathtaking views. His landscape is being recreated anew for the next 200 years.

Gatton Park was one of his most ambitious commissions, costing £3,055 – a small fortune in 1760. The park belonged to Sir George Colebrook, and he gave the maestro the go-ahead to rip out the formal gardens and work with the North Downs landscape to create magnificent panoramas to show off his estate. His efforts were so damaged and obliterated by time, though, that despite its scale, Gatton Park dropped right off the landscape radar.

According to Caroline Cliffe, the National Trust's curator, books on 'Capability' Brown did not mention Gatton Park at all. 'When he was working here,' she said, 'He was also involved with schemes for King George III and at Blenheim, so this was done in an important time in his career and Gatton should certainly be mentioned in any work about his landscapes.'

Eighteenth-century visitors would have entered the park at the top of Wray Lane via impressive gates and driven obliquely across the downs to the house along a track designed to provide maximum impact from the magnificent views. This carriage drive, the gates sadly long gone, now forms part of the 2 mile circular trail that gives the public access to the park without encroaching on the school, which occupies the site of the house.

The scale of the parkland restoration is vast and Andrew Wright, National Trust Head Warden for the North Downs East, knows his work in opening up the views and recreating 'Capability' Brown's designs is going to take a long time.

It has already involved major upheavals. A huge twenty-year-old hedge bordering part of the access trail, which cut right across one of the major vistas, has been grubbed up. Hedge lovers fearing a repeat of the great post-war desecrations need not be alarmed: this particular stretch was of no historical significance. A large tract of rough woodland blocking the view has also been totally removed and Hop Garden Pond has been dredged and remade. 'Capability' Brown liked his trees to grow in small clumps and it has been exciting to pinpoint the remains of his original planting in the sprawling woodland and clear the ground back to his design. Where only a few clues survive, whole new sapling clusters have been planted, and as a finishing touch to the eighteenth-century look, smart iron park fencing has been installed along the track by the pond. Modern wire stock fencing criss-crossing the pasture has also been removed and walkers can now get a real sense of sweeping grassland grazed by the attractive chestnut and white Ayrshire cattle from John Gray's herd at Polesden Lacy. The difference in the landscape is incredible.

The public access walk is just one part of the Gatton visitor experience. When Jeremiah Colman, of mustard fame, took over the estate in the late nineteenth century, he had horticultural aspirations of a high order. The house was already a stunning architectural jewel, with many rare kinds of Italian marble and ancient mosaics and the main hall was a close copy of the Corsini Chapel in Rome. But Jeremiah's passion was flowers, particularly orchids and carnations, and he spent a fortune remodelling the gardens, creating Japanese, Italian, rose and herbaceous sections, with several water features. He employed such a huge army of gardeners that he boasted there was not a single weed on the estate. 'He made it very labour intensive,' commented Caroline Cliffe. 'Now we are reliant on volunteers.'

Vertical Challenge

Like Colman, Richard Hull, who lived at Leith Hill Place, also wanted to impress. He was very much a man of his time, a mid-eighteenth-century landowner highly conscious of the dramatic setting of his estate and quite prepared to make a few deliberate alterations in order to enhance it. He wanted Leith Hill to be a nice round-figure landmark, and as its natural peak was 35ft short of the magic 1,000ft, he decided to build a tower. In the end he exceeded his goal with a 60ft folly, to create the highest point in south-east England, with views of St Paul's Cathedral and the English Channel. True to the Romantic Movement, it has a Gothic feel, helped by the nineteenth-century addition of the adjoining turreted feature. The tower has always provided good views, but the hilltop itself was encased in quite dense forest, preventing real appreciation of the landscape from ground level until the Inspiring Views Project set to work opening it all up.

The windows of open space are really effective. It might be a bit blustery up there by the tables, but picnickers now enjoy a fine 'roof of the world' experience. The Inglis Memorial at Colley Hill, adjoining Reigate Hill and Reigate Fort, has also been cleared. The power of landscape as a source of spiritual growth was evident at the ceremony to unveil a wall hanging created by special needs children. The specialist centre co-ordinator from Furzefield Primary School, Merstham, Nettie Lawrence, suggested that the children might like to show the audience the bits that they had contributed. 'We had children standing up in front of the whole school talking about it,' she said. 'One child, who never spoke a word until two years ago, stood up and told everyone what he had done.'

Preserving the Surrey Hills for the Public

Appreciation of landscape was largely the preserve of the rich until the nineteenth century, when the population became far more mobile. Remote rural areas became increasingly accessible thanks to the newly metalled roads and the arrival of the railway. Mobility created aspirations; why live in overcrowded, polluted urban misery when you could move to the country and commute? As developers advanced across the countryside, gobbling up farms and turning parks into housing estates, the Victorian philanthropists, Miss Octavia Hill, Sir Robert Hunter and Canon Hardwicke Rawnsley, created the National Trust to acquire threatened coastline, countryside and buildings and protect them for the nation.

The fact that so much of the Surrey Hills is owned by the National Trust is witness both to its aesthetic value and to the scale of the threat to its survival. Box Hill and Headley Heath, Denbies Hillside and White Down, Abinger Roughs, Piney Copse and Netley Park, Leith Hill, Limpsfield Common and Harewoods, Reigate Hill and Gatton Park, are all under National Trust protection and management.

Around 230 acres of Box Hill was gifted to the National Trust in 1914 by Leopold Salomons of Norbury Park, but since then, through gifts, legacies and purchases, the Trust's estate there has expanded to 1,200 acres. Leith Hill and its tower were given to the Trust in 1923 by Mr W. J. MacAndrew. The composer Ralph Vaughan Williams bequeathed Leith Hill Place and its estate in 1944.

▼ Leith Hill Tower, built to provide extra height to get the hill over the magic 1,000ft mark

The National Trust is now the largest independent conservation charity in the world, relying almost entirely on voluntary contributions. With some 612,000 acres of countryside, over 700 miles of coastline, and hundreds of historic houses and gardens, it is by far the country's biggest private landowner.

Surrey Wildlife Trust is another major player in the management of the Surrey Hills AONB, having taken over the running of Surrey County Council's Countryside Estate in 2002 and adding responsibility for five more open spaces in Mole Valley in 2007. The trust now manages eighty nature reserves covering nearly 10,000 acres of Surrey countryside. It also manages land under access agreements with private landowners.

So how do these bodies actually manage the AONB? The Surrey Hills Partnership Management Plan identifies eight areas of interest: farming; woodland; nature conservation; historic and cultural heritage; recreation and tourism; land use planning; traffic and transport; and community development and the local economy. It recognizes the need to support local food production to ensure that farming remains a viable and sustainable enterprise, balancing that commercial factor against the leisure demands of the public and the need to conserve diverse wildlife habitats. To an extent it has artificially chosen the landscapes it wants to perpetuate and experimented with ways of maintaining and enhancing them. Choosing close-cropped chalk grassland habitat when sheep are no longer municipal wealth creators is a deliberate decision that has coined a new term – conservation grazing. This means bringing in tough, often rare-breed, cattle and sheep, and even Exmoor ponies, to graze the right plant species to the right height. The heath and downland habitats are without doubt the most vulnerable, but even Surrey's valley landscape of irregular pastures, hedges, coppices and villages needs first to be recognized as something to treasure and then to be actively cherished. For example the Tillingbourne valley, so prized over the centuries for its pastoral beauty, is not entirely natural, being the result of very intensive water management. Harnessing the Tillingbourne has required the diversion of streams, the gathering together of meandering watercourses, and the creation of dams, fish ponds and mill races.

Farming

The way this pastoral landscape has been farmed has changed dramatically since the Second World War. There were massive, landscape-altering upheavals in previous centuries of course, for example the enclosure of common land and the rise of the wool trade, but never before change that threatened the very existence of farming. The concept of sustainability in agriculture has grown directly out of the fear that it could disappear, to be replaced by golf courses, pony paddocks, paintball adventure playgrounds or just housing. People now talk about landscape management as opposed to farming, with the different types of livestock there to act as specific varieties of lawnmower. One result of this is that Surrey now has the highest density of camelids – alpacas and llamas – in the UK, acting as attractive and low-maintenance paddock toppers for non-farmers with land to manage.

Historically, as an island, we were almost self sufficient in most foodstuffs, but the Second World War brought a reality check, showing up the country's enormous reliance on imports. In 1939, around half of the country's food, some 55 million tons, was imported by sea. As the German U-boats picked off the food convoys of merchant ships, the country sank into years of rationing, eased by a 'Dig for Victory' propaganda campaign to get people to grow vegetables on allotments.

▼ An aerial shot of Reigate Hill

Malcolm Pendrill

The war also inspired the drive to increase the productivity of the nation's farms. Intensive farming was certainly productive but at a high cost to the land and the livestock involved. In Surrey, the momentum was to produce milk and meat for the capital. Government statistics show that the number of cattle in Surrey increased from 40,000 in 1940 to 66,000 in 1980. There was an uninterrupted chain of dairy farms all the way from Guildford to Dorking, and in the 1950s Surrey also had the highest density of beef cattle in the country.

In the 1960s you could just about make a living from dairy with a couple of hundred acres and a small herd. I grew up in Wonersh and as a child helped out on a tiny dairy farm with a herd of beautiful Jersey cattle. Next to it was another, much bigger Hereford dairy herd. So many dairy and beef cattle, so much pressure to improve the grassland and keep them all fed. Not a single cow on either farm these days.

The history of the Poulsom family farms at Tongham is a good example of what happened to the dairy industry in Surrey. Percy Poulsom, born in 1880, was a good farmer and a shrewd businessman who quickly responded to the shortage of milk to supply troops mobilized at Aldershot and Farnborough during the First World War. He was first off the mark to apply for the army contract, acting as a processor and distributor for surrounding dairy farms, and he even managed to obtain a Royal Warrant, putting the Royal Crest on all his milkfloats – the only dairy business in the country to have this honour. By the time his grandson, Tony, was born, the family had acquired several local farms and business thrived.

It was the introduction of the hated milk quotas in the late 1970s that put the first nail in the dairy coffin. Tony responded to the threat by selling one of his farms before the situation really deteriorated, which it did progressively through the 1980s. A mix of quotas and rock-bottom prices forced him to sell all his milkers in 1991. They went to a good home on the Duchy of Cornwall estate. It is a story repeated across the Surrey Hills. There are now just two dairy farms between Guildford and Dorking. The statistics are stark. From a total county dairy herd of around 23,000 cows in 1970, numbers had plummeted by the year 2000 to just over 9,000 and the exodus from dairy has continued. The 2006 Department of the Environment, Food and Rural Affairs (DEFRA) statistics are revealing. Just 7,000 milkers were left in Surrey.

Dairy farmers across Surrey were at their wits end in 2003 because they were being paid around 10p a pint while the cheapest supermarket milk was retailing at two and a half times that amount – and that was without the cream which the processing plant skims off. The mark-up on doorstep deliveries was staggering. A doorstep pint was being sold for around 45p, four and a half times the amount paid to the actual producers. So in a most un-British move that smacked more of French tactics, they picketed the big milk processors in an effort to persuade them to raise prices. Surrey farmers travelled hundreds of miles to support the peaceful demonstrations organized by the Farmers for Action pressure group outside processing plants, blockading their gates and preventing lorries getting in or out. For most of them it was the first time they have ever taken action – a measure of their desperation. Nick Ranson, whose family has a dairy herd at Bowlhead Green, Hindhead, travelled as far as Nuneaton to join the protest.

The Hampton Estate at Seale is typical of many farms that decided the battle to keep the dairy business going was simply not worth the colossal daily effort: the Biddell family sold their beautiful Channel Island herd in 2004 and moved from intensive grassland management and the non-stop pressure of the milking regime to low intensity, low density, suckler beef production, in which calves are left with their mothers until they are naturally ready for weaning. The loss of the Hampton dairy herd was significant because of its size and milk quality. If it could not survive thanks to economies of scale, what hope was there for the small tenant farmer?

Finding a Niche for Survival

At least two small dairy tenant farmers are keeping going thanks to the entrepreneurial spirit of younger family members. Michaela Edge and Caroline Davies are farmers' daughters who were prepared to give up their non-farming jobs and careers to set up businesses adding value to the basic product. Michaela started making Norbury Blue Cheese at Norbury Park Farm in Mickleham in 2002 after watching her parents Michael and Lilian Frost struggle to maintain the dairy herd. She knew that if her son Lewis was to have a future inheriting the high quality Holstein Friesians, she had to do something. So she set about learning all about cheese.

The cattle that graze the rich Mole valley pastures beneath Box Hill are fed on home-produced fodder and the butterfat content of the milk is high at 4.6 per cent so it lends itself well to cheese-making. Michael feeds the cows to produce high levels of protein and milk quality. Michaela joined the Specialist Cheesemakers' Association, which subsidized her studies at Reading University. 'I picked people's brains and went around so many cheese dairies,' she said:

> but in the end, you have to decide who you go with. Michael Turner from the Traditional Cheese Company helped design the building where I make the cheese. My husband Paul did the building and renovation. It was originally the farm granary. We have installed a special viewing window so that visitors can watch the cheese being made from outside. I had a lot of help with the cheese-making from Val Bines, a cheese technologist from Devon: all the makers are so helpful. Everybody has been really friendly and nice.

The cheese is made with vegetarian rennet and has the greeny/blue veining that gives it its name, Norbury Blue. It is available at farmers' markets in Surrey and London, in local shops, pubs and by mail order. Michaela's son, Lewis, has gone on to agricultural college and his dream of carrying on his grandfather's farm might just become a reality.

South of the AONB boundary at Leigh, Colin and Christine Hamilton, their son William and daughter Caroline Davies have given their small dairy business a new lease of life by making Italian-style ice cream. 'All my brother has ever wanted to do is farming,' Caroline told me. 'My dad is past retirement age. We have lived through a frightful sequence of events over a very long time, with milk quotas and foot and mouth. It was now or never or we would have lost the farm and where would Mum and Dad have gone? We are only tenants here.'

These niche cottage industries are not just the only thing keeping farms in business, they are also enabling the next generation of farmers to enter the industry. The average age of farmers right across the country is perilously close to retirement age and if the Surrey countryside is to be nurtured, it needs to be able to offer young people a viable future here. The seed for the ice cream enterprise was originally sown by Fanny Maitland, who runs Fanny's Farm Shop at the top of Reigate Hill. She wanted a supply of local ice cream to sell and Caroline's brother, William, and Fanny's daughter, Nelly, are both senior members of Guildford Young Farmers' Club.

The need to keep farms economically viable is a key plank of the AONB management plan and crops up in every rural policy and grant scheme. Caroline's ice cream venture won the 2004 Surrey Business Link Farm Diversification Award, and diversification, not just into value-added agricultural products but into non-agricultural areas, is being promoted harder and harder.

Andy Marshall, chairman of Surrey County Agricultural Society during the 2007 foot and mouth outbreak, supplements his income from the 400-strong Jersey herd at Loseley, near Guildford, with a second career in agricultural consultancy. The Jerseys were famous in the 1970s and 1980s for the fabulous yoghurts and ice creams sold in the very best shops across the country and eaten by the thousand in theatre intervals. A Chinese student friend, Kwang-Fuh Lee, was a keen amateur photographer and he spent hours with these beautiful, delicately built cows in the 1980s, building up enough pictures to produce a slide show, including a sequence of a cow giving birth to the sound track of *Love Story*. It was breathtakingly simple and moving and won him an Associateship with the Royal Photographic Association.

I worked in the Loseley Dairy for a holiday job in

1975 and it was fantastic to be part of a completely natural, high quality, farm industry. The yoghurt was made in large metal churns, with generous helpings of real fruit stirred in. Staff were allowed to take churn scrapings home for tea – a real privilege as the yoghurt was delicious. My job was to man the machine that put the lids on the pots and to clean the churns, but the top job was making the exquisite ice cream gateaux that were hand decorated with wafer thin chocolate leaves. This was proper skilled work. That summer was incredibly hot and when the weather broke and it rained, the grass shot up and the milk seemed to double in creaminess overnight. Sadly the yoghurt and ice cream business had to be sold off in 1987. It had become bigger and more successful than a cottage industry could cope with and the levels of investment required tipped the balance.

Andy said:

> I couldn't make a living just from dairy farming and producing milk, but I get enormous satisfaction from running the farm. I do like working with livestock and Surrey is good for dairy farming. The clays of the Weald produce excellent grass, though they have a long winter when you have to feed supplementary fodder, and the sandy soils can parch in summer, but have a short winter. The soil has always grown good maize to feed the cattle.
>
> The main problem for dairy farmers in Surrey is that the holdings tend to be fragmented, with parcels of grazing in different places. And non-farming Surrey residents tend to be intolerant of mud and farm smells.

Where big dairy herds are replaced by beef suckler herds, the pressure on the land is suddenly eased. The farmer's workload is eased too. Historical field systems do not need to be changed so the visual impact on the landscape is minimal, but the great purpose-built dairy farm buildings become redundant, providing scope for diversification and vital new income streams. Suckler beef herds are not great wealth creators and farmers need something else as well. The buildings also need a new purpose, as by the time the dairy herd is sold, they are often in a poor state of repair because there was no spare money to invest. They need to pay their way if they are to survive. The supposed wealth of farmers is never quite what it seems, any more than the apparent wealth of Surrey folk in general. I commented to a local pub owner a while back that his clientele must include a lot of millionaires because the cars in the car park were very expensive – fast sports cars, top-of-the-range 4x4s, expensive saloons – but his reply was a snort of derision. They were all tax dodges, being paid for on the never-never, registered in the wife's name, and not the straightforward symbols of success they appeared to be.

Farmers who have 4x4s and tractors and live in big old farms down long tracks can be asset rich and extremely cash poor. If they rent the farm rather than own it, they are not even asset rich and their financial situation can cause profound anxiety and depression. National statistics show that farming is one of the professions most plagued by suicide. A farmer somewhere in the UK will take his own life on average every eleven days because he cannot cope any longer, and there are a number of charities specifically aimed at helping them before they reach crisis point. I was brought on to Surrey Rural Stress Initiative by the Rev Canon Geraint Meirion-Jones, then Rector of Shere, in 2002. He had begun his career as a farmer and understood the pressures, and founded the little charity even before the 2001 and 2007 foot and mouth outbreaks increased farming stress so dramatically. The aim of the charity is to raise awareness of the pressures weighing down on the wider rural community, including the farmers, and publicize the various helplines and advice organizations available.

One of the difficulties facing twenty-first-century farmers is isolation. Sixty years ago farms were large employers. The farmer had high social status because whole families in the local village depended on him for both permanent and seasonal work. But from the 1940s on, farming became increasingly mechanized. Horse teams were replaced by tractors and farming ceased to be a sociable activity. Tony Poulsom surveyed agricultural employment between Guildford and Farnham in the 1950s as a student project and found well over 400 people earning a living from farming. There is not one today.

Farmers can go all day without anyone to talk to and share their worries with, and traditional meeting places such as livestock markets have closed down. When I was a child my mother found me negotiating for a pen full of sheep at the livestock market on what is now the law courts and police station site in Woodbridge Road, Guildford. The market had already been moved out of North Street where it had been during the latter half of the nineteenth century. As Guildford experienced an orgy of redevelopment and expansion that included the new University of Surrey, the market, with its mud, straw and smells, became an anachronism so close to the town centre. In 1969 it was moved out of town to the Slyfield Industrial Estate at Jacob's Well, and closed altogether in 2000.

Diversification

The farm may have been excised from the town, but increasingly the town is moving out to the farm because the great empty dairy complexes have many possibilities. Diversification is bringing people, businesses, children even, back onto the farm. Manor Farm, Wotton, part of the huge Wotton Estate that has been in the Evelyn family for hundreds of years and is home to the Matthews family, took the down to earth approach. Laurence Matthews turned old poultry sheds and other redundant buildings tucked away behind Sheephouse Lane into the Surrey Hills Business Park, creating 25,000sq ft of business units including offices, retail and storage. Tenants include a large horse- and pet-food shop.

The redundant barns at Cross Farm, Shackleford, required more sensitive handling as they are right in the middle of the village, hard up against the road, and are an integral part of a very attractive village-scape. Richard Wyatt, who built the almshouses in Godalming, lived there in 1700, and in 1911 Sir Edgar Horne turned it into a model farm under the guidance of his friend, the architect Edwin Lutyens. His barns were converted into houses in 1996.

In the valley south of the Hog's Back at Seale nestles Shoelands Farm, part of the Hampton Estate. When the Thornton and Biddell families moved out of intensive livestock farming, its 1930s vintage farm buildings, ranged around a large farmyard, fell empty. The stables, granary, malthouse, dairy and milking parlour had also been built as a model farm. Shalford builders Marchant and Cheal restored the mix of brick and stone walls, left the broad welcoming doorways that once accommodated livestock, and converted the buildings into offices. Heating is provided by a wood chip burner fuelled by wood from the estate. This extremely green conversion won a ringing endorsement from the patron of the Area of Outstanding Natural Beauty, Penelope Keith OBE DL.

'The countryside does not take care of itself,' she told the guests at the opening of the offices in May 2006. 'We live in one of the most beautiful parts of the country but to look after that we desperately need farmers and they have been an endangered species for a good wee while now. They need to diversify. Imagine driving to work here. It would be wonderful.'

There are many examples of imaginative farm building conversions but among my favourites are ventures that are literally breathing new life into farms. Rob and Jeanette Walker of Penang Farm in Combe Lane, Chiddingfold, set up Barnkids in a specially converted redundant timber barn in 1996. It is utterly idyllic, a blend of the best modern facilities and play equipment in a safe environment surrounded by a working farm.

Jeanette, a former teacher, saw the potential for the barn to be turned into a nursery for three- to four-year-olds and from there she branched into after-school and holiday clubs. Popular request saw the addition of the Chicken Run, a building put up on the old chicken house site, for eighteen-month to three-year-olds. The name often takes some explaining, especially to prospective parents.

The staff take the children through the fields and into the woods, and they can see the sheep. Jeanette borrows

▲ The North Downs AONB between Puttenham and Seale, at Shoelands Farm

orphan lambs and the older children feed and look after them, while the younger ones can stroke them. Jeanette said:

> We love showing the children how food grows. We have a garden and the children grow beans and potatoes and they harvest the crops and eat them. We have a new day-care unit and we serve locally grown organic food every evening. The children adore watching Rob on his tractor picking up logs. We are getting a lot of people moving out of London and they get a better idea of the countryside here.

When Tony Isaac and his son Stephen sold their Guernsey and Friesian dairy herds in West Horsley, they knew they would have to diversify. For Stephen, a young married man with a very young family, who had been brought up as a traditional cattle farmer, it took a real leap of imagination to see where to go from there. In the theatre, they say one should never work with children or animals but Stephen has happily embraced both. 'We went looking for a full day-care nursery and we simply couldn't find anything local at all. It was all geared to term times and a little bell went in my head: if we couldn't find it ourselves, we could do it ourselves,' he said. They met a Norland-trained Montessori teacher through friends at a party who was interested in setting up a day-care nursery, and buoyed by her professionalism and enthusiasm, Stephen began making concrete plans.

Manor Farm had been a typical dairy unit. It had a slurry pit and cow sheds, lots of mud and barns, so the first challenge was to get planning permission for change of use. Evidence of genuine local need won the day and Footprints Montessori Day Nursery opened in 2005. 'We started with our son Ben and two babies,' said Stephen. 'But we can take up to fifty. The nursery is built on the site of the calf-rearing shed and the car park was the old slurry pit. The three- to five-year-olds room is the old beef building and the baby unit is in the Victorian barn that we absorbed into the nursery.'

The babies and toddlers have a completely enclosed grass courtyard to play in and safety has been built into every aspect of the nursery, yet at the same time, the children can go out and play on the farm. Mesh fencing enables them to say hello to the animals safely and there are special paths to keep children and vehicles apart. Like most Surrey farms now, Manor Farm is geared to environmental conservation and wildlife so just outside the nursery is Ben's Wood, a new mixed English woodland designed for public access all year round. It has pram paths too so that all the youngsters in the nursery can go for walks.

Stephen's new community venture is the conversion of another empty barn into a children's teaching pool for use by local schools: diversification need not always mean multi-million pound barn conversion houses.

The Environmental Movement

The poet John Keats's line 'The sedge is wither'd from the lake and no birds sing' is a powerful evocation of impending catastrophe. It taps into the deep-rooted human fear of something going irrevocably wrong with nature. Early man, lacking scientific explanations, focused this fear on the possibility of the sun failing to come up each morning. These days our knowledge of science does us no favours either. Our fears are not lulled by hard facts, they are fuelled rather by evidence of climate change and global warming. That idea of silence, the lack of birdsong, was taken up by natural history writer Rachel Carson in 1962, in her extraordinarily influential book, *Silent Spring*. Her warning that the post-war, gung-ho use of chemical pesticides, fungicides and herbicides was going to end up destroying the whole of nature, kick-started the entire environmental movement that is still shaping our countryside policy. Global warming is only reinforcing its importance.

The impact on the Surrey Hills landscape is subtle. Over the last forty years attitudes have changed most dramatically. What you see is less obvious and the most visible changes are driven more by EU policy than by consideration for nature – take the ugly acres of weed and neglect created by set-aside. Environmental policies are also having a profound effect on the countryside. Whether driven by belief in the new philosophy or by the pursuit of those elusive grants, most Surrey farmers have entered some kind of Countryside Stewardship programme over the last decade, which encourages low-chemical-input farming methods and an increase in wildlife habitat. Helped by organizations such as the Surrey and Hampshire Farming and Wildlife Advisory Group (FWAG), they work on projects such as hedge-laying, pond restoration, woodland coppicing and the creation of broad field margins left uncropped, but seeded with grass and wildflower mixtures, and managed for wildlife diversity.

Manor Farm on the Wotton Estate has been part of the Countryside Stewardship Scheme since 1999, with six different packages of environmental and conservation measures across the various farm holdings, all helping to encourage diversity of flora and fauna. Farmers Laurence and Paula Matthews have also signed up to the new Higher Level Stewardship Scheme. Manor Farm stretches from the scarp slope of the North Downs south into the Greensand Hills, incorporating chalk grassland, arable and woodland. Projects include the re-stocking of an English orchard, coppicing, ponds, field margins and returning arable land to natural grassland. Stubble is left to provide a habitat for ground nesting birds and crop spraying is restricted.

A few years ago I spent a day with a team of student hedgelayers as they worked their way down a length of overgrown hawthorn on Bert Broom's land close to Manor Farm, at Westcott. Bert is a rare commodity in Surrey – a young farmer on a family farm – but he supplements his farm income with a career in radio. A newly laid hedge is simply stunning but changes in the way grants are paid mean the incentive to adopt this practice may disappear. Bert Broom and Laurence Matthews have been laying their hedges for years now, and they have one of the best pockets of quality hedging in the whole county. In 2012, when Bert's ten-year Countryside Stewardship programme is completed, he will have 1½ miles of it, every foot painstakingly hand-crafted by members of the Surrey Hedgelaying Group and the South of England Hedgelaying Society.

The team happily learning their craft on Bert's thorn bushes that January day included retired professionals, bankers, gardeners, tree surgeons, men and women, young and old, all armed with a mix of traditional billhooks and modern chainsaws. Within just a few hours, the straggly 12ft trees had been tamed and turned into a work of art: laid, staked, clipped and woven. The craft probably dates back around 300 years to the enclosure movement. Between 1760 and 1830 Parliament passed the deeply unpopular Enclosure Acts which divided up common land and required landowners to fence their lands. Thorn bushes were the original barbed wire and Leicestershire farmers developed the technique of angling stems to make hedges completely stockproof. The technique spread throughout England, wherever the soil was deep enough for hawthorn. The alternative was the dry-stone wall.

Hedging and ditching were traditional winter jobs. Bert told me:

> Up until the 1940s we had two men doing it, and a lot of our hedges have not been touched since then. Hedges that were windward also took a hammering in the 1960s, 1970s and 1980s from chemical spray drift but where those hedges have been laid, they really bounce back. We had intentionally grown some high to enhance bird habitat and we discovered they were perfect for laying and off we went. We have 50 acres of neglected coppice that we are renovating off our own bat.

I love the vocabulary of ancient crafts. A pleacher is the name given to the stem once it has been cut and bent over. The twigs are brush or beaver, the binding ethering or heathering. The base of a stem is called a stub, a stool, a stovel, stoving or stobbing. A cant is a length of hedge marked out or an area of coppice, often delineated by a ditch. The distance between stakes is measured by the length of a man's arm from elbow to finger tip.

The secret of hedgelaying is to slice large, shallow wedges out of the stems just above ground level so that just the outer, sap-bearing layer is left intact. The stem is then flexed over, pointing up the slope if the hedge is on a hill. It looks quite brutal but is specifically designed to enable the living stems to create new shoots. Hawthorn is preferred, but surprisingly oak is also very tolerant of being laid. You can see quite a bit of laid hedging, some now neglected, some quite recent, as you drive along the A25 between Shere and Dorking.

Going around the Surrey Hills one might notice the characteristic steep angled stems of a laid hedge, and also the greens, mauves and yellows of the wildflower-rich field margins showing up against the solid gold of ripening crops. What takes longer to achieve is the conversion of overworked land back to natural pasture. Between Shere Heath and Pitch Hill there used to be several intensive horticultural businesses producing vegetables. The soil is very sandy and over the years the erosion was dramatic. Tons of soil, laced with chemical fertilizer and pesticide, would be washed into the Lawbrook valley. When the land was ploughed and it rained, 4ft deep gullies like miniature desert wadis would appear overnight, scoured out by rushing water. There were no rabbits – some would say a good thing – and no butterflies, though badgers and foxes abounded.

When falling prices drove the vegetable growers out of business, the land was returned to grass, some of it under Soil Association organic guidelines, and it has taken years to produce a self-sustaining, healthy greensward for sheep and cattle. Butterflies, bees and wildflowers have been slow to return; somewhat predictably, rabbits much faster.

Managing the 'Wild' Landscape

Some of the most precious habitats of the Surrey Hills are not strictly farmland *per se*: the top of the chalk downs and the sandy heaths, each with their own specific species of flora and fauna, are particularly vulnerable unless carefully maintained. They are not always enclosed and often have public access, and their importance as rare, open, wild habitat ironically depends on constant human intervention to prevent encroachment by scrub, trees, bracken, and even the 'Surrey weed', the naturalized rhododendron.

Until the mid-twentieth century people still exercised ancient commoners' rights on heathland. The main ones were: pasture – the right to turn stock on to the common to graze; pannage – the right to let pigs enter a wood to eat the acorns or beech mast; and estovers – the right to take wood or bracken for fuel, animal litter or for repairing fences or buildings. When I was a child, cattle from Hornhatch Farm in Chilworth were occasionally allowed to graze the unfenced commons.

National Trust and Surrey Wildlife Trust countryside rangers have experimented with a number of different breeds of grazing animals to see which have the most beneficial effects on the land and its smaller inhabitants – not the pampered commercial varieties that produce quick meat for the supermarket, but ancient, often rare breeds known for their hardiness. They are slow to fatten, so discarded by modern farmers. Just as well then that a few visionary souls took the trouble to preserve the bloodlines.

It is not only when disasters like foot and mouth happen that the importance of a diverse gene pool suddenly becomes obvious. The National Trust manages much of the North Downs and huge areas of heath at Hindhead and its rangers have been experimenting to find the best browsers of scrub and grazers of invasive coarse grass. It was a tall order. They need to be fully winter hardy, tolerant of steep hills, and dog-proof. Ideally they should not have a taste for rare wildflowers, be aggressive to walkers or be difficult to handle. Rare breeds come closest. A combination of belted Galloway, Dexter and Highland cattle, Exmoor ponies, Soay and black Welsh mountain sheep, as well as a local herd of goats worked well, but the sheer numbers of cattle needed to keep the downs cropped and the demands of animal husbandry has led to a pioneering arrangement with Wotton farmer Lawrence Matthews; his commercial herd, as well as some rare-breed belted Galloways, will graze a vast area of the downs from Dorking to Albury under a huge Higher Level Stewardship scheme. A role as a conservation grazer could be the salvation of the Exmoor pony, the oldest of our native breeds, which is known to have roamed England in the Bronze Age. The upper slopes of Denbies Hillside at Westcott, where grass is poorest, is grazed by a small herd of semi-feral stocky Exmoors. They did a professional job, eating scrub and grass and leaving the flowers. It is a Site of Special Scientific Interest (SSSI) with rare butterflies like the Adonis blue, whose breeding sites are small and isolated

from each other. The ponies graze round the orchids and the vetch, which the butterflies live on.

Former head warden John Cranham appreciated that their selective grazing, which included the invasive newcomer, the coarse tor grass (*brachypodium*), provided a variety of habitats for insects and other wildlife. Lower slopes are being turned back into chalk grassland by Dexter cattle from Badger's Farm at Effingham. National Trust volunteers have helped the restoration process by collecting hay from established meadows and raking it across the fields to seed them. They were rewarded with a display of bee, pyramidal, common spotted and twayside orchids and cowslips making new homes amongst the grass.

At Box Hill and Headley Heath, Dartford warblers and woodlarks have returned to the woods and acid heathland as a result of grazing by belted Galloway and Highland cattle and linnets are on the increase. Andy Wright, National Trust Head Warden for North Downs East explained that the cowslip derives its name from its habit of setting seed and growing in the muddy scrape where a cow has slipped on the chalk. Just by walking about on the hills, cattle make little pockets in the soil with their hooves, where seeds can grow. Andy has kept belted Galloways on Colley Hill at Reigate since 2001, along with a flock of not-so-rare but very tough black-faced sheep. His favourites are the 'belties', stocky furry black cattle with a broad white cummerbund round their middles that originate in the exposed uplands of south-west Scotland and so are well suited to rough, steep grazing. They have a double coat to protect them from the elements, a long-haired outer layer which sheds the rain and snow and a soft undercoat for warmth. Chalk grassland has poor nutritional value but these cattle thrive, not being fussy but eating everything. They chomp their way through tree seedlings and the tough, tall grasses that would otherwise flop over, create a matted thatch and choke the more delicate species.

Headley Heath and Gibbet Hill at Hindhead also have herds of statuesque Highland cattle. It is as well not to get too close on account of their magnificent pointed horns, but like the 'belties' they have gentle natures. The situation is particularly sensitive on sites like Box Hill, where the very specialized habitat hosts some endangered species. The man and musk orchids, the small blue butterfly and the straw belle moth are only just hanging on thanks to conservation grazing of the grasses.

The heaths also need managing in order to protect areas of heather and maintain habitats for threatened species like the sand lizard. This maintenance is done by humans because sites like Blackheath or Frensham Ponds would be impossible to graze now, owing to the sheer numbers of people, dogs and horses and the proximity of roads, so they cannot be managed 'naturally'. One can therefore see signs that birch and bracken have been sprayed and that millions of baby fir trees have been pulled up by the roots, or even that a grove of stately pine trees has been

Peter Haynes

◀ Exmoor ponies are among the oldest breeds of pony in the world and can survive extremely tough conditions. They are ideal for conservation grazing and are used to keep scrub at bay on the North Downs at Ranmore

▶ Adonis blue: chalk downland butterfly

clear-felled. This is not the Amazon rainforest. The forests and heaths of Surrey have to be managed in the interests of good woodland practice and biodiversity.

The Most Wooded County in England

The management of Surrey's woodland has been rising rapidly up the priority ladder thanks to the increasing interest in sustainable fuel sources. In Surrey, wood is very sustainable provided our climate continues to deliver a good amount of rain every year. The management of woodland, however, has fluctuated wildly over the centuries, ranging from rapacious consumption to near-terminal neglect. The Romans and the Tudors were very demanding. They needed huge quantities of wood to power their iron-making industries and right up until the twentieth century there was an incentive to manage and conserve woodland as a source of domestic and industrial fuel and of building materials. London was greedy for wood and Surrey could provide it. The River Wey was only the second river to be made navigable in the whole of the UK, its canal sections built in the seventeenth century during the Commonwealth Parliament, more than 100 years before the great era of canal building in the late eighteenth and early nineteenth centuries. It was the brainchild of Sir Richard Weston of Sutton Palace, and cost a fortune at £16,000 as over half the distance from Guildford to the Thames consists of artificial cuts, but it finally opened in 1651. It was successful, made money after a rocky start and much talk of fraud and scams, and was extended to Godalming in 1763.

▼ Highland cattle are hardy, docile grazers used to maintain plant and habitat biodiversity both in the River Mole floodmeadows and on the North Downs

Records for 1664 have details of 14,000 horse-drawn barges of timber using the navigation, as well as corn, flour, coal, chalk, bark for tanning, rags for paper-making, barrel-hoops and other ironwork, sugar and groceries, and until after the First World War, even gunpowder from the powdermills at Chilworth.

The Wealden woodland was also extensively used to create charcoal until the seventeenth century, when James I banned charcoal burning out of concern that there would not be enough timber left to build ships for the navy. Charcoal was one of the prime fuels driving local manufacturing, and whole industries, such as glass-making at Chiddingfold and Alfold, died out when coal replaced wood as the new industrial fuel. Glassmaking in Alfold ended in 1618. According to local historian Pat Green, of the Balchin Family Society of Alfold, the worn slab of marble in Alfold churchyard by the war memorial is believed to cover the grave of Jean Carre, one of the last of the French glassmakers, who was buried in 1572. He introduced glassmaking from Lorraine into Surrey in 1567 and traces of old glass can still be found in Sidney Woods.

The management of woodland went hand in hand with agriculture. Pigs feasted on acorns and beech mast, and farmers and landowners pollarded trees at around 8–10ft high, enabling cattle to graze beneath the canopy without damaging the regrowth, which was then harvested for fuel and building materials. These ancient pollarded trees, often oaks, can still be found in Surrey, and although their crowns have been neglected for years, their shapes are clearly recognizable.

This system was known as pasture wood and the proper name Pasture Wood survives near Abinger. These grazed woods were open, in contrast to the enclosed woods, which were protected from livestock. A lot of the surviving old woods were originally managed as hazel coppices. The trees were cut to ground level in a seven-year rotation, producing crops of hazel for use in hurdle-making and fencing. Neglected coppices are identifiable by the way all the trees appear to have multiple stems growing from single stools. It is quite possible to restore coppices, and apart from the crops of hazel wands, the reward on clay and loam soils is a carpet of primroses, and on more sandy soil, bluebells in Spring. Research by landscape archaeologist Dr Nicola Bannister on the cultural heritage of Surrey woodlands shows that whereas

▼ Oaks were commonly pollarded (their leading shoot cut and limbs regularly reduced) so that the branches could be harvested for timber and fuel, while cattle were able to graze below. Pollarded oaks that are around 400 years old can be seen in parkland, such as Netley at Gomshall

around 40 per cent of the county is now covered by trees, only 12 per cent is actually ancient woodland. Everywhere you look are traces of abandoned managed woods – derelict choked coppices that have not been managed for decades and have become high forest. Much of the woodland of Surrey is actually self-sown, neglected scrub that has grown up unchecked and gradually engulfed formerly open land. Plantations, even mature commercial conifer plantations, have been allowed to become suffocated and overgrown. Some Surrey pine woods are so dark and menacing that all they need is a Victorian street lamp to conjure up images of Narnia. The pine plantations take advantage of the sandy soil of Blackheath, Hurtwood, Winterfold, Leith Hill and the Elstead area. They self-seed so readily that recently cleared areas quickly take on the appearance of a tree nursery and the battle to reinstate heather instead of trees is extremely time-consuming and often involves working parties of volunteers.

Ernest Shepard, who illustrated the Winnie the Pooh books, lived in Shamley Green and as a child I always imagined Eeyore mooching about among the dark and gloomy pine woods at Farley Heath. I was equally convinced the river meandering beneath rustic bridges through the watermeadows behind Lords Hill in Shamley Green was where Christopher Robin played pooh sticks.

Up on the chalk downs, old Victorian plantations survive despite the ravages of storms like that of 1987, which left an extraordinary trail of havoc, particularly in the beech woods. The shallow, spreading beech roots wrenched vast roundels of chalk from the ground as the trees fell and for years they stood out like great white tombstones against the dark of the forest. Box Hill and Mickleham are unusual in being colonized by box and yew, though Dr Bannister believes they are the remnants of much larger forests.

It is notable that one of the first English people known to have written about woodland management was the seventeeth-century diarist John Evelyn, who lived at Wotton, between the North Downs and the slopes of Leith Hill. He published *Sylva; or a Discourse on Forest Trees and the Propagation of Timber* in 1664, advocating the replanting of trees to replace the timber being plundered to fuel the glass and iron industries, not to mention his own family's business – gunpowder – which was manufactured in the Tillingbourne valley. He claimed to have influenced fellow landowners to plant millions of trees, and from his scientific observations was able to note how the removal of brushwood for the Tillingbourne industries improved bio-diversity in the forests.

There has to be a powerful motive to manage woodland, whether industrial or financial, and the neglect of the twentieth century is largely down to money. If there is no attractive financial return, there is no incentive either to plant or to harvest timber. Plantations go in only when grants are available and, coppice aside, timber is a very slow crop with a twenty- to thirty-year wait for maturity. It is only in the last few years that people in the

▼ John Evelyn of Wotton, author of the treatise on forestry: *Sylva, or a Discourse on Forest Trees and the Propagation of Timber in His Majesties Dominions*

Surrey History Centre

UK have started to look at wood as a sustainable fuel with full green credentials.

Scandinavia and Germany are streets ahead of us with established technology for burning chipped and pelleted wood, but Surrey is starting to catch up. In 2005, the Surrey Hills Wood Fuel Group was set up with support from DEFRA under its Bio-energy Infrastructure Scheme. The partnership's goal was to create a market for wood for chipping, with the wood producers sharing resources to enable cost-effective processing of wood to fuel local heat-and-power projects. The partnership included the energy charity the Energy Centre for Sustainable Communities (ECSC), local authorities in the Surrey Hills AONB area, Surrey Wildlife Trust, local farmers and forestry contractors. The project won support from Surrey Hills AONB, the South East England Development Agency (SEEDA) and Guildford Environmental Forum.

Wood chip and pellets sounded radical in 2005, but the sustainability of fossil fuels was also taking a knock, and the arguments for harnessing a renewable local resource were starting to look very attractive. The advantages include the fact that wood fuel is carbon neutral, likely to remain cheaper than gas or oil, can produce heat and hot water and, most importantly, need not run out. Managing woodland to produce wood chip helps with nature conservation and boosts the rural economy with jobs. It also provides a sustainable use for wood waste produced by tree surgeons and landscape maintenance contractors. Ben Oubridge, who launched the wood-fuel group, called it a 'chicken and egg situation. We need people to have the confidence to put boilers and stoves in, so we can supply the fuel and then we can start to raise the quality and value of the woodland. We just need to find the local end users so we can supply them with heat.'

The Surrey Hills AONB Partnership used its Sustainable Development Fund to support new rural wood-based businesses. Consultant woodland manager Laurence Crow from Capel won a grant to install a kiln for drying timber. Fuelled by wood waste, it artificially seasons logs to create a clean, efficient fuel that can be used quickly in a variety of different ways, as 'eco logs', chips or pellets. This is real green technology. Drying the wood reduces the emissions when it is burnt, which means less carbon dioxide going into the atmosphere. It makes it more efficient, so its heat conversion is better and it creates a market for wood that is not high-grade construction or cabinet-making timber – and that accounts for almost all of Surrey's woods. A dominant species is the hornbeam, a wood with a very high calorific value that was traditionally used for iron smelting.

Cutting wood for fuel, either by felling and replanting or by coppicing and waiting for regrowth, is good for the environment, because if managed intelligently, trees can be net consumers of carbon dioxide or at least carbon-neutral. Growing trees absorb carbon dioxide, and if they are harvested and burnt cleanly, the planet will benefit.

The Hampton Estate in Seale caught on to the idea of home-grown fuel very quickly. As we have seen, the Thornton family converted all the redundant farm buildings at Shoelands Farm into an award-winning set of office suites heated exclusively by timber from the estate. The giant wood-burning unit is essentially a district heating system that provides heat not just for the new office complex but also for two farmhouses and several cottages nearby. Called a sustainable biomass heating system, it is a fine example of British-made green technology from Talbotts Ltd in Stafford, the leading UK biofuel and waste-to-energy specialists. The wood chips are fed by auger into a combustion module, which generates lower emissions than a domestic gas boiler. It is a revolutionary system for a small business park, although it has been successfully pioneered for hotels and estates, and the result is a sustainable energy source plus a market for estate timber. Everyone wins, especially the environment. The conversion won the South East regional award, celebrating the centenary of the Country Land and Business Association.

'This is the first time a wood-burning central heating system has been used for a commercial office complex,' said Bill Biddell, the Estate Manager. 'Normally people developing offices aim to sell on as soon as possible.

We are in it for the long haul. We are running it. The heating system gives us a market for our wood. We can start harvesting our trees and even supply other people with wood chips.'

The Hampton Estate has 850 acres of award-winning woodland, and it is one of the few estates to have produced a twenty-year forestry plan that includes public access, felling and thinning programmes, and management of biodiversity and habitat. The estate still practises coppicing, and the wood produced in this way is used for fencing. Businesses that relocate to Shoelands are buying into a whole philosophy of rural sustainability and environmental conservation, so much so that the offices were officially launched by the patron of the Surrey Hills AONB, Penelope Keith OBE DL. She was full of praise for the way the buildings had been given a future tied in to the management of the estate's woodland.

Laurence Crow sees Surrey's woodlands enjoying a twenty-first-century renaissance, enhancing the AONB with vistas of bluebells and primroses, neat crowns and luxuriant growth, hedges and wildlife – genuine working woodlands. 'Surrey's woodland is suffering from benign neglect,' he said, 'but if you burn wood that has been harvested and dried in a modern stove, then more trees will be grown and you then get more growth and more carbon dioxide is absorbed. Trees are definitely good.'

Another woodland project to attract sustainable development funding is Norbury Park Wood Products, based at a Surrey Wildlife Trust sawmill near Mickleham, which specializes in manufacturing outdoor furniture. Surrey Wildlife Trust manages many of the woods in Norbury

▼ Bluebells thrive on forest floors where the trees have been thinned to allow winter light

Park to provide timber. Some trees are coppiced for fence poles and charcoal-making, and where trees are felled, the trust replants with trees native to chalk such as beech, yew, ash and cherry. The Norbury sawmill uses its waste to power another Talbot boiler which heats its wood workshop. This system is automatically fed and can take shavings, chips and sawdust for fuel. This piece of logical self sufficiency could be a lifesaver for Surrey sawmills, as across the UK around 40 per cent of mills have closed down. Only in Northern Ireland, where tons of sawmill waste are purchased by a local wood-pelleting factory, have all the mills survived.

According to James Little, who co-ordinates the Surrey Hills Wood Fuel Group, Surrey is buzzing with interest in sustainable energy. The two main types of wood fuel – chip and pellet – are both poised for major production in the Surrey Hills, wood chip on the North Downs at Shere and pellets in the woods at Tilford. LC Energy, run by Mark Lebus, launched in 2007 with the aim of making Surrey the largest provider of alternative sustainable energy in the South-east. The Forestry Commission is a key partner, and it calculates that Surrey could supply more than 500,000 tons of timber a year to be converted into wood chips to fuel boilers. The proviso here is that woodland owners take advantage of the commercial opportunity by managing their woods to supply the chipper, rather than neglecting them. At present only about 50 per cent of the woods are managed, so there is massive scope for increasing supply.

The chipper is based at Scotland Farm, next to the Surrey Hills Brewery, on the Duke of Northumberland's Albury Estate and it will process timber from within a 10-mile radius. Mark Lebus reckons that this catchment alone would produce enough sustainable fuel to heat 2,500 care homes or 1,000 large schools. In its first year it supplied a primary school in Richmond, a care home in Bramley and a new housing development in Chobham. It now supplies Stansted Airport.

Mike and Oliver Barnsley of Long Life Timber at Tilford are working on the manufacture of wood pellets. According to James Little, there is substantial interest in both chips and pellets, many of the inquiries coming from London. Southwark Council plans to heat its new offices with pellets, and a lot of new buildings specify sustainable fuel. Surrey Hills district councils are all keeping tabs on developments and with the cost of energy, going over to wood could make sound financial as well as environmental sense. When you think of all the wood ravaged from roadside trees during the winter hedge-mangling season, there must be a good supply of wood waste just asking to be turned into something useful too. Surrey is rightly proud of its wooded nature but that pride would be even better justified if its trees were healthy, loved and productive.

If only it were that simple. Fuzzy logic and misplaced sentiment mean that many people prefer to see neglect: wild woods, tangled undergrowth, romantic decay. They recall slogans such as 'Plant a tree in '73, plant some more in '74', worry about the loss of the rainforests and associate any tree felling with rape of the countryside. This makes it very difficult for landowners to manage woodland, particularly where it is accessible to the public. The Hurtwood is a classic example. There was considerable opposition to the creation of fire breaks, to the opening up of the landscape on Holmbury Hillfort and to the felling of mature conifers in this expertly managed tract of countryside dedicated to the public for air and exercise. It comes down to a lack of understanding of the broad principle that the countryside in Surrey is not 'natural' or wild, but needs managing.

The Holloways and Drove Roads

One of the most beautiful features in the woodland of the Surrey Hills is entirely man- and animal-made. The holloways running north–south through the sandy hills are really magical on a sunny day. Created by the hooves of herds and flocks moving from summer to winter pasture and by the trains of smugglers' pack ponies, these ancient tracks and drove roads are kept open now by thousands of walkers, horse-riders and mountain-bikers. Some of the best are to be found around Leith Hill, characterized by near vertical sandy banks grasped by a tangle of knotted tree root fingers, the trunks and branches arching over the track to provide a green vaulted roof. It does not matter what the season, these deeply sunken lanes are always stunning – thick snow dramatic, the warm sage green of branches in early spring full of expectation, summer throwing its dappled sunlight through the near black of the leafy tunnels and achingly beautiful drifts of red-gold autumn leaves.

These are the short-haul livestock routes. The long-haul drove roads took animals hundreds of miles to market, and the main livestock highway across Surrey followed the line of the downs. The sense of keeping traffic to high ground becomes very clear when one explores old eighteenth-century roads like the one from Wonersh to Cranleigh. This is now just a bridleway through Lord's Hill as the lord of the manor rerouted the road round the edge of his new deer park. The soil is clay, and in winter the old road would have been an impassable quagmire.

Names like The Drift and Halfpenny Lane are often associated with drove roads. Halfpenny refers to the cost of overnight grazing for each head of cattle or sheep in the drove. The Drift occurs in Horsley were you can still see the line of old drove roads through the village, and there is a Halfpenny Lane just off the downs on the edge of the Guildford Gap.

Hindhead and the Punch Bowl

Every so often, the transport lobby rears its head and swathes of countryside are scooped up, pushed about, resculpted and buried under asphalt to create new

motorways. The M25 sliced its way across the North Downs at Reigate in an eleven-year project from 1975 to 1986 costing £909 million. But set to beat that is the Hindhead Tunnel, one of the largest and most expensive road projects in Europe.

The A3 historically crossed the Greensand Hills at Hindhead on the way from London to Portsmouth docks, a difficult and dangerous mountain pass because of the terrain and the lawless natives, and its exact route has altered several times over the centuries to make the going a bit easier. The original route went up Gibbet Hill, named for the gibbet at the top, where criminals were hanged and their tarred bodies left to rot in an iron cage as a ghastly warning to anyone tempted by a life of crime. The advent of the motor car dictated a lower traverse of the hill but, as generations of transport engineers have discovered, when you have Gibbet Hill on one side and the Devil's Punch Bowl on the other, there is really not much room to manoeuvre. Beautiful protected landscape enjoyed by thousands of people was cut brutally in two by a traffic jam in a bottleneck and crossing by horse or bicycle was not for the fainthearted.

The Hindhead crossroads traffic lights have been a horrible anomaly in an otherwise modern highway. Jams were a daily occurrence, particularly when convoys of continental container lorries converged on the junction. The need for a bypass round Winchester, which just happened to involve carving a multi-lane groove through another treasured chalk landscape at Twyford Down, sparked the roads protest movement of the 1990s, and there was a great deal of opposition to proposed solutions for Hindhead that involved similar landscape vandalism. The livid white scar at Twyford Gap is still a constant reminder of a worst-case scenario. A tunnel always seemed the sensible solution – sending long-haul traffic inside the hill and spewing it out the other side, to continue its motorway-style journey unimpeded.

The current scheme was first mooted in 1993 and eventually, after years of protests and inquiries, politics and pressure, the tunnel is finally being built. There is an irony about the fact that the final spur to action was quite likely the sudden demands of the 2012 Olympic Games: its water sports scheduled for the south coast. And the tunnel's cost? The Highways Agency estimated £371 million. Drilling began in early February 2008 with Transport Secretary Ruth Kelly ceremonially helping to start up the boring machine. The project creates a new 4-mile dual carriageway plus additional underpasses to the south and north, and following the precedent of Twyford Down, with the old road unceremoniously ripped up.

Highways Agency

◀ A typical sunken lane carved out of the sandstone over the centuries at Abinger

▶ This is the massive scar created at the start of the Hindhead Tunnel project. The photograph shows the view of the North Portal taken in 2007

Highways Agency

▲ This is an artist's impression of what the North Portal of Hindhead Tunnel will look like

The Highways Agency uses the Global Positioning System (GPS) to plot the course of the two ends of the tunnel and make sure that they end up meeting in the middle. It is essentially the same system used by cars' satellite navigation, but the Highways Agency is confident that it is rather more accurate. The GPS receivers concentrate on the tunnel survey stations for an hour at a time and, when the data is processed, it gives accuracy down to a centimetre – global positioning for cars is within 5–10 yards. After all the drama, the delays and the general frustrations, the tunnel project is now a tourist attraction in its own right, with a visitor centre and viewing platform.

Failing south coast-towns may see it differently, as an upgraded A3 is their lifeblood for regeneration, but this project is really a £371m landscape conservation scheme bringing incalculable benefit to the Surrey Hills AONB. For the tunnel and the closure of the old A3 enable the two sides of this fabulous piece of 'little Switzerland' to be reunited, a car-free zone accessible safely to walkers, horse-riders, cyclists, Highland cattle, butterflies, deer and all the rest of the region's flora and fauna. The prospect is glorious. The countryside emerges the clear winner.

Freeing the Devil's Punch Bowl from traffic will make a tremendous difference. The National Trust cites a local legend that says the Devil lived on three small hills near Churt and provoked Thor, the god of thunder, who lived at Thursley (Thor's Leigh) by jumping from hill to hill. Thor retaliated with a few lightning bolts and the Devil scooped up a handful of earth from the heath and threw it at him. The depression he made is the punch bowl. The more prosaic truth is that this spectacular landscape feature was not created by the Devil, or even by a meteorite, bomb-blast or quarrying. It was the unbelievably powerful, slow, steady seeping of water from springs that shaped the bowl, making it the largest spring-made

Highways Agency

▲ Hindhead Common was highway territory, but thanks to the new A3 tunnel it will be one vast tract of stunning countryside with full public access

feature in the whole of the UK. This process of erosion is still in progress around the springs at the bottom.

The steep wooded hills, the second highest in the county, are a watershed in the climate of the south of England. As well as snow – far more than in the rest of Surrey – and dramatic clouds, the area attracts dangerously swirling mist, and it may have acquired its name from the way the mist gets trapped in the bowl and then flows over its rim, as if it is a pot boiling over.

When not heavy with fog, the air on the hills is clean and fresh, and it is this healthy environment that inspired people to follow the railway and come and settle at Hindhead in the nineteenth century, turning it into a fashionable rural idyll for wealthy intellectuals and artists. The National Trust actually started life in the countryside around Haslemere and Hindhead, as is described in Chapter 3. Since then the area has been designated a SSSI for its flora and fauna, and it is also a Special Protection Area under the EU Directive on the Conservation of Wild Birds. When the decision was taken to reunite the two sides of the common, the National Trust, the Surrey Hills AONB Partnership, the Highways Agency, English Nature, the Countryside Agency, the SEEDA, Surrey County Council, Waverley Borough Council and Haslemere Town Council all got together to form the Hindhead Together Partnership with the aim of optimizing the community, economic, landscape and ecological benefits to be gained from such a rare opportunity to restore rare lowland heath. The Director General of the National Trust, Fiona Reynolds, who visited Hindhead in 2006 to celebrate the centenary of the purchase of the Commons by the Trust, commented on the significance of the restoration on a European level. Praise indeed.

History

Mammoth and woolly rhinoceros, wild boar and wild ox, these wild beasts – all extinct now except for the boars which are making a comeback – were dangerous enough to keep early settlers hugging the high ground, just venturing into the dense Forest of Anderida on hunting forays. Clues to the lifestyles and the numbers of these hunter-gatherers are few and far between. A large pit with post holes and hearths is all that remains of Mesolithic huts in Abinger and Farnham, built around 5000 BC. Badshot Lea had, until 1936, a Neolithic long barrow dating from *c.* 3000 BC and there are the remains of flint workings at East and West Horsley and Redhill, and a long barrow at Newlands Corner. Bronze Age burial mounds dating from 2500 – 70 BC are visible at Box Hill, and there are tumuli on Thursley and Frensham Commons and at Reigate. However there is nothing to compare with Stonehenge, or the Avebury Rings.

The first substantial evidence of our Surrey ancestors comes with the organized labour of the Iron Age, when huge earthworks were created on strategic vantage points by people who had probably migrated from northern France and the Low Countries. The forts at Anstiebury, Holmbury, Hascombe at Dry Hill, Lingfield, may have been for defence, or used as stockades for livestock and centres for communities. There is also a prehistoric fortification on White Hill at Blechingley on the crest of the chalk downs, 770ft above the sea, and there may have been a fort on the top of Hydon Ball near Hascombe. Local historian and writer Eric Parker was sure there was one there because of the deep field banks surrounding the hill, but it has not been excavated.

The Roman Occupation

The local people would certainly have retreated to the hillforts for safety at the time of the Roman invasion in the first century AD, when Caesar took his force through the North Downs at Godstone and Dorking. It was he who built a Roman road north-south through the otherwise impenetrable Wealden forest. Stane Street linked the old Thames crossing at Southwark with Chichester, passing by Langley Vale on the Epsom Downs, running through the Roman station at Dorking to South Holmwood and on to Pulborough – a line used now by the A29. It passed through Ewell, Dorking and Ockley. Parts of the A29 and bridlepaths close to Ashtead and across the Mickleham Downs near Box Hill still follow its route. Originally built to enable the Roman army to move at speed around the newly conquered territory, it quickly developed into an important trade route. A branch road led off from Stane Street at Rowhook and crossed over Winterfold, past the villa at Rapsley, on its way to the temple at Farley Green. Other smaller Roman roads joined Stane Street, such as the road from the villa and brick and tile works at Ashtead. So when Saxons and Danes were rampaging across the country a few centuries later, they were able to take advantage of a very basic network of usable roads. There is evidence to show that another Roman road ran alongside the Hog's Back from Guildford to Farnham, probably close to the Romano-British temples at Wanborough, but archaeologists are still trying to establish its exact route.

F.E. Green, writing of his delightful ramble round the Surrey Hills in 1915, described the farming that developed under the Romans: 'Those long furrows which were the beginnings of the three-field system and the foundation of the manor, which, coming under the protection of some fighting lord or thane, has lasted so long in the history of our land. It was the slopes of the downs on which were scored the first birthmarks of English agriculture.'

Green takes a long view from a democratic perspective, and one suspects that his green idyll, his Surrey golden age, was not the centuries of agricultural prosperity for rich gentry, when country labourers starved, but an earlier age when families enjoyed security under a local lord. It is a romantic idea easily dispelled by thoughts of dirt, disease, slavery and early death, but the feudal pact between the people and the lord did require an element of responsibility and obligation on both sides, and the old feudal manors have survived remarkably intact down the centuries along the Tillingbourne valley. I have always believed that the estates at Albury, Shere, Abinger and Wotton started life as Roman farmsteads, and my hope is that archaeological excavations will eventually substantiate my theory. There is certainly a villa at Abinger, as well as at Ashtead, Ewhurst and Walton, and the fact that so many village churches – St Giles, Ashtead, St Nicholas, Compton, Holy Trinity, Rudgwick, St Mary, Fetcham, and St Peter, Walton-on-the-Hill, to name just a few – have Roman tiles incorporated into their fabric, indicates that our current understanding of Roman Surrey significantly underestimates the real level of activity.

The Roman villa on Ashtead Common was excavated in 1924–9 by A.W.G. Lowther. The site is a rare type of corridor villa, with a bathhouse and clay pits and tileworks, and it is now a scheduled monument. Remains of a Roman bathhouse with paved rooms and tiled walls have also been found at Pendhill, Bletchingley. The villa near the stables of Abinger Hall was first excavated in 1877. Three rooms paved with coarse red tiles were uncovered, and finds included coins and Samian and other pottery. Subsequent excavations during the twentieth century revealed brick and tile, a statue of Bes and blue glass beads, evidence of a hypocaust system and the design of a mosaic floor.

The early work on the villa was not helped by the involvement of Charles Darwin, who used the uncovered mosaics to observe earthworms – a project aided by his niece, Miss Wedgwood of Leith Hill Place. Darwin often stayed at Abinger Hall in the 1870s as the guest of Thomas Henry Farrer. He wrote up his activities in his paper on *The Formation of Vegetable Mould*. He described how the old farmyard had been dug out in the autumn of 1876 revealing ancient remains and how the owner of Abinger Hall ordered the ploughland next to the yard to be searched and a trench dug. Darwin calculated from the dates of the coins found that the buildings uncovered had been inhabited over a long period.

> I was present during the commencement of the excavations (August 20, 1877) and Mr Farrer had two deep trenches dug at opposite ends of the atrium, so that I might examine the nature of the soil near the remains.

Roman buildings in Surrey are mostly associated with industry, religion and roads. The villa at Rapsley in Ewhurst is linked to the tileworks at Wykehurst, the two Walton villas straddle the ancient North Downs highway, and the one at Ashtead is associated with the tileworks at Epsom. Religion was significant with Romano-British temple sites at Farley Heath, Wanborough and Titsey. Some scholars believe these temples marked the boundary between neighbouring tribes: at Farley Heath, between the Regnenses of Sussex and East Surrey and the Atrebates of Hampshire, and at Titsey between the Regnenses, the Cantiaci of Kent and Catuvellauni to the north.

The Victorian antiquarian Martin Tupper from Albury, famous for romanticizing the legend of Stephen Langton, excavated the temple at Farley Green and described the scene in his autobiography *My Life as an Author*. Having watched a professionally organized late twentieth-century dig of the site by county archaeologists that revealed nothing at all, I find his account of an enthusiastic amateur barging blindly and destructively through what was obviously a hugely significant amount of untouched history extremely distressing.

Some of our finds were very curious, e.g., we were digging in the black mould of the burnt huts round the wall-foundations (all above ground of said hectagonal wall having since been ruthlessly utilized by parochial economists in making a road across the heath), and found amongst other spoil a little green bronze ring, – which I placed on the finger of our guest of the day, Mrs Barclay of Bury Hill: oddly enough it had six angles exactly like one of gold she wore as her wedding-guard. Again; we had picked up some pieces of pottery decorated with human finger-tips, – just as modern cooks do with pie-crust; a son of mine said, perhaps we shall find a dog's foot on some tile, – and just as he said it, up came from the spade precisely what he was guessing at, the large footprint of dog or wolf stamped fifteen centuries ago on the unbaked clay. Again; I was leaving for an hour a labourer in whose industry and honesty I had not the fullest faith. So in order to employ him in my absence, I set him to dig up an old thorn bush and told him to give me when I returned the piece of money he would find under it. To my concealed but his own manifest astonishment, he gave me when I came back a worn large brass of Nero, saying with a scared face, 'However could you tell it was there, sir?' I looked wise, and said nothing.

Among the rarest copper coins was one of Carausius (our English Carew), with two heads on it symbolling the ambition of our native usurper to assert empire over East as well as West, and among more treasure-trove was a unique gold coin of Veric, – the Bericus of Tacitus; as also the rare contents of a subterranean potter's oven, preserved to our day, and yielding several whole vases. Mr Akerman of numismatic fame told me that out of Rome itself he did not know a richer site for old-world curiosities than Farley; in the course of years we found more than 1,200 coins, besides Samian ware, and plenty of common pottery, as well as bronze ornaments, enamelled fibulae, weapons of war, household implements, etc., both of the old British and the Roman, the Anglo-Saxon, and more recent periods; Farley having been a praetorian station on the Ikenild highway.

At least the finds were largely saved and deposited in the British Museum. Wanborough Temple, just north of the Hog's Back, which was discovered via a similar surfacing of coins, suffered a fate far worse than the thoughtless hacking of Tupper's dubious labourer with his spade. In 1983, two metal detectorists found gold and silver Iron Age coins in a lane in Surrey and declared them to Guildford Museum. The antique coin market was then flooded with an influx of Roman coins which undermined their value and prices dropped. It sparked a treasure inquest at Surrey Coroner's Court in Guildford and the location of the find was accidentally revealed. Nighthawks – the dramatic name given to a ruthless minority of metal detector-wielding antiquity thieves – swooped on the site after dark and ransacked it. An estimated 10,000–20,000 mainly Iron Age coins were looted, and just the odd nighthawk was caught. I reported the main trial and remember the distress of the archaeologists at the vandalism and loss of heritage. It became famed as the Battle of Wanborough Temple and there were calls for metal detectors to be banned. Luckily this was avoided in favour of creating better liaison between archaeologists and detectorists. It prompted a landmark change in the Treasure Act, making all artefacts found with coins considered treasure.

After the Romans left, Surrey had to endure a pretty dismal Dark Ages because it did not even have its own identity. It was pushed and pulled and fought over by rival tribes for centuries. Invading Saxons pushed the Britons slowly back towards the west and Wales. Odd Celtic British communities held out, identifiable by the place names – Walton-on-Thames, Walton-on-the-Hill and Wallington – but Saxon tribal infighting left the county a cultural backwater, any Roman prosperity evaporated. It was never a centre of power or government and was even the last area of England to be converted to Christianity.

Saxon Surrey

The name Surrey is derived from the Saxon *Suthrige* meaning south region. In the sixth and seventh centuries it fell to Wessex, then to Mercia, and was reclaimed by Wessex again in 823 after a decisive battle. It is small wonder that there is little evidence of Saxon civilization in Surrey, but towns like Guildford were probably settled some time during the upheavals after 500. The town's attraction was the ford, the route to London through the North Downs gap and the boundary between two local sub-tribes, the Godhelmingas and the Woccingas. The earliest evidence for them in Guildford occurs in the late fifth- and sixth-century pagan cemetery on the Mount, found in 1929. Thirty-five sixth-century skeletons were excavated, and it is thought that there may be others there, still undiscovered. Another group of skeletons was found down the hill in Mount Street. The Guildown cemetery contained a wealth of finds, from iron spears to dark handmade pots that may have contained food or drink, fine glass beakers, brooches, beads and rings. Part of the downs at Albury is known as Harrowshill, which may indicate an Anglo-Saxon holy place and St Mary's, West Horsley, may have been built on a pagan holy site, as it is separate from the village. All the other churches and manors in the area follow the old Iron Age road along the spring line on the dip-slope of the North Downs, and the early West Horsley settlement called Stroud was situated on the old road at Wix Farm. St Mary's is the only church not on that road line and local historian Pam Bowley, who has thirteen books on every conceivable aspect of West Horsley to her credit, argues that its position on the site of two springs away from the road might indicate that it was deliberately built in the eighth or ninth century over an existing pagan sacred place.

Dark Ages bloodshed worsened with the arrival of fierce Danish invaders who threatened to conquer the whole of England, and the chaos is well documented in the *Anglo-Saxon Chronicle* records for 851:

> This year Alderman Ceorl, with the men of Devonshire, fought the heathen army at Wemburg, and after making great slaughter obtained the victory. The same year King Athelstan and Alderman Elchere fought in their ships, and slew a large army at Sandwich in Kent, taking nine ships and dispersing the rest. The heathens now for the first time remained over winter in the Isle of Thanet. The same year came three hundred and fifty ships into

▼ Was this the ancient battlefield where Anglo-Saxon warriors fought off the Danes under the brow of Leith Hill?

> the mouth of the Thames; the crew of which went upon land, and stormed Canterbury and London; putting to flight Bertulf, king of the Mercians, with his army; and then marched southward over the Thames into Surrey. Here Ethelwulf and his son Ethelbald, at the head of the West-Saxon army, fought with them at Ockley, and made the greatest slaughter of the heathen army that we have ever heard reported to this present day. There also they obtained the victory.

King Ethelwulf of Wessex was the father of King Alfred, and he hurried to intercept the Danish army as it headed for Winchester, marching his West Saxon troops along Stane Street, which was already hundreds of years old. The two armies clashed south of Dorking at Ockley. Whether the battlefield itself was the long village green or the levels at the foot of Leith Hill is unclear, but the name given to the site of the slaughter was Aclea and according to the bloodthirsty chronicler, none remained alive to bury their dead.

This battle of Aclea is one of the few decisive and overwhelming victories by the English over the Vikings recorded during the first phase of Viking invasion between 793 and 865. The battle was said to involve 15,000–20,000 men on each side – a huge confrontation – and 'rivers of blood' were reported to have flowed down the hillside. In 1882, in a field near Ockley, a large number of ancient human bones were found, fuelling rumours that it was the graveyard of the battle's dead.

The first written record of Guildford as a settlement occurs in King Alfred's will of about 880, in which he left a property there to his nephew. After *c.* 920 it is probable that the town was developed as a defensive and commercial centre because of its strategic position controlling access along the river and through the downs. The High Street was laid out with a ditch enclosing it on either side which continued over the river to include the ford in the defences. There may well have been a bridge there by this date and the stone tower of St Mary's Church in Quarry Street may also have been built at this time. The town's new importance is certainly underlined by the presence of a royal mint.

In 1036, Alfred the Atheling, brother of the man who became Edward the Confessor, came to England from exile in Normandy. He and his followers were massacred by Earl Godwin at Guildford, and when the pagan cemetery on Guildown was excavated, nearly 200 other skeletons were found, mutilated and randomly heaped in pits. It was long assumed that they were the victims of this massacre, but archaeologists now believe they were the bones of convicted criminals who had been hanged on a gallows on the site of the pagan cemetery.

By the time of the Domesday Survey in 1086, Guildford was the principal town in Surrey, held by the king and containing seventy-five plots and supporting 175 heads of households.

The Pilgrims' Way

The Pilgrims' Way stirs the romantic within us: this beaten path, which follows the ridge from Winchester to Canterbury, is loaded with history, infused with religious ardour and poetic inspiration, an umbilical cord linking us with the earliest human settlers in southern England. Local historian Eric Parker felt the power of its imagery when he wrote in his book *Highways and Byways in Surrey* in 1908:

> Of all English Roads, it has the longest pageant. It saw the beginnings of English history; for four centuries it was one of the best known highways in Christendom: the vision from its windy heights is one of the widest and most gracious of all visions of woods and fields and hills. By the trackway they made upon the ridge came the worshippers to Stonehenge; Phoenician traders brought bronze to barter for British tin, and the tin was carried in ingots from Devon and Cornwall along the highway to the port of Thanet; Greeks and Gauls came for lead and tin and furs and the merchants rode by the great Way to bring them.

When Caesar swept through Surrey on his second landing, his legions marched over the Way before he turned north to the Thames. When the Conqueror drove fire and sword through Southern England, he went down to Winchester by the chalk ridge and when the great lords under the Conqueror and Rufus, Richard de Tonebrige and William de Warenne built their rival castles, they built them to command the highway; so did Henry of Blois build his castle at Farnham; and so was Guildford Castle built.

Following it along the Hog's Back and on from Newlands Corner to Dorking, with ancient track beneath one's feet, ancient yews along the way and staggering views to catch the breath, it is easy to share his misty-eyed enthusiasm. One can imagine the busy thoroughfare of heavily laden trains of pack animals and livestock trudging through the mud all the way from Cornwall to the Kent coast long before the Romans came. It was already an ancient way by the time Chaucer's pilgrims jogged along it *en route* to Canterbury. It only became known as the Pilgrims' Way in 1174 when the faithful began trekking to Canterbury to the shrine of Thomas Becket after his murder at the cathedral altar. They partly followed the old Way on the top of the ridge, partly created new tracks or used existing ones across or below the downs, travelling from inn to inn and church to church by different routes but in the same general direction. A whole economy developed and thrived on pilgrims. St Catherine's Chapel outside Guildford and St Martha's Church, both isolated chapels perched on

▲ Chilworth Manor gardens still have the stew ponds that once provided fish for the monks who lived there pre-Reformation

hilltops, would both have been busy, as would all the inns along the route. The name St Martha is quite possibly a corruption of St Thomas the Martyr, or of Martyrs' Hill, indicating an early anti-Christian backlash.

Chaucer immortalized the track in his *Canterbury Tales*, and John Bunyan's *Pilgrim's Progress*, though written before he knew Surrey from his stays in Quarry Street, Guildford, and Horn Hatch, on Shalford Common, gives every appearance of having been based on first-hand knowledge of Shalford and St Martha's Hill. It is all part of the romance.

The Pilgrims' Way and the ancient Way are still well trod today; much of the route is now known as the North Downs Way. Modern Christian pilgrims still follow it from Winchester to Canterbury, but its main purpose now is leisure rather than religion or commerce. Mountain-bikers, horse-riders, dog-walkers, orienteerers, joggers, courting couples, thieves and ne'er do wells, picknicking families – all human life is there, just as it has been for thousands of years.

Church and State, Rivals for Power

Castles and cathedrals were the status symbols of medieval England, representing the competing powers of State and Church. The Normans built castles at Farnham, Guildford, Betchworth, Reigate and Bletchingley – parallel with the downs – and there were priories at Tandridge, Reigate and Waverley, and a Dominican friary founded by Eleanor, queen of Henry III, at Guildford. There was also a monastery on the site of Chilworth Manor – the land had been granted to Odo, Bishop of Bayeux after the Norman Conquest. The Church was a major landowner in Surrey in the eleventh century and its influence on the rural communities can be seen today in surviving tithe barns and village ponds for the compulsory Friday fish. The late Lady Heald of Chilworth Manor, who died just before her hundredth birthday, told

▼ Farnham Castle, architectural hodgepodge of great character and antiquity. Still in use today though no longer home to the Bishops of Winchester

me that the lakes in the gardens there were stew ponds to provide fish for the monastery. 'I'm not sure I believe the story,' she said, 'but if you go to the cloak room by the front door there is a passage that goes down. I say it only went to the pond for the monks to get the fish but other people say it was a passage to the church. The old farmer's daughter said she went halfway up it when she was a girl.'

Farnham Castle managed to combine both Church and State, and is still very much in use today. A great wide market street leads straight up to the magnificent rambling building, a collage of architectural additions and embellishments to the original twelfth-century keep. Vast stone fortress walls, timber-framed Tudor domestic wings and brick towers with neat crenellations are all interwoven together. Walls may cut right across old archways, and wings show scant regard for minor details like window levels, but the overall effect is wonderful. It is a magnificent hodgepodge castle that is still alive, vibrant and functional after 900 years. This is probably the oldest, most continuously inhabited building in the entire country.

The castle keep dates from about 1138 when Henry de Blois, William the Conqueror's grandson, was enthroned as bishop, and while Church and State were closely entwined Farnham flourished. For more than 800 years the castle was the residence of the bishops of Winchester, who were immensely powerful.

The Surrey castles had their first taste of military activity in 1216 when the French Dauphin invaded at the invitation of rebel barons and occupied first Reigate, then Guildford and finally Farnham. They stayed for a few months, and then withdrew back to France.

During the Civil War, Farnham Castle changed hands several times, and there was vandalism but no bloodshed. It had the distinction of being held at different times by two poets, one for Parliament and one for the King. The Roundhead was George Wither and the Royalist was Sir John Denham. The Civil War temporarily severed the link between Church and State and Farnham's dual role ceased altogether when it became part of the new Diocese of Guildford in 1927. The castle was no longer required for the bishop and it was leased in 1962 to Farnham Castle International Briefing and Conference Centre. Since then, thousands of ex-patriates have benefited from the wisdom and experience of the Farnham Castle tutors who have prepared them for the language, culture, food and customs of the countries where they were being sent on tours of duty by the Government or international companies.

In contrast to Farnham, Guildford Castle is still quite an enigma. All that remains above ground is the keep and a few ruined walls, but for a very brief period in the thirteenth century, it was one of the most sumptuous, avant-garde examples of royal palace architecture, décor and wealth in Europe. Its flowering was extremely short-lived, however, and Guildford Museum and Surrey County archaeologists have worked hard to piece together what it was like at its peak and what happened to it. For successive years in the 1990s, professionals and volunteers took part in three-week excavations. It was such an exciting project that in its first year it attracted more than 150 helpers, and each year volunteers had to be turned away as the site was packed. Hundreds came to watch and have guided tours.

The excavations concentrated on the grounds outside the great tower, and archaeologists stumbled on the original bailey ditch that pre-dated the larger twelfth-century boundary. The expansion was to create space for a palace for Henry II, a project that blossomed under his son Henry III. He died in 1272 and just 100 years later this opulent set of royal buildings, featuring rooms painted green and spangled with gold and silver, were being dismantled. Rob Poulton, of Surrey County Archaeological Unit, who led the excavation in partnership with Surrey Archaeological Society and Guildford Museum, believes its decline started long before that.

In 2004, attention turned to the keep, for a major restoration project which led to some exciting discoveries, sparked by a report by Guildford Museum archaeologist John Boas on the serious condition of the stonework. The Assistant Curator, Mary Alexander, had just completed a doctorate on the history of the castle, and with Professor John Ashurst and archaeologist Catherine Woolfitt from Ingram Consultancy, they were able to interpret each new discovery. The real eye-opener was that the castle had once had proper battlements. Every child who draws a castle or makes a sandcastle automatically includes battlements – they are the defining architectural motif of medieval castles – but Guildford's ruinous tower had no sign of ever having them until the conservators started removing the old mortar around the stonework. Bits of whitewash and rendering were still visible.

This shed new light on what the castle would have looked like in medieval times. Instead of the familiar raw stone and flint walls, the whole of the tower would have been neatly rendered smooth and painted white. It might even have had a mock stone effect created by drawing red lines on the whitewash.

Earlier conservation work in 2000, on the inside of the antechapel, revealed traces of red, yellow and black paint, so the whole castle effect would have been bright and colourful. The absence of a latrine had been a puzzle, the little chamber in the north wall of the keep had always been assumed to be a garderobe where clothes and other personal belongings were kept; but during the project an in-filled shaft was uncovered: the *en-suite* royal privy had finally been unblocked.

The twelfth-century dating links it directly to King Stephen, during the Civil War with his cousin, the Empress Matilda. And that would make Guildford Castle unique – the only surviving stone building in the country connected to Stephen. The detective work cast doubt over the function of castle keeps. Were they defensive or just symbols of power?

By the mid-thirteenth century it was only being used as the sheriff's court and county gaol, but Mary Alexander's research uncovered a domestic phase in its history, when the local keeper of the gardens modernized it with brick windows and fireplaces in the sixteenth century, but the tower was completely abandoned around 1630 and both roof and floors removed. By the eighteenth century it was merely a garden feature, and when the council bought it in 1885, the public used it primarily as a viewing platform.

Betchworth Castle, built around 1377, is one of Surrey's few medieval buildings and therefore significant. Now reduced to ruins, it was once a fortified house built on a sandstone spur by Sir John Fitzalan, Marshal of England. It is believed to have been built on an earlier castle erected by Richard FitzGilbert after 1066 on land granted to him by William the Conqueror.

▼ The main tunnel beneath Reigate's Norman keep, showing beautifully shaped roof, and side pits gouged by later sand diggers

Nick Catford

The second Earl of Surrey, William de Warenne, built Reigate Castle soon after 1088, sitting the keep on top of a soft sandstone mound. It was surrounded by a dry moat, with timber buildings and defences on the mound, or motte. In the twelfth or thirteenth century, the timber structures were replaced with stone ones and the castle was extended to include an outer bailey with a second moat. It eventually fell into ruin in the sixteenth century although, like Farnham Castle, it made a convenient billet for troops of both sides in the Civil War. All the stone above ground has since been robbed for other buildings, leaving just the mysterious Baron's Cave, a professionally carved Gothic arched tunnel, believed to date from the eleventh century, leading from the keep right down through the mound to the moat. A rather unlikely rumour has it that the barons held a secret meeting at the cave on their way to Runnymede to sign the Magna Carta. Steep, straight and sandy, with a side gallery large enough to harbour several hundred people, the tunnel's purpose is unclear except as a refuge in time of siege.

The lords in their draughty towers may have thought they held the reins of power, but until the Reformation the Church was a formidable rival. The Benedictine Abbey of St Peter at Chertsey, founded in 666 by Frithwold, the Viceroy of Surrey, owned land all over the county including at Clandon and Effingham. There are the remains of a series of public fish ponds at West Horsley whose construction was probably influenced by the monks and their insistence on fasting and ritual; everyone had to eat fish on Fridays or suffer the torments of hell.

Waverley Abbey, 3 miles south of Farnham, was built in 1128 as the foundation house in England of the new Cistercian order, which encouraged its monks to do manual work. It proved popular and continued to grow until late in the fourteenth century. It was an important part of the social fabric, both hotel and hospital, providing shelter for pilgrims and an infirmary for the sick. The village of Elstead, a rural patchwork of farms and mills, was tied to the abbey; it has no manor house, just working families whose fortunes ebbed and flowed with the price of wool. The abbey has long gone, but the village is still a workaday community without a local aristocracy.

Reigate Priory was founded for regular canons of the Order of St Augustine during the thirteenth century, and it is probably the only one of Surrey's religious houses to have survived at all. After the dissolution of the monasteries in 1535, Henry VIII gave the estate to Lord Howard of Effingham, who converted it into a beautifully furnished Tudor mansion. The Howard family, including the Lord High Admiral who fought off the Spanish Armada, lived there for about 140 years. The priory was modernized during the eighteenth century and is now home to a museum and middle school, set in 65 acres of parkland, with gardens and a lake. The eighteenth-century staircase was described by Niklaus Pevsner as 'the best of its date in Surrey and, in its combination of painting and architecture into a homogeneous and satisfying space, one of the best in England'.

The site of the friary in Guildford has had a very varied history. Only the name lives on now, with more than a touch of irony, as a temple to fashion and materialism, the Friary Shopping Centre. When I was a child, visits to Guildford meant being overwhelmed by the pungent smells of brewing beer as the site was then occupied by the Friary Brewery. I hated the smell then, especially when it mingled with the smell from the Market Street fish shop: I suspect I might rather like the brewery smell now.

The friary was founded by Eleanor of Provence, widow of Henry III, in late 1274 or early 1275, when records show that Edward I gave the friars a road from the town to Guildford Park to enlarge their property. Eleanor founded it, possibly in memory of her husband or of her grandson Henry, who died at Guildford in October 1274, aged six. Henry III was buried in Westminster Abbey and his heart was later preserved in the friary church, probably in the chapel on the north side of the chancel.

When the friary was excavated, traces of an earlier construction were found under the Dominican building, with pottery dating after 1250. This is probably the house of the Friars de Ordine Martyrum, the only house of their order, which was probably merged into the Dominicans.

▲ St John's Church, Wotton, nestling in the Evelyn Estate

It was quite a small establishment, with around twenty-four friars. After the demise of the palace, the friary was often used as a royal hotel. In 1403 Henry IV is recorded as having to pay 40 shillings to cover the damage caused by his hangers on. It was even used by Henry VIII in 1534 to sign a treaty with the Scots but, however useful the lodgings, the King did not spare it from closure four years later. Its buildings seem to have lasted until the early seventeenth century, when a mansion was built there. In 1818 it became an industrial site and is now a completely modern mecca of retail.

Before the Reformation, the Church had very long tentacles; many places in Surrey have names that have no local connection whatever and only make sense when one unravels the ecclesiastical threads. Take Gomshall for example: Netley House gets its name from the Cistercian Abbey of Netley in Hampshire because in 1243 the West Gomshall manor was given to the abbey. Towerhill in Gomshall gets its name from the Abbey and Convent of St Mary of Graces near the Tower of London, which was given the land at East Gomshall in 1389.

Elysium Britannicum – The Manors of the Tillingbourne Valley

In this era of lightning change, technological revolution and mobility, it is incredible that at least three families, two in the Tillingbourne valley and one just on the Godalming side of Guildford, still occupy estates that have been in their families for hundreds of years. Add to that Albury, which despite change of ownership in the mid-nineteenth century, is still intact as an estate, and you have an extraordinary continuum of feudal society. Of course it has changed, and continues to evolve, but it makes the Tillingbourne valley special. John Aubrey, writing in the seventeenth century, called it 'little romancy vale', and William Cobbett, 'one of the choicest retreats of man'.

▲ The eighteenth-century Italian gardens at Wotton, recently restored to their full glory

The Evelyn family, whose fortune was founded on gunpowder manufacture, has owned the Wotton Estate for more than 400 years. Henry Owen, a descendant of Owen Tudor, sold it to George Evelyn of Long Ditton in 1579. Since then, Evelyns have been hugely influential in Surrey, in England and in Maryland, America. The most famous member of the family was John, who was born in 1620. The seventeenth century was extremely turbulent but it was also a very exciting time for men of an intellectual and inquiring bent. John Evelyn was not only involved in national affairs but he was also a great writer, and his first-hand accounts of events, set down in his diary and letters, are among the most important archives used by historians all over the world. It is interesting that he was a close friend of another brilliant diarist, Samuel Pepys, but he also wrote to other great men of his day, including Sir Thomas Browne, Grinling Gibbons, Robert Boyle and Sir Christopher Wren, so he was very much at home among the movers and shakers of his time.

As the Civil War raged around him, the young John Evelyn decided to go abroad, travelling through Italy and France and spending enough time in Paris to find a wife. The most important result of his travels, however, was that he educated himself very widely, so that when the monarchy was restored under Charles II he became a founder member of the Royal Society. Unlike today, the age of the tunnel-vision, in-depth specialist, the seventeenth century was the age of Renaissance Man, when it was possible to explore and experiment in a wide variety of subjects encompassing both arts and sciences. He wrote copiously on topics ranging from London pollution to theology and cookery. Aside from his diary, probably his most famous work is *Sylva, or Discourse on Forest Trees*, written in 1664 to encourage landowners to plant trees to provide timber for the navy.

Evelyn was no mere academic theorist, pontificating in prose. He enjoyed putting his ideas into action, and his interest in landscape was not confined to Wotton; he also designed the gardens and grounds for Albury House. Amazingly, after nearly four centuries, his plans for both Wotton and Albury are not only still visible, but being actively restored and maintained. He may even have had a hand in the moated gardens of Great Tangley Manor in Wonersh. His name and the date 1641 are certainly scratched in the glass of one of its windows.

The Wotton garden is believed to be the first Italian-style garden to be built in England, and so is of national importance. It nearly did not survive, however: the twentieth century saw Wotton follow the pattern of so many grand country houses in Surrey, ceasing to be a family home and struggling to adapt to institutional service. It was billeted during the Second World War, then used as a fire training centre, fire service college and latterly BT offices. In 1986 the lease was handed back to the Evelyn family and the house was left empty until Hayley Conference Centre Group took it on and embarked on an ambitious programme of restoration and development. Huge new wings have been added to provide accommodation, and they have been marvellously successful in blending the new brickwork with the old. The extensions, with their brick and stone architectural details following the style of the original house, fit in extraordinarily well. It was a monumental project and the restoration of the gardens, which are officially listed along with the house, took eighteen months.

In a twilight recess behind some overgrown rhododendrons, a Buddha smiles a shy smile. His private meditation probably goes unseen by conference delegates, more interested in their coffee break, but luckily the gardens are opened to the public on several days during the summer under the National Gardens Scheme. They certainly deserve to be appreciated by a wider public. The south-facing formal gardens at the back of the house feature a spectacular centrepiece, a vista straight from Renaissance Italy transplanted into the heart of the Surrey Hills. The Buddha in the shadows is just a gentle reminder that, however stunning the centrepiece, the most interesting gardens do not yield up all their secrets at first glance.

The South Garden is dominated by John Evelyn's steep, artificial terraced mount, topped by a classical temple that he built in the mid-seventeenth century to a design inspired by the principles of Italian Renaissance gardens that he visited between 1641 and 1645. Evelyn was a naturalist and philosopher who believed that 'the air and genius of gardens operate upon human spirits towards virtue and sanctity'.

The Tillingbourne rises on Leith Hill very close to Wotton House, and provides almost a moat round it, as well as supplying a number of fountains and spouts. Evelyn conceived the idea of an *Elysium Britannicum*, and was immensely proud of his garden, saying it 'far surpassed any else in England'. Thankfully, his descendants kept the basic design intact over the centuries, modifying it here and there but retaining the basic Italianate features. Little paths lead through the overgrown shrubbery past statues like the serenely smiling Buddha, and all sorts of other little forgotten architectural features can be spotted half buried in soil and bushes. But the major features have been cleaned and restored, the fountains brought back to life and the beds replanted with purple sage, santilena, rosemary, periwinkle, catmint, lavender, euphorbia, honeysuckle and bergenia. The planting is subtle and muted, the geometric patterns edged with box hedging which contrasts superbly with the stone chip paths. The water system is complex, involving five lakes and a variety of pumps and sumps, pipes and spouts, tunnels and chimneys – Heath Robinson feats of eighteenth- and nineteenth-century engineering designed to propel the water round the different features and allow people to get inside to attend to its maintenance.

An iron gate leads you through a wonderful old wall, not into a traditional vegetable and fruit garden, but a severely classical garden with a second temple-like structure and formal pond with fountains – this time rectangular rather than round – which was used to house a collection of terrapins. It is reputed to be the only one of its kind in existence and it has been fully restored –

except for the terrapins. House guests were once able to watch them frolicking in the pool from the roof of the tortoise house. The walls must originally have been covered with climbing plants or fruit trees, as the old vine-eyes are still there, but planting is being strictly overseen by English Heritage.

The Evelyns were not just sold on Italiana. They were also into grottoes but they did not plot these features on a grand landscape scale, as at Claremont; they liked them close at hand. The temple mount itself is also surprisingly close to the house and the grottoes are even closer. One is practically outside the back door.

John Evelyn was regarded by historians as the greatest man Surrey had ever produced. Robert Southey called him 'the perfect model of an English gentleman'. His self-judgement – or was it false modesty? – was that he was 'a plain husbandman and simple forester'. He certainly knew his mind and so do his descendants. The Victorian, W. J. Evelyn, was a Home Ruler, and as a ground landlord in Deptford he would invite members of the Irish League to bring their families down to Wotton for a day's holiday, providing meals for all. He allowed the people of Deptford to use the grounds of Sayes Court for recreation and eventually handed it over to the county council.

His descendant Patrick Evelyn, the current owner of the estate, is equally outspoken. He resigned as Vice-Chairman of Surrey County Council on the eve of taking over the Chairmanship in protest at Conservative plans to extend the right to buy legislation to private landlords in the 1980s.

Albury Park

Evelyn made use of the Tillingbourne again when he laid out the terraced gardens for Henry Howard, later 6th Duke of Norfolk, at Albury. His plans are again very formal and architectural. The key feature is a 60ft wide canal. The seventeenth-century antiquary John Aubrey, described a bridge across it with a hole through it for watching the water. He wrote in *The Natural History and Antiquities of the County of Surrey* that water

▼ The gardens at Albury Park were landscaped by John Evelyn and his terraces, walks and water features are still maintained

from the spring was rerouted to erode sandstone for landscape effects.

The Silent Pool, just north of the A25 in Albury, a spot much loved by romantics, was made larger and deeper, and a second, lower, pool was dug out by Evelyn's work-force to supply the water for the garden features. The Silent Pool is certainly atmospheric but it is largely the result of this practical seventeenth-century engineering.

Clear water attracts myth and legend, however. There is a legend at Buckland near Reigate that tells of a pure maiden who when deceived by a wicked gentleman, fell dead and became a stream. This is not dissimilar to the tale that the Victorian poet and author Martin Tupper embellished in his romance *Stephan Langton*. The basic story is of a beautiful girl who was accustomed to bathe naked every day in the Silent Pool. One day she was spotted by a man on horseback, who rode after her into the water. She backed away until the water was too deep and, faced with capture or drowning, she chose the water. Tupper went further. He made the rogue into King John and made the girl's brother drown too, trying to rescue her. She would never have drowned in the real Silent Pool. Recent dry summers have periodically dried up the springs that feed it and left it temporarily a shallow, dessicated mud flat – very unromantic.

Writing a little later, Eric Parker was more impressed by the speed of Tupper's inventions than by their quality. In *Highways and Byways in Surrey* (1908), he wrote:

> He set out to write a historical novel dealing with Guildford in the days of King John, weaving into it various legends and a love-story of an abbess and an archbishop. He 'began the book on November 21, 1857, and finished it in exactly eight weeks, on January 21, 1858, reading for the work included.' The list of books which he consulted in Mr Drummond's library at Albury must be read in full for the mere physical labour of the business to be appreciated; but after such abstruse searchings, to have crammed into ninety thousand words of solid print such a concatenation of murders, arsons, slayings, swoonings, drownings and burnings must always remain a considerable achievement. The story itself is sad stuff.

The Silent Pool has survived Tupper's extravagance and eventually copes with droughts. When the aquifer is replenished – it takes some three months after heavy rain for the water to penetrate the chalk – the springs gurgle back to life and the magic returns.

The mature gardens fed by the pools were impressive enough to inspire William Cobbett to a lengthy description in his *Rural Rides* a century and a half later.

> At the back of this garden and facing the yew-tree row is a wall probably ten feet high, which forms the breastwork of a terrace; and it is this terrace which is the most beautiful thing I saw in the gardening way. It is a quarter of a mile long, and, I believe, between thirty and forty feet wide; of the finest green sward, and as level as a die. The wall, along at the back of this terrace, stands close against the hill, which you see with the trees and underwood upon it rising above the wall. So that here is the finest spot for fruit trees that can possibly be imagined. At both ends of this garden the trees in the park are lofty, and there are a pretty many of them. The hills on the south side of the mansion-house are covered in lofty trees, chiefly beeches and chestnut: so that, a warmer, more sheltered, spot than this, it seems impossible to imagine.

The Finch family lived in Albury manor-house for most of the eighteenth century, and in 1782, the fourth earl sold it to his brother, Captain William Clement Finch, who acquired his fortune by capturing a Spanish ship. At this time fashion dictated that the lord of the manor's mansion should to be private, surrounded by parkland, and not, as at Albury, jostling for space around the church with a lot of cottages. The message was clear: riff-raff keep out. The captain obtained magistrates' orders in 1784–5 to close or reroute a number of roads out of the park, enclosed the village green, incorporated part of the churchyard into his grounds, and generally harassed the locals. Many of them escaped to the relative calm of the hamlet next door, called Weston Street.

After a little lull in hostilities, Albury was once again thrown into upheaval by the arrival on the scene of banker and MP Henry Drummond, a man both eccentric and rich, who decided to sever the last links between the park and the people by closing the medieval church. It was by then in severe need of repair, and in 1839, Drummond applied to the Bishop of Winchester for its closure. In return he offered to build a new church at Weston Street, where most of the parishioners were by then living. The old church was closed by an Act of Parliament in 1840 and the last service was held in December 1841. It was the last straw for the old settlement of Albury, and the name was transferred to the new settlement at Weston. The name Weston, which dates back to the fifteenth century, is perpetuated throughout modern Albury. The estate offices are in Weston Yard and the lakes are named Weston Fisheries.

Drummond's sons died young and when his daughter married the Percy heir, Albury passed to the Northumberland family of Alnwick Castle. Like the Evelyns of Wotton, they no longer have the mansion, which has been used as an idyllic sheltered housing scheme, but the Northumberland estate is still the central pillar of the community in Albury and its green and cream livery can be seen throughout the village. Hall, shop, pub, lakes, even new village housing, are all part of the estate and the Northumberland family wields considerable local clout. When the village hall needed refurbishing, the estate was there to help, and when the village shop was threatened with closure, it stepped in to save it. But then the estate also sanctioned the huge Albury sand quarry and landfill site, and gas and oil exploration and harvesting.

It is a sad reflection on village life that the butcher, the baker, the haberdasher, the chemist, the garage, the dairy, the men's tailor, the photographer, the grocer, the blacksmith, and the undertaker, all successful businesses in Albury, have now left, leaving just the one convenience-store-cum-post-office. Surprisingly though, the village is far from moribund. The shops may have gone but Albury has found a new role as a rural business centre, many companies finding homes in redundant buildings on the Albury Estate. The model farm on the bypass, converted houses in the street, back rooms, old sheds and redundant farm buildings on the downs opposite are buzzing with commercial activity. The Surrey Hill Brewery is at Old Scotland Farm and a new woodchip business in the barn. When the postmistress helped organize a children's Christmas party a few years ago, she was able to approach twenty-nine businesses in the village for sponsorship.

The Northumberland family came down to Albury Park Mansion every Easter holiday until the 1960s, children, ponies and all, but the mansion was sold when the old Dowager Duchess died and the family now uses Clive Lodge by the Tillingbourne as a base instead.

▼ Henry Drummond, Victorian owner of Albury Park, who built two new churches in the village

Surrey History Centre

Shere Manor

Albury's neighbour upstream along the Tillingbourne is the Shere Manor estate which has been in the Bray family since the fifteenth century. The 500th anniversary of the lordship of the manor was celebrated in 2005. Sir Reginald Bray reputedly discovered Richard III's crown in a thorn bush after the Battle of Bosworth in 1485 and gave it to Henry VII; 'Shiere', which at that point was forfeit to the king, was his reward. In fact Sir Reginald was only granted half of the original medieval manor as by then it had been split in two – Shere Vachery and Cranleigh, and Shere Eborum. He was given Shere Vachery.

Sir Reginald was a statesman, holding the position of Lord Treasurer of England and directing Henry VII's great building operations at St George's Chapel, Windsor, and Westminster. According to H.E. Malden's *A History of the County of Surrey*, Shere Vachery had a sitting tenant, Lord Audley, who paid Sir Reginald £10 a year in rent. His son James inherited the tenancy and is recorded as receiving the profits of the manor in 1497, at his camp of Cornish rebels at Blackheath. He probably led the rebels through Shere *en route* from Guildford to Kent. After the rebellion, the king confiscated the manor again but handed it back to Sir Reginald. It passed to and fro among Bray descendants down the centuries, its owners including the Surrey historian William Bray and High Court judge Sir Reginald More Bray. Since 1771, the two halves of the original manor, Vachery and Eborum, have been reunited. The manor house of Shere Vachery was situated south of Cranleigh, because Cranleigh and Ewhurst were part of the medieval *vill* of Shere. The Bray family lived there and also at Baynards nearby but they now use High House beyond St James's Church, the principal house in Shere Eborum, as the main family home.

▼ Albury, looking south over Albury Heath to Blackheath, showing the new parish church built for the uprooted villagers by Henry Drummond

In 1926, the Lord of the Manor, Reginald Bray, dedicated the Hurtwood manorial and common lands to the public 'for air and exercise'. This was the time when people were really waking up to the importance of the country landscape and public access. The National Trust, established just thirty years before, was beginning to flourish but the opening of the Hurtwood was still a magnificently far-sighted move, and one that has been enormously successful. Thousands of people still come for their 'air and exercise' through the magical steep-sided forests and over the heaths, where Tolkien would have felt at home.

There was definitely a spirit of philanthropy in the lordship. Louisa Bray and her friend Laura Lomax founded the village school, a gipsy school was situated on the Hurtwood near Wicket's Well, one of the many springs there, and in the 1930s a barn at High House was converted into the Barn Theatre, home to the Otherwise Club, where Peter Ustinov and Herbert Lom made their theatrical debuts. Ustinov was seventeen years old and the play was *The Wood Demon*.

The present Lord of the Manor is Handa Bray, who continues the family tradition of working to sustain the village community. She inherited the estate in 1964 and arrived with a romantic vision of benevolent patronage, fuelled by memories of visiting tenants with her grandfather and Thomas Hardy-esque parties for everyone on the estate.

'I hadn't the slightest idea of what it would entail,' she said, 'I was twenty-five years old, expecting my first baby. I would have been really frightened if I had been aware of all the problems and pitfalls. But I was hugely aware of the privilege and responsibilities.'

Handa's policy of letting her cottages to local people at affordable rents has helped ease the housing crisis in villages like Shere for a few lucky tenants. 'Once I sat in church on Mother's Day and saw four generations of a family in the pew in front,' she said. 'That seems to me to be what it is all about. One tenant moved in on his wedding day and celebrated his diamond wedding there sixty years later.'

Shere is probably Surrey's main honeypot. Easily accessible from London, it is always clogged with traffic and parked cars, but the advantage is that the community and the local economy is kept alive. How many other villages of this size can boast a church, a school, a museum, a post office in the Co-op store, a greengrocer, a bakery, a flower shop, a tearoom, two pubs, a gift shop, an interior décor shop, a forge shop, a fashion boutique, a kitchen designer and even a 4x4 dealer? It was one of the first villages in England to have a piped water supply and it even boasts its own open-air heated swimming pool. Run as a members' club, it buzzes with activity all summer.

Christine Carpenter, Anchoress of Shere

The story of Christine Carpenter, an apparently normal fourteenth-century village girl, daughter of William, the carpenter of Shere, who asked to be walled up for life in a cell in the church, is tantalizingly enigmatic. What was going on inside her head, or inside her community, that being incarcerated in a confined space with no amenities, let alone creature comforts, appeared preferable to life in the village? It is impossible to see it now through fourteenth-century eyes. The decision by medieval women to become nuns and live in convents is understandable. Women were expected to marry young, usually with no personal choice, they had few rights, and they could expect to spend most of their adult life pregnant and probably die in childbirth. Mother Church might look like a much safer, cleaner, more companionable option. But to be walled up alone in your parish church – that is much harder to comprehend. Christine's enigma is compounded by the record showing that for four months in 1332 she lapsed from her vows and returned to her life in the village. The questions hang in the air, unanswerable.

It is a fact, however, that during the Middle Ages, throughout Europe, living as a hermit was quite fashionable with numbers peaking in the thirteenth to the fifteenth century, just when Christine was drawn to join them. They lived in caves and remote rustic huts and some, like Christine, chose to be next to the church. They were called anchorites or anchoresses, from the Greek *anachoretes*, meaning one who lives apart. The cells they inhabited were called an anchorholds and they were usually built on the dark side of the church in order, quite deliberately, to starve the hermit of sunlight.

The decision to be enclosed was extremely serious and the enclosure ceremony, presided over by the bishop, was like a funeral, as the anchoress was considered to be dead to the world. Sometimes they were literally walled up but it was more usual just to lock them in. Occasionally they would spend some time in the outside world without incurring punishment, but it was more usual for them to remain secluded, watching church services through an internal window and communicating with the world via a small external window.

A letter from the Bishop of Winchester to the Dean of Guildford in July 1329 shows how serious the whole business was. It is eminently sensible, though devoid of human detail. The Dean was charged with organizing a meeting, attended by Sir Matthew, the Rector of Shere, and members of the parish who knew Christine and her family, to investigate her motives, lifestyle and character, in order to assess her suitability as an anchoress.

> You shall apply yourself to seeking the truth diligently, as to whether the aforesaid Christine is of such good life and conversation that she is likely to make a success of this proposal for a more saintly life, and whether she is free or espoused to anyone or joined to marriage, and whether in the opinion of the Rector or the parishioners or of anyone else who may contribute in any way.

The meeting took place quickly and Christine obviously passed the tests with flying colours. Her purpose was described in the bishop's next letter the following month as 'praiseworthy' and she was ordered to be shut away so that 'laid aside from public and worldly sights, she may be enabled to serve God more freely in every way, and having resisted all opportunity for wantonness may keep her heart undefiled by the world.'

She managed four years and then left her cell. What happened? What had gone wrong? The consequences of breaking religious vows, especially ones taken so publicly and with such high Church authority, could be dire. Excommunication was extremely serious in the fourteenth century. Christine spent four months in the outside world and then asked to go back to her cell in St James's, raising more unanswerable questions. The bishop wrote back to the dean:

> His sister Christine..., now with God's help changed in heart, wishing to return to her former abode and calling, she has humbly petitioned us that she may be treated mercifully by the Apostolic See in this matter. Therefore we, who strive for the salvation of the soul of her and of all mankind with fervent longing, wishing to take care of her soul send you, according to the form of the church, absolution for her by the authority of the Lord Jesus Christ that in the manner of good father of a family rejoicing in the finding of a lost sheep, and the said anchoress having come to you humbly within the space of four months from this our order, you shall cause her to be re-enclosed in the same place, or elsewhere if she would not be secure there, lest by wandering any longer about the world she be exposed to the bites of the rapacious wolf and which, heaven forbid, her blood be required at your hands. And after she has been re-enclosed there and has for some time conducted herself in a worthy manner, you shall enjoin upon her by the said authority, a salutary penance in proportion to her sin; if however she neglects to come to you within the aforesaid time, without any legitimate excuse, henceforward she shall relapse into the sentence of excommunication and these present letters shall be absolutely no moment.

There is a veiled threat here of punishment by death.

If you go into the church you can see the quatrefoil and squint, through which Christine took part in services, but this is all we actually know about her. The letters and stone window were enough, however, to excite local journalist and author Paul Moorcroft to spin a steamy psychological yarn around them. Poor Christine, I cannot think she would have approved.

Loseley Park

The Brays of Shere were briefly connected in the sixteenth century to another great Surrey Hills family, the Mores, subsequently More-Molyneux, of Loseley Park. Reginald Bray's second wife was Elizabeth Roper, daughter of Meg Roper and Sir Thomas More's granddaughter. The Mores had been at Loseley since 1508 when Sir Christopher More bought the estate with its medieval house situated on what is now the south lawn. His sister married Sir Thomas More's father after his first wife died.

The present Tudor house was built by Sir William More, who inherited the estate in 1549. He was one of Queen Elizabeth I's advisers and, according to James More-Molyneux, the twentieth-century custodian of Loseley, the queen dropped him a very heavy hint about upgrading his home. She indicated that she would like to come and stay with him, but that his house 'was not mete for her to tarry at'. It was just the spur an enterprising Renaissance man needed. He took on the project and ran it, using stone from the then dissolved Waverley Abbey. These stones had already been part of the abbey for 400 years and have now been part of Loseley for more than 400 so the whole structure has an incredible atmosphere. It is wholly appropriate that the house is still one of prayer and meditation, with its own chapel. James certainly feels the influence of the centuries of Cistercian prayer, and Sir Thomas More would feel entirely comfortable there. The queen stayed there four times, once commenting that it needed to be cleaner than the last time she was there.

William's son Sir George played host to James I and his wife, Anne of Denmark, and the gilding in the Great Hall is believed to date from its redecoration in their honour. His daughter Anne secretly married the poet John Donne, causing a huge row which ended in Donne's imprisonment. When the angry father finally relented, the couple had twelve children before Anne died young, aged just thirty-three, leaving Donne heartbroken. Sir George built a new wing at Loseley, incorporating a chapel, a riding school, a picture gallery and staff accommodation, but when the family fortunes declined in the eighteenth century, the building fell into disrepair and was demolished in 1820. William More-Molyneux, who inherited the estate in 1874, made his contribution to Loseley by building the Nursery Wing, which now allows different generations of the family to live harmoniously side by side, 'semi-detached at Loseley' as James described it in his book *The Loseley Challenge*. James's father, Brigadier General Frank More-Molyneux-Longbourne built up the herd of Jersey cattle and started the Loseley dairy business, but when James returned home at the end of the Second World War in 1946, he found the house in a woeful condition. 'Five years without staff, windows shattered by bombs, no heating, dust and cobwebs covering the well-polished furniture of my memories; war had taken its toll.'

His parents had kept the house alive against all odds – cold, uncomfortable, empty, with no electricity and no piped hot water. They had refused suggestions that they should move out to one of the smaller, more modern homes on the estate because they knew that Loseley would not have survived if they had abandoned it. James cast around for ways of creating an income to restore the estate to its former glory. He built up Guildcrete, a concrete building blocks company, but the financial situation was rocky and it was faith that made him keep going and expand into timber framed houses with Guildway. For years Loseley was the centre of entrepreneurial activity – the famous ice-cream and timber homes each played a part in helping to restore the house and estate to health. It now looks at its best, loved, polished and lived in. Since James's son Michael began taking up the reins, he has steered it down a different path to survival, making this fabulous Tudor family home pay its own way as a venue for grand occasions.

Visiting stately homes has been a favourite public activity for centuries, so throwing Loseley open to visitors and wedding parties is following an established tradition. The house was originally used for royal visits so its impressive reception rooms are perfect for special events. Most modern solutions to keeping big houses in the family require an astonishing tolerance of the general public, and features shared by their owners include a strong sense of personal privilege coupled with a desire to share their good fortune with other people. There is a generosity of spirit here as well as a keen understanding of the importance of generating an income.

'I think Johnny Depp was behind me in the breakfast queue the other day,' commented Michael More-Molyneux after seeing a photograph of the screen idol. Depp filmed *Finding Neverland* with Kate Winslet at Loseley. But when Michael's daughter Katrina later tried to ask for the star's autograph, a bevy of bodyguards materialized from nowhere to protect him. Alternately rubbing shoulders with celebrities and being seen off by minders is one of the perks, or hazards, of the game when you open your doors to film crews. Over the years, a string of famous names, from Felicity Kendal to James Mason, have acted in films using Loseley as an authentic historic backdrop, and Hampton at Seale was used for episodes of *Poirot*. It is one of the more exotic ways of making great Surrey houses pay in order to keep them in the family.

'I think for a house of Loseley's size, it's terribly important that it is lived in,' said Michael.

> Otherwise it tends to become a museum and loses its spirit. It needs people doing all the little details like opening and closing windows and putting flowers out in order to create the atmosphere of being loved.

We are here to safeguard the house, not just for the family but as an important piece of history, and all our enterprises have been done to keep it all together. We were one of the first houses to start opening to the public in the 1950s, and now we open the gardens and have different events like concerts, fairs, shows and ploughing matches. It's developed from a few wedding receptions a year to about eighty receptions and forty actual weddings here and it's expanding all the time. There are always new things going on. A few years ago there was a craze for murder mystery evenings.

Outside we have an off-road course and we host a lot of conferencing awaydays. We also do a lot of Christmas parties and dinner dances. The family feels very strongly that Loseley should be shared and people are very appreciative. I am very excited at the prospect of having two sons in the future working at Loseley.

Meg Roper, Sir Thomas More's daughter, famously rescued her father's head from a spike outside the Tower of London, but another famous head, belonging to the Elizabethan adventurer and erstwhile court favourite Sir Walter Raleigh, is believed to be buried at West Horsley. When he was executed, his wife bribed the executioner to avoid his head being displayed on a spike. She waited below in her carriage and his head was wrapped in his cloak and thrust through her window. She had to decide quickly what to do with it. She was obviously a lady of strong stomach, for she had it embalmed and it accompanied her everywhere. After her death it was kept in a corner cupboard in the hall at West Horsley Place which had passed to her family, and when Raleigh's son later suffered a major family bereavement in an epidemic, he buried all the victims in the church, and laid his father's head to rest there too. It is assumed it is still there.

◀ The moat at Loseley Park

Highwaymen, Smugglers and a Notorious Murder

The sparsely habited heathlands of Surrey were dangerous for travellers. During the seventeenth and eighteenth centuries, Bagshot Heath was a haunt of notorious highwaymen like the Golden Farmer and the Frenchman Claude Duval, and the lights from the lone coaching inn at Hindhead must have been a very welcome sight for travellers braving the desolate heaths *en route* from London to Portsmouth or Chichester. But this was also a bad spot for highwaymen who would melt into the Punch Bowl mist after snatching their loot. William Cobbett described Hindhead as 'the most villainous spot God ever created' and I have heard several twentieth-century ghost stories about people stopping on the A3 to give a young woman a lift, only to find she vanishes from inside their car while they are driving. This area was dangerous and still is spooky; disappearing hitch-hikers are at best unsettling.

The wide open country of the North Downs at Epsom and Banstead were also haunts of highwaymen. Richard Wyatt JP recorded a rather genteel highway robbery, in the report of Surrey Quarter Sessions for 2 February 1775.

> Information [witness statement] of Daniel Harvey, driver of common post chaises, of Staines, Middlesex: About 2 months ago he was stopped by a man on Bagshot Heath near a house called Bromwell Hutt in Surrey, between the hours of 2 and 3. The man ordered him to stop, which he did. The man then went to the side of the chaise he was driving, in which were 3 women, and said to them 'Pray, ladies, don't be frightened. I am in distress and money I must have.' Informant did not see him take anything from them, but heard him say to them, 'Divide her money between yourselves.' The man then left the chaise and gave informant one shilling. The women told him that they had been robbed of 2 or 3 guineas, and desired him to drive on to the Taunton stage coach which was in sight.

The penalties were severe, however, with most men sent to the gallows like the one on Gibbet Hill. Until the railway brought the prospect of relatively safe freight travel in the mid-nineteenth century, heavily laden coaches were regarded as fair game by the highwaymen, and if possible people travelled by water for safety. The Thames was a major alternative thoroughfare.

But while legitimate travellers were grateful for the turnpikes and coach roads for their greater speed and comfort, other less law-abiding folk preferred the sunken winding lanes that threaded north-south through the hills, away from prying eyes. Smuggling was big business and people did not mess with smugglers. They did as they were told and enjoyed the odd reward of brandy or lace. The smugglers transported contraband from the coast to London. They crossed the Weald and then followed the narrow drove roads across the Surrey Hills.

Alfold – The Story of a Surrey Village, written in 1935 by F.W. Cobb, tells of Dame Tickner of Rosemary Lane, who was born in 1764. She told Miss Sparkes, the Rector's daughter, that in her youth, she knew of several smugglers operating in the area.

> When in bed she would hear them splashing down the lane on their powerful horses laden with spirit kegs. They turned up Mary Magdalene Lane, now a disused grass track. The smugglers' kegs were hidden in farm houses in Sidney Wood, where recesses in the great chimneys received them. If a farmer allowed the smuggled goods to be hidden in his farm, he would always find a present of spirits left behind for him.

Even the rector of Chiddingfold was a member of a local smuggling gang that met at Chantry House. Puttenham was also notorious for smugglers. They would ride through the village on their way to the wilds of Bagshot Heath which was a well-known smugglers' rendezvous. Local farmers would leave food for men and horses at places such as Puckstool Bottom at Rodsall in return for some contraband comforts.

The lanes and woods of Shere, Peaslake, Abinger, Coldharbour, Wotton, Holmbury St Mary, Holmwood, Hindhead and Haslemere were perfect for smuggling and there are lots of tracks still known locally as Smugglers' Lane. In the seventeenth and eighteenth centuries, squatters moved into the hills and heathland, building small cottages and making subsistence smallholdings. They scratched a living from the poor, sandy soil, and supplemented their incomes with broom-making, sheep-stealing and smuggling. The tax system in the eighteenth and early nineteenth centuries made smuggling worth the risk. Their targets were French wines, silks, satin and brandy which they sold on at a vast profit in London. One of the families known to be involved in smuggling gangs were the Tickners, who operated across Surrey, Sussex and Kent.

Even if not involved directly in smuggling, most humble folk turned a blind eye. Tax avoidance and the cash-driven black economy still enjoy a widely sympathetic hearing. But *The History of the County of Surrey* records how William Dudley of Coldharbour, who died in 1902 aged nearly 101, recalled that a man with whom he worked had been a witness when the turnpike keeper at Holmwood 'boldly refused to open his gate at night to a body of smugglers with kegs of brandy on their horses'. So there were a few upright people around after all.

Broom-making was associated particularly with Hindhead and the smallholders in the Punch Bowl, who went by the name of broom squires. Their brooms were made from the local silver birch trees and heather, and they had royalty and gentry among their clients, with their brooms going to grand houses including Hampton Court Palace and Windsor Castle. Makers of hand-crafted besoms and brooms are still known as 'broom squires', even apparently if they are female. The Hindhead 'broom squires' were immortalized by the Victorian author Sabine Baring-Gould, who wrote a novel about them inspired by the real murder of an anonymous sailor on Hindhead Common by three men. In his book *The Broom-Squire*, he imagines that the sailor was carrying a baby daughter, and that she survived the ambush.

This murder became very famous. It took place on 24 September 1786. An unknown sailor fell in with three men as he travelled to Portsmouth to join his ship. He paid for their lodgings in Godalming and they continued on their way south down the A3. Whether they quarrelled or whether the men had been preying upon him and were just biding their time is not known, but as they approached Hindhead, they killed him, stripped him and dumped his naked corpse in the Punch Bowl. His body was quickly discovered, however, and in the hue and cry that followed the murderers were caught just a few miles away in Rake, trying to sell his clothes. They were hanged on Gibbet Hill, their bodies left to rot inside iron cages as a deterrent to footpads. The sailor, identity still unknown, is buried in Thursley churchyard.

A large memorial called the Sailor's Stone was set up by the road, inscribed: 'Erected In detestation of a barbarous Murder Committed here on an unknown Sailor On Sep. 24th 1786 By Edwd. Lonegon, Mick Cagy & Jas. Marshall Who were all taken the same day And hung in Champs near this place. Whoso sheddeth Man's Blood by man shall his Blood be shed. Gen: Chap 9:Ver 6.' It was a gruesome tale that typically appealed to Charles Dickens, who wove it into his novel Nicholas Nickleby. Nicholas and Smike passed by the spot and read the inscription.

Remains of the gibbet were recorded as still standing in 1827, along with a plausible reputation for the place being haunted. Sir William Erle erected the present Celtic cross on the site of the gibbet in 1851 to reassure passers by with a message of hope and consolation. It read, in Latin, 'After death, safety; in death, peace; in life, hope; after darkess, light.' All very well, provided the traveller was capable of translating it.

William Cobbett

William Cobbett, the Farnham-born commentator on agricultural and social conditions, conservationist, politician and human rights activist, saddled his horse in 1822 and set out on the first of his famous *Rural Rides*. He was by then already an authority on farming practice and he looked at the countryside from a farmer's perspective. He liked land to be neat, orderly, well pruned and well husbanded, and the people who worked it to be properly paid, housed and educated. And he did not mince his words when he found ugliness, injustice, exploitation and the erosion of traditional skills. Today he would be a member of Greenpeace, the Campaign for the Protection of Rural England, the Surrey Hills Society and the Tenant Farmers' Association, and he would be shouting loud for the preservation of the countryside, affordable housing and a better deal for farmers from the European Union.

His descriptions of the Surrey Hills concentrate on the state of the roads, the quality of the timber and the health of the crops. Riding from Godalming to Guildford, after a nightmarish saga of misdirection trying unsuccessfully to avoid Hindhead, he wrote:

> I came here to meet my son, who was to return to London when we had done our business. The turnips are pretty good all over the country, except upon the very thin soils on the chalk. At Thursley they are very good, and so they are upon all these nice light and good lands round about Godalming.

▼ The memorial to the murdered sailor at Gibbet Hill, Hindhead

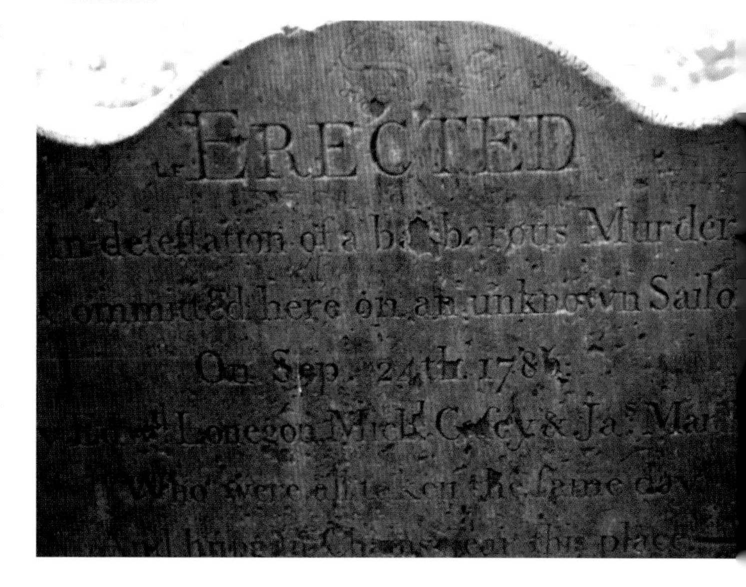

> This is a very pretty country. You see few prettier spots than this. The chain of little hills that run along to the south and south-east of Godalming, and the soil, which is a good loam upon a sand-stone bottom, run down on the south side, into what is called the Weald. This Weald is a bed of clay, in which nothing grows well but oak-trees. It is first the Weald of Surrey, and then the Weald of Sussex.
> November 29. Went on to Guildford where I slept. Everybody that has been from Godalming to Guildford knows that there is hardly another such a pretty four miles in all England. The road is good; the soil is good; the houses are neat; the people are neat: the hills, the woods, the meadows, all are beautiful. Nothing wild and bold, to be sure, but exceedingly pretty; and it is almost impossible to ride along these four miles without feelings of pleasure, though you have rain for your companion, as it happened to be with me.

Cobbett returned to Surrey after a spell as MP for Oldham in Lancashire and settled at Normandy Farm in Ash, where he died in 1835. He was buried in his home town of Farnham. It is completely appropriate that Farnham should cherish its Cobbett connection as the town's wealth was founded on agricultural bounty – corn, wool and hops.

Sanctuary for French Evacuees

The proximity of the Surrey Hills to London, especially when toll roads began to make travel less exhausting, brought a stream of literary, artistic, political, musical and generally cultured and interesting people to live in the villages. Mickleham at Box Hill played host to a particularly unusual set, not so much avoiding London smog or seeking an accessible rural idyll as escaping the Parisian mob and the guillotine. The story begins in 1784 when an officer in the Royal Marines, Captain Molesworth Phillips, a heroic survivor of Cook's last voyage, retired to Mickleham. His wife Susan was the sister of Fanny Burney, lady in waiting to Queen Charlotte and author of *Evelina,* the first novel published by an Englishwoman. Fanny would visit Susan when she was able to get away from court and the two would socialize at the nearby Norbury Park with William and Frederica Locke. Locke was by all accounts a thoroughly good man.

In 1792 France was entering Robespierre's Reign of Terror and the revolutionary hotheads were turning on those more liberal members of the French aristocracy who had initially supported the movement for change. They fled for their lives and found sanctuary at Mickleham and Westhumble. Ronald Shepperd, in his book *Micklam, the Story of a Parish*, quotes from a letter from Susan Phillips to Fanny Burney: 'We shall shortly, I

▶ William Cobbett, whose *Rural Rides* took him back and forth across the Surrey Hills

believe, have a little colony of unfortunate (or fortunate since they are safe) French Noblesse in our neighbourhood. Sunday evening, Ravely informed Mr Locke that two or three families had joined together to take Jenkinson's house Juniper Hall and that another family had taken another house at Westhumble.'

These were the liberal minded aristocrats and they included Narbonne, who had been Minister for War, Montmorency, the young reformist who had overseen the suppression of titles of nobility, Talleyrand, Bishop of Autun, and Mme de Stael, whose banker father had failed to rescue France's finances, all installed at Juniper Hall, and Mme de Broglie and family at Westhumble. By the time Fanny Burney finally met them all at Norbury Park in 1793, they had been joined by a recent escapee from the guillotine, General d'Arblay, who had been adjutant to General Lafayette.

Fanny and the dashing general hit if off immediately and within weeks he had proposed. It was a romantic story, one which Jane Austen could have easily used as a plot for a novel. D'Arblay had lost his fortune by leaving France, so although he was dashing and good company, everything one could hope, he had a serious drawback in that he was penniless. And he was a Catholic. Fanny relied on a royal pension of slender means dependent on good relations with the Protestant monarch, and the scene was set for a classic battle between heart and head. Despite sound advice as to the misery of wedded poverty, her heart won and they married at Mickleham on 31 July 1793. Some of the happiest years of their marriage were spent in their little house, Camilla Cottage in Westhumble, where the general launched into vegetable growing and amused his wife by attempting to prune the hedge with his military sword.

It is typical of Mickleham that the grand house where Fanny was courted by the general should be put to such a different use now as a Field Centre for Environmental Studies; another is now a school. These great houses in the village survived the ravages of military occupation during the last war, their histories peppered with extraordinary characters, and continue to contribute extraordinary added value to the life of the community.

Until recently, the elegant plaster mouldings of Juniper Hall's Templeton room made an almost surreal backdrop for the plastic clutter and noisy clatter of a student canteen. Luckily the building of a new dining room means it is now enjoying a more civilized existence as a meeting room. The field studies centre has been at Juniper Hall since 1947, providing courses for all ages from nursery level through to the University of the Third Age, taking up to eighty-five residential students plus 100 on day courses. Biology, geology, photography, history, flowers, insects, birds and butterflies – there are courses for all interests.

Surrey History Centre

▶ Early English novelist Fanny Burney who lived at Mickleham

If Juniper Hall students were accustomed to eating under a gilded ceiling, down the road at Box Hill School, pupils still enjoy the ornate Tudor-style panelling and mock-Gothic decoration of Dalewood House, built in 1883 by D.H. Evans, the Oxford Street department store owner, as a wedding present for his daughter.

Box Hill School was founded in 1959 by Gordonstoun housemaster Roy McComish, on the principles laid down by the pioneering educationalist Dr Kurt Hahn. It used to be known as the school with the cold showers and the morning run. All these schools have a less spartan regime now, but Box Hill still keeps the holistic approach. It is a big presence in the village and takes its social role seriously. The village uses the hall and the first school uses the grounds and theatre facilities. The parish priest is the chaplain.

Mickleham has for centuries been linked with the extended families of the Wedgwoods and the Darwins. The first Wedgwood connected to the area was the famous potter Josiah Wedgwood. He was elected a fellow of the Royal Society in 1783, in recognition of his invention of the pyrometer to measure kiln temperatures. When his long-term business partner died, he asked his friend Erasmus Darwin for help and his daughter married Darwin's son. Their son was Charles Darwin, the naturalist who formulated the theory of evolution. Charles and his sister Caroline also married a Wedgwood sister and brother. Caroline's husband, Josiah III, moved to Leith Hill Place in Tanhurst Lane, Coldharbour, in the second half of the nineteenth century and Caroline planted its famous rhododendron garden. Charles spent several holidays with them there, visiting his relatives and conducting his experiments.

The current Lady Wedgwood's parents came from very old Mickleham families too, the Gordon Clarks and the Lawrences. Her great grandfather, Sir Trevor Lawrence, was prominent in the Royal Horticultural Society and they were also friends with the Darwins. Sir William Lawrence was writing on evolution long before Charles took up the theme.

Poets in Residence

The dramatically brooding, black-cloaked figure of Alfred Lord Tennyson loomed over Haslemere but he was not the only poet to find inspiration and peace in the Surrey Hills. The poet and playwright Richard Brinsley Sheridan bought Polesden Lacey in 1804 and used the house as a great country social venue, where he could let his hair down away from his political and theatrical career in London. The house was in need of renovation but he never got round to rebuilding it. He did, however, create the impressive long terrace known as Sheridan's Walk with its great wall, which visitors still admire.

John Keats sought out the romantic landscape of Box Hill in 1817 to fire his imagination so that he could complete his epic poem *Endymion*. Over several days at the Fox and Hounds Inn, now the Burford Bridge Hotel, he wrote the final section, referring to the landscape that surrounded him in the poem. He wrote in a letter of climbing Box Hill and watching the moon.

Some fifty years later, George Meredith wrote of his life at Flint Cottage at the bottom of the Zig Zag: 'I am every morning at the top of Box Hill – as its flower, its bird, its prophet. I drop down the moon on one side, I draw up the sun on t'other. I breathe fine air. I shout ha ha to the gates of the world. Then I descend and know myself a donkey for doing it.' Meredith's poetry is muscular and spiritual with a pervading sense of the oneness of nature and he deserves to be better known.

Composer in Residence

Ralph Vaughan Williams was Caroline Wedgwood's grandson, and he lived at Leith Hill from the age of three until he left college. He grew up in one of the oldest and most noteworthy of the grand houses there that make the most of the spectacular panoramic views from Leith Hill across the Weald. It is unusual in that it dates back well beyond the nineteenth-century railway boom to around 1600 but with substantial eighteenth-century revamping. The enterprising Richard Hull lived here in the eighteenth century before the arrival of the Wedgwoods. Coldharbour has managed to avoid the

Surrey stockbroker belt makeover, emerging seamlessly out of dense forest, its rough grass very roughly cut, and churchyard paths thickly mossed. Drives are not all tarmac and paving with electronic gates. There is even some mud. Vaughan Williams spent his childhood deep in this beautiful countryside, with its blend of grandeur and rustic simplicity, teeming with wildlife and birdsong, and one senses how profound the effect has been upon his wonderfully evocative music.

He moved back to Dorking in 1929 on account of his wife Adeline's ill-health, throwing himself wholeheartedly into the musical life of the town, and in 1933 he bought White Gates, an eccentric house built on the lower slopes of Ranmore Common, since demolished. He used an enormous circular bay window as his study. Maybe it was the very remoteness and cultural poverty of the village he had grown up in that encouraged him to start a network of choral societies in Surrey's rural communities, choirs that welcomed everyone from the dairymaid, the cowman, the parlourmaid and the butler right through the social hierarchies to the gentry in the big houses. White Gates was perfect for the task of training these amateur gatherings as it had a huge central room perfect for choir practices.

These choral societies are still flourishing today, many of the original ones still taking part in the annual Leith Hill Music Festival in Dorking, founded in 1905 by his sister Margaret and Evangeline Farrer, who lived at Abinger Hall. Vaughan Williams was its conductor for nearly fifty years, stamping his inimitable personality on the event. The festival was set up to bring music to the villages, to people who had no experience of choral singing. Surrey was probably the only county with serving girls and gardeners happily singing madrigals under the baton of an internationally famous composer. Its motto was 'Music won the cause', taken from Dryden's *Alexander's Feast,* set to music by Handel. This work was appropriately featured in the festival's centenary programme.

Vaughan Williams was a friend of the novelist E.M. Forster, who from 1925 to 1946 made his home in Abinger Hammer, just up the road. Forster wrote *Aspects of a Novel* and *Abinger Harvest* while living at West Hackhurst. He must have felt part of the community, for in 1934 he wrote a pageant to be performed in aid of the Abinger Church Preservation Fund. Vaughan Williams, who was in the middle of composing music for the English Folk Dance and Song Society Masque, provided some music for the pageant as well and Forster included the pageant programme in *Abinger Harvest.* They collaborated again a few years later.

One gets a strong sense of convivial social networking in the Tillingbourne valley, almost a Surrey Hills Bloomsbury Group. Forster knew the Farrers and George Meredith through his great aunt. His university friend R.C. Trevelyan was living at Abinger – Forster had travelled to India with him in 1912. Trevelyan and Sylvia Sprigge, who moved to Abinger a bit later, produced a literary magazine called *The Abinger Chronicle,* which contained poems, essays and stories. The Barn Theatre at Shere, where Peter Ustinov made his theatrical debut, was also flourishing in the 1930s, so culture in the Surrey Hills was positively humming.

Vaughan Williams died in 1958 and memories of him are still vivid. At the centenary in 2005, the choirs he had founded competed as usual in the Dorking Halls that he had helped design. His spirit is no doubt still inside on the conductor's rostrum, but a bronze statue of him conducting stands in mid baton-wave outside the hall.

Rachel Farden was a member of the Dorking Oriana choir and she recalls Vaughan Williams taking rehearsals as an old man, growing increasingly deaf but still the absolute perfectionist.

> I remember Ralph Vaughan Williams. I did shorthand and typing for him just after the war. His study, where he composed, was a hexagonal room with benches round the window and I would have to clamber over piles of manuscripts to get to one of the seats to take notes. 'Kick them out of the way, m'dear,' he would say.
>
> Later I kept a riding stables and when I took the horses up the road I would meet him in his

bedroom slippers and pork pie hat tottering down to post a letter. He was quite solemn, with bushy eyebrows and his thoughts kept deeply inside him. Maybe he was composing music inside his head.

In 1944, Vaughan Williams left Leith Hill Place and its surrounding area, which had passed down to him through his family, to the National Trust, and the gardens of Leith Hill Place are now open to the public. The Trust already owned Leith Hill itself so the whole area is now protected.

The Arrival of the Railway

The second half of the nineteenth century and the turn of the twentieth witnessed so much social change in England that it is hard to work out what came first and what influenced what. Of huge significance to the physical development of Surrey was the arrival of the railway. But it was the invention of the bicycle and workers' leisure time that brought day tourism to the hills. The possibility of a better, healthier life outside the dirty, smoggy city could be appreciated by all sectors of society and pressure to build houses and sanitize muddy tracks with asphalt became almost unstoppable.

The Waterloo–Portsmouth and Victoria–Dorking main lines, the 'slow' line from Guildford to Waterloo via Clandon, and to a lesser extent the little Reading to Tonbridge line, opened up the Surrey Hills to commuters and the transformation of rural communities into dormitory suburbs. It brought the middle classes and new money, eager to escape the pollution of the capital, but in the early days it also brought novelists, painters, scientists, composers and poets. And it happily signalled the end of the highwaymen who had made travel such an uncertain experience. Smart money took the train, and pistols could be left at home. The changes were reflected in the works of Charles Dickens: by the time he was writing his final, unfinished novel *The Mystery of Edwin Drood,* his protagonists were hopping casually onto omnibuses to get to the railway station and catch a train to London.

The railway reached Guildford in 1845, Godalming in 1849 and Haslemere in 1859. Until then, there was little there bar the odd coaching inn on the rural stretches of the old turnpike from London to Portsmouth. The fact that towns and large villages were the safest places to stop is clear from the number of inns that used to crowd Guildford, Dorking and Ripley.

Soon Alfred Lord Tennyson was installed in his rural retreat at Blackdown, and by 1884 the eminent scientist and mountaineer Professor John Tyndall was enjoying country living on Hindhead Common. Tyndall did not need to fear the footpads any more and he was able to appreciate both the wild remoteness of Hindhead and its health and purity. He saw it more as a spa. He was fascinated by the movement of glaciers, the radiant property of heat and the acoustic nature of air. He succeeded Michael Faraday at the Royal Institution of Great Britain, where some of the major scientific discoveries of the last two centuries have been made. It was Tyndall who discovered why the sky was blue, and it is easy to see how Hindhead, with its racing clouds and dramatic storms caught his imagination. He and his wife lived in a hut among the heather complete with its own well until Hindhead House was built. He died quite tragically; he had married very late and as an old man found sleep elusive. His wife accidentally gave him an overdose of chloral, and he realized what she had done before he died.

Haslemere was still referred to as a village when retired surgeon Sir Jonathan Hutchinson fell in love with it. By 1875 he was living there full time, commuting to the London Hospital during the week. But when his wife died in 1887, he threw himself into his hobby of collecting archaeological finds. His collection became Haslemere Educational Museum, a pocket-sized British Museum with a completely eclectic collection of things garnered from all around the world. His haunting of London auction houses produced an amazingly diverse range of specimens, from fossils to stag heads, rock crystals to butterflies and it is hard to find a local artefact apart from some second-century cemetery ware.

The museum reflects Victorian philanthropy and a belief in the value of public education, and its philosophy still holds true today. Hutchinson was very advanced for his time; he believed museums should not be places where people just looked, but where they were encouraged to think and learn. He was very keen on getting adults in for what would now be described as lifelong learning, and the museum carries on that tradition. When he died, there was a real risk that the collection would be disposed of and lost, but luckily his friend and former patient Sir Archibald Geikie, a renowned geologist and fine watercolourist, stepped in to save it and he set up a trust. Haslemere Museum now boasts superb facilities for workshops, lectures and projects. Arthur the stuffed bear, which is at least eighty-four years old, was even given a session with a specialist hairdresser during a Heritage Lottery Fund refit.

Thanks to Tyndall's and Hutchinson's promotion of Hindhead and Haslemere, a steady trickle of famous writers, poets, musicians and wealthy gentry arrived. They sought out the most impressive settings for their grand architect-designed houses. You can look across the valleys to the hills and see these mansions perched on steep wooded slopes, tucked into folds in the forests and hugging hilltops as they gaze out at the magnificent views across the Weald; there is a feeling of space. The railway did not just bring the wealthy, however. It also sparked the creation of new, more utilitarian settlements around the stations, for example at Weyhill. When big houses required staffing, artisans' and workers' accommodation, shops and craftsmen's workshops had to be provided too.

Professor Tyndall died just as the crime writer extraordinaire Sir Arthur Conan Doyle arrived on the scene, determined to give his consumptive wife Touie the best chance of survival by building a house where the air was pure. It worked; Undershaw was situated in a sheltered, dry valley south of the Hindhead crossroads and Touie confounded her prognosis of a few months to live by surviving for thirteen years. Sir Arthur saw the beginning of another revolution in transport – the private motor-car. There was reputedly great excitement at the arrival of the author in his new car. He swept into the drive, lost control, rolled it and broke his leg.

Queen Victoria and the Volunteer Review

Probably the most important event in Chobham's history occurred in 1853 when the British Army camped *en masse* on Chobham Common. It was a spectacular event. Queen Victoria reviewed the troops and watched mock battles; it sealed the future of Surrey Heath as a military area. It still is. Luckily for Blackheath, however, the Volunteer Review of Easter Monday, 28 March 1864, was probably the most important event in Blackheath's history, but it failed to have any long-term significance other than to confer the name the Volunteer on the pub built in the village a few years later.

The event was extensively covered in the *Illustrated London News* of 9 April 1864, complete with a detailed illustration of the action and the grandstand where Queen Victoria sat and watched the mock battle unfold. The accompanying plan of the whole exercise shows that trains were laid on to bring spectators from Southampton, Lewes, Hastings, Brighton, Chichester, Winchester, Croydon, Reading, Maidstone, High Wycombe, Kingston, Chatham, Rochester and London. They would have taken the trains to Guildford and Dorking and changed to the Tonbridge line to Chilworth, then a substantial station with a connecting rail link to the gunpowder works. They would have walked up Sampleoak Lane to the heath. Blackheath was probably chosen for the review because the 22nd Surrey Royal Volunteers had their rifle range just off Littleford Lane.

The grandstand was erected on Rosemary Hill, then bare heather, and an area was set aside for spectators along Littleford Lane. Refreshments were set out on the heath to the west of Sampleoak Lane where the friary was built twenty-five years later. Visibility would have been much better than it is today because there were no trees on this part of the heath. The battle was between troops advancing from Albury and units drawn up to defend the area near what is now the cricket pitch, but it became rather muddled and the spectators were caught between the two sides. The worst incident occurred when one soldier accidentally left his ramrod in the barrel of his gun.

It shot across the heath and killed the Vicar of Blackheath, the Rev. W. Earle.

The Volunteer pub was built opposite the cricket ground and in the 1960s was a small, quiet pub with a sawdust-strewn bar floor, frequented by the cricket team. When as a child I rode past on my donkey, the cricketers would cajole him – surprisingly willingly – inside, where they would feed him soft drinks and arrowroot biscuits. He became adept at drinking neatly from a bottle. The pub could not escape change for long, however. Several makeovers later, it is now called the Villagers – a somewhat ironic name change, as it is used more by hungry ramblers than locals. It is also one of the few pubs with a hitching rail for horses, which makes it a favourite with thirsty horse-riders.

Technology and the Quest for God

The nineteenth century was an age in love with technology and the possibilities of engineering. In 1881, the world's first public electricity supply was switched on in Godalming – the UK's first hydroelectric power station, driven by water from the River Wey. This breakthrough was prompted by council thrift, however, rather than a love of new technology – and maybe that is what prevented it from being an unqualified success. Electricians Calder and Barrett of Lambeth undercut the Godalming Gas & Coke Company's quote to provide street lighting, which until then had been fuelled by gas. The electrical engineers harnessed the power of two Poncelet waterwheels at E & J Pullman's Leather Works at Westbrook Mill and produced a somewhat uncertain electricity supply, bright at the mill, a bit weak in the town centre. Alexander Siemens, who had supplied arc lights, provided more expertise, plus a traction engine to give more consistent power, but it was a bit of a nine-day wonder. The new-fangled electricity supply turned out to be expensive. The townsfolk were cautious, Siemens was not convinced of its long-term viability with such limited public support and he declined to tender for the next contract. Godalming's pioneering foray into public sector technology was snuffed out; the council went back to gas. But no one can deny Godalming's claim to fame as the first town to install public electricity.

The Churches at Albury

Balancing the nineteenth-century drive towards technological advance and material progress was a concern for the spiritual, partly contained within the mainstream Anglican and Catholic churches but also splitting off into fringe churches. The Catholic hierarchy in England and Wales had been re-established in 1850 and was anxious to set up institutions for training people for the priesthood and the Oxford Movement of high Anglicans was looking to establish the links between the apostles and the Church of England. Surrey villages were also alive with a variety of non-conformist churches.

The story of Albury, for example, is one of intense religious faith and heavy-handed bullying. It is the story of how a little community with barely enough people to fill one church, came to have three: the Saxon church in Albury Park, unused since 1843; the unusual red-brick Victorian parish church on the hill overlooking the modern village; and the very ornate Catholic Apostolic church in Sherbourne, mothballed to await the Second Coming.

My favourite is Albury Old Church which was recorded in the Domesday Book – golden honey stone, with a seventeenth-century bulbous shingled cupola finishing off its tower, and inside a chapel ablaze with glowing decoration by Pugin and dazzling stained glass. There is a real sense of the continuum of worship here over 2,000 years and thanks to the strong ties that even modern villagers have with the church, services are still occasionally held there. They are worth going to. The church had been abandoned to decay for eighty years before a service was held there in 1921, and now there is one every year at midsummer and a very special candle-lit carol service at Christmas.

▶ Albury Old Church, the much loved 'redundant' medieval church in the grounds of Albury Park

The Old Church was rescued by the Churches Conservation Trust which rebuilt the chancel at the east end, and the Old Church Committee keeps it in good heart. It is ideal for historical film sets because it is surrounded by beautiful, unspoilt country, approached via a narrow drive through the park over a cattle grid. There are no intrusive signs of the twenty-first century here.

The conversion of the Old Church into a private mortuary chapel for the Drummond family more or less finished off the depopulation of Albury Park. Henry Drummond, a wealthy banker and MP, was also a fervent follower of a radical Christian sect led by Edward Irving, a Scottish preacher who had been thrown out by the Presbyterians for his wild pronouncements, and who had started his own church in London. He had been a friend of Thomas Carlyle, but the speaking in tongues and bizarreness and hysteria of his services in London put an end to that. Irving was a forerunner of the charismatic movement and his teaching was based on an interpretation of Revelation. Drummond was fascinated and held discussion groups at Albury that initially included the rector, the Rev. Hugh McNeile as well as other Anglican clergy. As Irving's Catholic Apostolic Church got up steam, the clergy backed off and eventually Drummond and the Rev. McNeile parted company completely, with the rector actually preaching against the sect. Drummond meanwhile embarked on a flurry of mock-Medieval ecclesiastical building. In 1839, the young architect Augustus Pugin was detailed to decorate the newly designated mortuary chapel in the old Saxon church while William McIntosh Brookes was commissioned to build an exquisite neo-Gothic church in Sherbourne, complete with matching chapter house, for the new sect. A Romanesque church was commissioned on the steeply sloping Rudge's Field above Weston Street for the parish.

The sect believed in modern-day apostles but this proved tricky. When the last one of the sect died in 1901, the congregation dwindled and died. The church is now closed to the public, although it is meticulously maintained.

The only fully functioning church in Albury now, is the parish Church of St Peter and St Paul. Tradition has it that Drummond was shocked to return from a trip abroad and find that, in his absence, the church had been constructed not from stone as he had planned, but from very red brick. Perhaps he had not allocated sufficient funds. The brick is certainly eye-catching.

The Cokelers

During the 1840s, shoemaker John Sirgood, who had moved to Kennington from Gloucestershire, came under the influence of the non-conformist preacher William Bridges, the founder of the south London sect, the Plumstead Peculiars. While he was finding his feet as a preacher, Sirgood stayed around London, but in 1851 he and his wife Harriet moved south into the countryside, with their worldly goods in a handcart. He preached along the way and for a while they stayed at Lord's Hill in Shamley Green before settling in Loxwood, just over the border in Sussex.

Sirgood found his niche in the agricultural community, particularly among farm workers. He rejected the authority of the established church and concentrated on the individual's relationship with Christ, and soon he was able to set up small religious communities. Formally

▲ The extraordinary Catholic Apostolic Church built by Henry Drummond at Albury and now mothballed to await the Second Coming

▲ The new parish church for Albury, built by Henry Drummond after the villagers were forcibly resettled in what had been the hamlet of Weston

known as the Society of Dependents, because they were dependent on Christ for everything, the sect was more commonly called Cokelers, though no one knows for sure quite where this name came from. There are several theories. One is that it derived from Sirgood's preference for cocoa instead of beer, as the sect was teetotal, and another that it came from Coke's Hill, where they built a chapel. A third theory is that it is a corruption of 'cuckolders'. The sect preferred people not to marry on the grounds that family life got in the way of communion with Christ, but the women, who wore distinctive black straw bonnets and their hair plaited and bound up in a bun, were required to be housekeepers to the men, with the obvious opportunity for gossip and slanderous innuendo. The gossip was probably unjustified, as the chapel dominated their lives and the rules were strict.

As well as being teetotal and opposed to all frivolity such as singing and dancing, they were conscientious objectors and the ideal life was one of celibacy. They were unusual in that both men and women preached, often outside or in farm buildings. They attracted hostility from the establishment and support from the poor. As the communities became established they were accepted in the villages, especially when they started to open shops. Shamley Green historian Marion May traced the Cokeler stores to 1879. They sold everything from soap to suspenders, bacon to bootlaces as well as homegrown vegetables. They were known for their kindness to the poor, and profits from the shops were often used to help people in need. Like the Shakers in America, they also made furniture.

The last service at the Lord's Hill chapel was in the 1960s. At the height of Sirgood's ministry the Dependants numbered 2000; by the end of the 1980s they had dwindled to thirty. This verse from a Dependent hymn was found by Northchapel historian Pamela Bruce:

Christ's Combination Stores for me
Where I can be so well supplied,
Where I can one with brethren be
Where competition is defied.

Love and Death

The story of Holmbury St Mary and its picturesque little Victorian Gothic Revival church is underpinned by tragedy. In Medieval times Holmbury Hill was common land, where local people grazed animals and gathered fuel. It was wild country, settled in the seventeenth century by folk driven out of London by plague and fire, and the area gained a reputation as a nest of sheep stealers, smugglers and poachers. Many of the old cottages have large cellars that were used for storing contraband. In the early nineteenth century the hill was still just a scattering of tiny hamlets – Felde, Sutton and Pitland Street.

In 1849 the Redhill – Tonbridge railway line opened up the Greensand Hills to commuters, and when the eminent Victorian ecclesiastical architect George Street visited friends in one of the new big houses that had been built on the slopes of Holmbury Hill, he described the area as 'heaven's gate'. He set about designing and building a house for himself and his wife Mariquita called Holmdale. But before it was finished, she died. Work on the house came to halt but after a few years Street found himself a new young bride called Jessie Mary. His misfortune now escalated to tragedy. Jessie Mary caught a fever on their honeymoon and died just eight months after their wedding. A man with a deep love of thirteenth-century English Gothic architecture and a career in church and public buildings – one of his most famous achievements was the Royal Courts of Justice – George Street found solace by building his own memorial to his young bride. It took the form of a Gothic Revival church, built at his own expense and dedicated to the Virgin Mary, named in memory of his wife, whose tomb is on the outside wall of the chancel. Twice widowed and overworked, the poor man suffered a stroke in 1881, and died at the age of 57. He would probably have liked to be laid to rest next to Jessie Mary, but he was such an eminent architect that he was buried with full honours in Westminster Abbey.

There is an interesting aside to this sad story: churches need parishes and there was none for his church before he started building, so the three little hamlets were drawn together under the new name of Holmbury St Mary, combining the names of church and hill.

Quaker's Orchard

There were Quakers in Surrey from the mid-seventeenth century, with communities in Dorking and a small group in Peaslake. Quaker's Orchard in Lawbrook Lane, Peaslake, is a rambling house dating back to the sixteenth century. *Peaslake – Story of a Surrey Village,* edited by local historian Jenny Overton, records that from 1532 the house was owned by Thomas Seaman. It passed down through his family and in 1660 was owned by another Thomas Seaman, one of the early Quakers. According to local legend, he built the stone part of the house as a meeting hall and gave over a plot of land in the garden, believed to be within the small walled orchard, as a burial ground for the Quaker community. There are records held at the public record office in Kew of twenty-six burials from 1671 to 1716 at the 'Shere Burying Place of Friends'. Thomas Seaman died in 1699 and the Quaker community gradually dwindled, but the house was still known locally as 'the Burying Place'.

The conductor Sir Adrian Boult also left his mark on the house. He built a large and ugly music wing during the Second World War, and incidentally also upset the village by swapping the recreation ground that abutted his music room for a piece of land he owned on the other side of the road. Apparently the noise of villagers playing put him off his music. The exchange was a disaster. Too far from the village centre, the new ground is barely ever used except for a monthly clay pigeon shoot.

The Friary at Chilworth

On the edge of Blackheath overlooking Chilworth stands the friary of the Franciscan Order of Friars Minor. The Rev. Dr Arthur Wells bought the 10-acre site from George Henry Drew in 1889 for £960 and he became

▼ Chalets, some Swiss style, some looking unexpectedly like ones from the Raj era in Indian hill stations, dot the steep sides of the Greensand Hills

the founder of the friary and the church, which was built in 1892 as a novitiate house – the place where novices were trained in preparation for their final vows. The overall cost of building the friary (£7,000) was met from the legacy of Mrs Marry Alliott, Wells's aunt. It is interesting to note, however, that while Surrey wealth would endow stone and mortar, it was reluctant to support the running costs of the friary and in the early years the friars lived in genuine poverty and physical discomfort through lack of a generous Catholic population nearby. It was the cash-strapped parishioners from the inner-city Franciscan parishes who were most supportive.

The sense of spiritual tranquillity, both within the grounds and inside the friary and its beautiful church, is almost tangible, with a real sense of the continuum of worship and communion with God. This atmosphere is helped, no doubt, by the presence in the cloisters of a yew tree struck from a cutting of an ancient tree growing in the quadrangle of the friary in Killarney. This tree in turn originated from Muckross Abbey, which founded in 1430. Since its foundation in 1892, more than 800 men have passed through the friary, seeking to find out if they had a vocation for the Franciscan way of life. It is the much-loved focal point of the Roman Catholic parish and is used by school and parish groups for day retreats and longer periods of recollection, as well as for weddings and concerts and the popular annual fête. Where else would you find fully robed friars running a coconut shy and organizing children's races and a dog show?

Quite by accident I one year provided donkey rides for the fête. I was taking my old donkey for a walk on the heath with a group of friends, dogs and my pet sheep, when we saw that the fête was on and decided to go and have a look round. A friar rushed up to me with a look of utter relief on his face: 'Thank goodness you have come,' he said, 'the pony rides have not turned up. Could you do them for us?'

The sheep was tethered to a tent post, the dog was entered for the dog show and the donkey performed a sterling service all afternoon.

▼ St Mary's Church, Holmbury St Mary, lasting memorial to a lost wife.

▲ Chilworth Friary on the edge of Blackheath overlooking the Tillinbourne valley was built for the Franciscan Order and forms the centre of the local Roman Catholic community

Franciscan friars were never meant to live a strictly monastic life. The order was founded to work among the people and has a tradition of hospitality that the Franciscan community is keen to foster. Like many religious communities, it is having to adapt to a changing world. There are just a few friars living there now. The novitiate has moved to Ennis in Ireland and Chilworth takes postulants instead – people who are considering whether to enter the novitiate.

'One of the big challenges now is to decide what our life is about,' Father Juniper told me before retiring as Guardian of the Friary and parish priest.

> A lot of young adults are still seeking a spiritual life and a community but they don't necessarily see the way we live our lives as attractive. What we have to offer, however, from St Francis and St Clare, is highly attractive. Our job together is to explore the potential here, see how we can develop Chilworth and get more and more people involved.
>
> The Friary is a unique place of prayer, hospitality and space: a place to engage with youth particularly. What matters to us is people's humanity.

St John's Seminary

The neighbouring Roman Catholic institution, St John's Seminary in Wonersh, was designed by the same eminent Victorian architect as the friary, Frederick Walters, who tackled the projects fresh from designing the rebuild of the demolished medieval monastery at Buckfast Abbey. It must have been an exhilarating time for this prolific architect. He relied on a 1734 print of the Buckfast ruins, and the discovery of the medieval foundations under the vegetable plot to recreate the abbey in mid-twelfth-century ecclesiastical style. He studied the thirteenth-century ruins of Greyfriars in Reading and St Andrew's Hall in Norwich as inspiration for Chilworth Friary. At the same time he was drawing on red-brick Dutch Jacobean architecture as inspiration for St John's Seminary, just the other side of Blackheath. The result is two stunningly different institutions built within a couple of miles and a few years of each other.

The seminary, just outside Wonersh, was founded in

1891, at the same time as the friary, to train students for the Roman Catholic priesthood. In the 1950s and 1960s, the students used to be sent out for fresh air and exercise in threes. The pavements were not wide enough for three abreast, so the trios of men in black walking along in a V formation, deep in conversation, were instantly recognizable. As children we called them the 'corbies' – the country name for crows. The seminary today is an associated institution of the University of Surrey and as well as serving dioceses in the south of England, it also caters for students from dioceses further afield and members of religious orders. Since 1985 it has also offered university courses in theology for lay (external) students.

The 'Nest of Peaslake Suffragettes'

This wonderful phrase, conjuring up a tightknit community of intellectual feminists was the invention of Edwin Waterhouse, founder of the accountants Price Waterhouse, who lived in a splendid country house he had built for his family at Feldemore in Holmbury St Mary. He was very concerned that a group had settled in neighbouring Peaslake, of 'fourteen ladies there of very advanced views, among them Mrs Brackenbury and her two daughters, all of whom were convicted recently of breaking shop windows in London for the purpose of advertising themselves and their cause.'

His principal anxiety appeared to be the way their houses and behaviour lowered the tone of the area, but such unusual women tucked away in an isolated little hill village, whose historical claim to fame was smuggling, excited the imagination of two current Peaslakers, Joan Mant and Jenny Overton. They set about discovering who they were and how they came to be there. 'Who were these fourteen ladies, arriving like the bad fairy at the birthday ball: uninvited but potent guests, accomplished, well turned out – and threatening disruption?'

Their booklet, *A Suffragette Nest,* sets out the fruits of their research, and it makes fascinating reading. The Brackenburys of Brackenside, for example, were both politically motivated and artistic, and they moved in quite exalted artistic circles. Their friend Flora Shaw knew the Vaughan Williamses of Leith Hill and Charles Brackenbury was a friend of the poet George Meredith of Box Hill. The suffragette movement interested Jenny Overton because she was related to Mary Overton who worked by the Brackenburys. It interests me because my family includes Elizabeth Garrett Anderson, the first woman to qualify as a doctor, her doctor daughter Louisa, and her sister Millicent Garrett Fawcett, president of the more peaceful and rational National Union of Women's Suffrage Societies. Hilda Brackenbury and her daughters Georgina and Maria, along with Mrs Emmeline Pethick-Lawrence, however, joined Mrs Pankhurst's much more militant and confrontational Women's Social and Political Union. Peaslake was probably home to both suffragettes and suffragists. I imagine hot debates among the pinewoods of the Hurtwood.

Peaslake was positively buzzing with intellectual and artistic women, some independent and single – there were more than ninety independent women in the village in 1919 – some married to long-suffering menfolk. Amongst the community were: Helen Gordon Liddle of Mackie's Hill, who endured force feeding in Strangeways Gaol; Emmeline Pethick-Lawrence's husband, one time Secretary of State for India who supported his wife's cause and went to prison, who was made the first Baron of Peaslake; and Alice Bell le Geyt

▼ Miss Le Geyte, one of the wealthy female intelligentsia who monopolised Peaslake in the early twentieth century

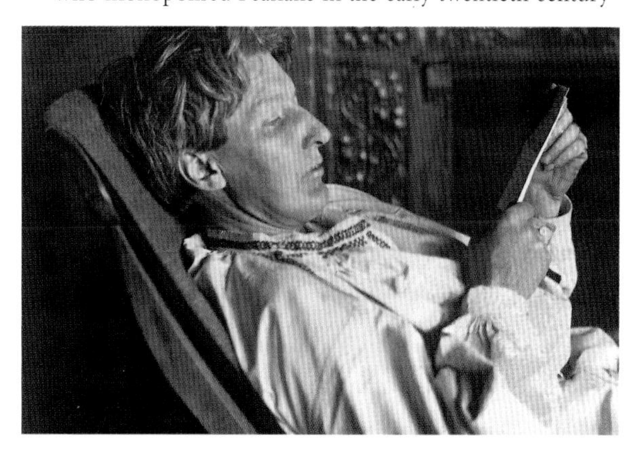

who lived at the Chalet opposite Peaslake Church. She was a novelist and coppersmith and the house was full of her handiwork. Some of it is still there.

The Birth of the National Trust

The Surrey countryside changed dramatically with the influx of wealthy, educated intellectuals and artists from London. They were a threat with their enthusiasm for bricks and mortar, but they also had an aesthetic appreciation of the landscape and the clout and the funds ultimately to organize to protect it. It happened very quickly – just fifty years from the arrival of the newcomers on the newly opened railway to the creation of the National Trust.

The Open Spaces Society, its forerunner, was set up in 1865 because people who had moved to the country to enjoy the landscape were concerned about the enclosure of the common land they loved. It is Britain's oldest national conservation body and its founders and early members included Sir Robert Hunter and Miss Octavia Hill, who with Canon Hardwicke Rawnsley went on to found the National Trust in 1895, to 'act as a guardian for the nation in the acquisition and protection of threatened coastline, countryside and buildings'. The trust is now one of the biggest landowners in the Surrey Hills so the organization is hugely important for the survival of the AONB. A stone seat was erected by Octavia Hill's family on Hydon's Ball after her death in 1912, as a monument to her achievement in preserving the hills. Parts of the Welsh coastline, the Cambridgeshire fens, the Lake District and Stonehenge were the first major triumphs in its property portfolio.

With Sir Robert living in Haslemere, it is no surprise that threats to Hindhead and the Devil's Punch Bowl were watched with alarm. By the 1880s, the wealthy arrivistes were bubbling with concern at the insensitive activities of the lords of local manors. The Lord of the Manor of Frydinghurst was enclosing part of Hindhead Common and among the commoners urging action to protect the land was Jonathan Hutchinson of Haslemere Museum fame. Sir Robert Hunter had already saved Epping Forest from enclosure with the help of the Liberal MP Henry Fawcett, the husband of the suffragist Millicent Garrett Fawcett, and he suggested that local people form the Haslemere Commons Committee to campaign to keep the heaths open. They realized that they needed strong local support, a sound knowledge of law and good maps – probably the three most important elements for any conservation campaign. Their aim was also to get the landowners to accept statutory regulation. The modern word for this is partnership – the fundamental element of all conservation work on the Surrey Hills today.

Thanks to the committee's efforts, the lord of the manor of Frydinghurst eventually accepted that the freehold tenants of the manor were entitled to rights of common, of pasture, of turbary (turf cutting) and of estovers (gathering wood for fuel or house or tool repair), and the lord was prevented from 'enclosing or digging gravel'. The locals had won and the Haslemere committee lapsed, its members taken up with the newly established parish councils, until a new bad boy appeared on the scene.

The self-made Anglo-American millionaire, J. Whitaker Wright of Witley Park, started rooting up shrubs and trees on the common for his garden. The *Surrey Times* headline for 13 May 1899 was 'Despoiling Hindhead Common' and with delicious understatement quoted residents being 'not a little annoyed, and certainly very much grieved', at his cavalier treatment of the Punch Bowl. He apparently pleaded ignorance. He could not plead ignorance in his financial irregularities, however, and despite evasive tactics – moving first to Paris and then to America – in 1902 he was brought back to stand trial in England. Sentenced to seven years in gaol, his response was to commit suicide inside the courthouse: he swallowed a cyanide capsule, asked for a cigar in a final gesture of sang-froid and died.

Following his death, his estate was auctioned and the manorial rights over the Hindhead commons, including the Punch Bowl and Gibbet Hill, were offered as one 750-acre lot. It seemed a golden opportunity. The

Commons Preservation Society appealed to the locals to raise the money and Sir Robert Hunter stepped forward again to chair a fund-raising committee to buy it. There was a worrying moment during the auction, when the bidding went hundreds of pounds beyond their guaranteed funds, but the committee held their nerve. They bought it for £3,625, just over £4 10s (£4.50) an acre, and local people donated the outstanding balance. A local committee was formed to take over its management and Sir Robert became chairman. The committee transferred the land to the National Trust in 1906. The *Surrey Advertiser* broadcast that Hindhead was safe and 'preserved in perpetuity for ever'. The paper was right, as in 1907 the National Trust Act gave it the right to call its land 'inalienable', safe from compulsory purchase. If the Government wants any of it, it has to pass an Act of Parliament first.

Hindhead was the first Trust property in the country to be managed by a local committee. Over the years, further land was acquired nearby, including some in neighbouring Sussex, and in 1908 the large expanse of Ludshott Common in Hampshire was added. This unusual arrangement continued until quite recently, when the Trust took over direct control. The Director General of the National Trust, Fiona Reynolds, visited Hindhead in 2006 to celebrate the centenary of its acquisition of the commons. 'This was the birthplace of the amenity movement,' she said, 'The people who bought this land and gave it to the Trust were visionaries with enormous prescience.'

Sir Robert Hunter was driven to found the National Trust because he knew that Victorian legislation was inadequate to protect land and property. In 1884, the owner of Sayes Court, a seventeenth-century manor house at Deptford, had wanted to donate it and its grounds to the public, but there was no authority in place, either to accept or to maintain it. It took Sir Robert over ten years to set up a new company with the power to buy and hold land and property for the benefit of the nation, too late to save Sayes Court, which was demolished in 1930. The manor had been part of the Evelyn Estate. The acquisition of property by the Trust was still a very difficult issue. However, when Sir Robert died in 1913, his campaign and his achievements were well appreciated by the public, and in 1919 the ponds and valley at Waggoner's Wells, next to Ludshott Common, were bought with money collected by public subscription, as a memorial to him. A stone of Iona granite stands at the head of the top pond with the inscription: 'In grateful memory of Sir Robert Hunter KCB and his lifelong work for open spaces, Waggoner's Wells were purchased and dedicated to the public by his friends and neighbours, December 1919.'

It was not until the National Trust Act of 1937, which enabled the Trust to accept the gift of country houses with endowments in land or capital, free of tax, that opportunities opened up for private owners to avoid punitive death duties and save precious buildings and landscapes for the nation. This was a hugely significant piece of legislation for Surrey and a number of properties were made over to the trust at this time, including the areas around Leith and Box Hills.

The National Trust had really caught the public imagination by this time. It was still a small, personal organization and stories about it abound. One concerns the Robertson Bequest, named after William Alexander Robertson, whose two younger brothers died in the First World War. William left a legacy to the Trust on his death in 1937 that would give his brothers a lasting memorial. He stipulated that the money should go towards buying interesting land or buildings in the south-east, match-funded by the Trust. The Trust was delighted to oblige. Netley Park at Shere is one of the properties bought with his legacy, marked with a memorial to the brothers: 'Norman Cairns Robertson, Capt 2nd Batt Hampshire Regt, who died twentieth June 1917 at Hanover, Germany, and of Laurance Grant Robertson, 2nd Lt 2nd Batt, King's Own Scottish Borderers, who was killed in action in France during the Battle of the Somme in or near Delville Wood, 30th July 1916.' The exact specification of the memorials, which were to be erected at each site bought with the legacy, was set out in his will. Other parcels of land were acquired at Frensham Common, Hindhead, Inval and Weydown Commons, Hydon's Ball and Hydon Heath. There is a nice little rhyme connected with Hydon's Ball, but why is a mystery:

> On Hydon's Top there is a cup,
> And in that cup there is a drop.
> Pick up the cup and drink the drop
> And place the cup on Hydon's Top.

Octavia Hill's stone seat is there and morris dancers sometime frolic on the summit on May Day. In August 1989, ramblers noticed a circle burnt into the turf which gave rise to rumours of a witches' coven. It was also spotted by Wonersh geologist Dr Peter Llewellyn, who speculated that it had been created by pouring metholated spirits in a circle and lighting it. The low blue flame would not have been noticed except by people close to the circle, he said.

The Ferguson Gang

This account of an extraordinary group of high-born, highly educated female philanthropists who helped the fledgling National Trust acquire a number of properties, comes from architect and *Oldie* cartoonist Brian Bagnall. He knew them all personally as he lived at Shalford Mill, where the gang had their secret den, until his death a few years ago.

> In 1931, a young woman in her mid twenties was staying for the weekend with the Godwin Austen family who were living in a house near Ewhurst. They owned most of Shalford. On the Sunday evening Arthur Godwin Austen took the young woman back to Guildford to take the train to London. As they came through Shalford, she happened to look down the lane and the evening sun lit up the tiles on the mill and it was very beautiful.
>
> It has a magical, clear luminescence and she said how pretty and as they had some time before the train, they walked down the lane and saw the dilapidated mill. The Gramshaw family, then a very, very good furniture restorer, wanted to buy the mill for all its timber but Arthur Godwin Austen was reluctant and he said to the young woman: 'If you can think of a use for it I will give it to you.' It was a burden to him financially.
>
> She went back to London and got hold of some chums and they met. It was a group that had started three years earlier as a result of a book by Clough Williams-Ellis to defend England from what he called the Octopus. They called themselves Ferguson's Gang but nobody knows why.
>
> It was just a name and they were all women who met at Oxford and they limited themselves to eight members and they all adopted noms de guerre. The young woman staying with the Godwin Austens was Sister Agatha, who became a luminary in the British Red Cross. They were very idiosyncratic. Bill Stickers was a great niece of Gladstone and the first woman to take a double first in Sanskrit and Oriental Languages at Newnham, and she did everything wholesale. She was quite a good artist and within a year had staged a one man show. She married the 'Captain' and went to live in Cornwall. She became a Catholic and was in the Guinness Book of Records for having created the longest tapestry illustrating the Narnia stories by C.S. Lewis.
>
> Red Biddy, another of them, was the daughter of a major general and she was a paediatrician. She cared so much about children that when she felt that one was being neglected she abducted it. She was imprisoned for 18 months. It was a very strange group of people and they went to the National Trust and said 'we want you to have this mill'. The National Trust said they must establish whether it was worth keeping and what needed to be done to it and consulted the eminent architect John MacGregor, the most important expert on the protection of ancient buildings. He went to see the mill and said it was absolutely marvellous and should be kept, recommending that it be lived

in. At that time the trust had almost no buildings, just land. Shalford Mill was among the first three they accepted.

The Trust said a shed like that would be very difficult to let and he said, 'Try me for size' and it was agreed that if someone could live there part time and they could raise the funds through Ferguson's Gang they would accept it. The gang collected over £300. Everything, including repairs and conversion cost £450 in 1932 and that is the point at which we became involved. John MacGregor was my wife Joanna's father, and Joanna went to live there with her family in 1932. The gang, primarily Bill Stickers, called Joanna's father, the architect, the 'artichoke'. She talked in a mock Cockney accent. She was very well born but it was her quirk. I have letters that are most extraordinary in the way they are worded and expressed in Cockney.

Anyway, they asked the artichoke whether he could make a private room for them to meet between the house part and the public part of the mill. He made this tiny room about 12ft by 12ft and it had a small deal table, four simple chairs, a Belfast sink, and an Aladdin stove which took three hours to boil a kettle. The R101 crashed at Beauvais in 1931 and the R100 was dismantled and one of the gang had a brother who was part of the airship programme and they managed to buy two of the bunk beds from the gondola and brought them down.

They would bound into the National Trust offices fully masked – their masks were gym knickers with holes cut for their eyes – and hand over a goose stuffed full of coins. Their deposit for Shalford Mill was £100 in silver coin. Their message was:

We ain't so many – we ain't so few;
All of us has this end in view –
National Trust – to work for you.
Green grass turning to bricks and dust –
Stately homes that will soon go bust –
No defence, but the National Trust.
Looking at rural England thus –
George and Dragon is changed for us,
Into St Clough and the Octopus.
Ferguson's Gang has paid its debt;
Ferguson's obligation's met,
Ferguson's Gang has more for you yet.

They would come down and take out a Fortnum and Mason hamper and two or three bottles. If our children were around Bill Stickers would hide under the bunk bed as she wasn't keen on children. By 1965 the gang had stopped using the room, they had dispersed and married and three of them came and formally handed the room over to Joanna and myself.

Joanna and her sister Penelope were brought up at the mill during the warmer months and they still live – all year round now – in the mill and the cottage next door. As children they were told not to stare when the gang came down and to be on their best behaviour. They recalled how they would arrive and start cooking with ingredients such as garlic, which seemed exotic to children in the 1930s. They would listen to them yelling their battle cry as they struck the millstone, and chanting in Latin, dancing in flowing robes and staying up all night to greet the dawn. To the children they were fascinating and a little shocking.

Joanna and Brian made the mill their full-time family home in 1952 despite the cold and damp, and their children and two of their grandchildren were born there. Brian Bagnall died in 2004. His final cartoon for *The Oldie* was sent from his hospital bed just three weeks before his death.

Brian illustrated the 'Dear Bill' column in Private Eye from 1984 to 1990 and his cartoons also appeared in *History Today*, *Boz*, *Spectator*, *Punch*, *Oldie*, *Observer* and for many years, the *Surrey Advertiser*. A Catholic with a sharp wit and gritty humour, he declared that he would 'draw until the tumbril arrives'. He practically did.

Shalford Mill was just the first of the Ferguson's Gang's purchases for the Trust, and the secretaries grew accustomed to their antics. Their messages were signed by Bill Stickers, Sister Agatha, Red Biddy, 'Erb the Smasher, See Mee Run, Gerry Boham, their spiritual head, the Right Bludy, the Lord Beershop of the Gladstone Islands & Mercator's Projection, Silent O'Moyle and others. Their escapades were all recorded with relish in their minute book called the Boo, which is now in the Trust's archive. The Trust appeared to enjoy doing business with the gang. After all they shared Clough Williams-Ellis's loathing of the Octopus – the uncontrolled sprawl of post First World War ribbon and urban development that seemed to have no appreciation of England's heritage. And they raised an incredible total of £4,500 between the wars – a huge sum for the time, especially as not all the members of the gang were well heeled. Sister Agatha's father was a socialist who did not believe in inherited wealth and she earned her living as a hospital almoner.

▼ Sisters Joanna Bagnall and Penelope Adamson, who still live in and next door to Shalford Mill, where they grew up as children

Fox's Arboretum

In 1952, Dr Wilfrid Fox, a specialist in dermatology, handed to the National Trust a rather special piece of the Surrey Hills that he had nurtured for some fifteen years – his arboretum at Hascombe. This is not natural Surrey countryside but a magnificent collection of trees from all around the world and it is a fabulous place to visit, especially in spring when the azaleas are in bloom, and in autumn when the leaves flame into colour. The hillside site was bought by Dr Fox in 1937. He lived nearby at Winkworth Farm, later the home of wildlife artist David Sheppard, and he had long enjoyed the piece of neglected woodland that was then part of the Thorncombe Estate. For him it epitomized the English landscape – a mix of pastoral and woodland, with hedgerows full of wildflowers and great views. And it also gave him the space and opportunity to indulge his hobby of collecting trees and shrubs. When not working in London hospitals, he was campaigning to improve the urban environment through the planting of trees in streets. He was a founder of the Roads Beautifying Association in 1928, and like many people passionate about their hobbies he became an expert on trees and was a close friend of W.J. Bean, Curator of the Royal Botanic Gardens at Kew. He donated 62 acres, including the Upper Lake to the National Trust in 1952 and the Trust bought another 35 acres with the Lower Lake in 1957. He continued to help manage the collection, now known as Winkworth Arboretum, until his death in 1962.

Feathercombe

Not far from Winkworth, across the hills in Hambledon is another piece of living history, a house and a fabulous shrub garden that has been in the ownership of one family since it was built nearly 100 years ago. Twelve acres of painstakingly created terraces and parterres, walks and vistas have survived two world wars and the social revolution that all but destroyed other gardens. But unlike Heligon, the famous Cornish garden eventually reclaimed from its long sleep, Feathercombe was never totally abandoned to nature; it simply evolved.

Eric Parker, local author and journalist, who built the house on the slopes of Hydon Ball looking out over panoramic views from the Hog's Back to Hindhead and Blackdown, would still recognize the garden he created in 1910. But he would be amazed that Ion Campbell, his granddaughter Muriel's husband, should have become sole gardener, managing the estate with just a few hours' help a week. It originally occupied the time of six gardeners, working full time, tending herbaceous borders and propagating and bedding out thousands of annuals. It must have been a riot of colour in summer.

Eric Parker is not widely read these days except by people interested in old Surrey, but his name should strike a chord with more observant Guildford shoppers as the plaque in the wall by Holy Trinity Church in the High Street bore a quotation from one of his books, entreating passers by to help keep Guildford 'a beautiful city'. His book *The Gardener's England*, which he wrote in the 1930s, described how he planted the garden and brought in tons of local Bargate stone to make the retaining walls for the terraces. These terraces, flights of steps and rockery still provide the hard structure of the garden, but nature has also put up a hard fight for supremacy. Ion has had to hack back monster rhododendrons to expose old walls and give smothered plants a chance; Eric Parker admitted that if he had known how aggressive rhododendrons would be, he would never have planted them. Wherever one looks in this wonderful old garden, one sees his planting at full, mature stature. In spring, the densely planted, massive shrubs covered in flowers are spectacular. Saplings that he planted round a splash pool for the children are now 60ft monsters lowering over the pool's ghost, a slight depression in a dark glade.

Feathercombe has something of the feel of an arboretum, partly because the disappearance of the garden staff has forced a change away from labour intensive cultivation. Annual bedding plants are definitely out. Trees and shrubs are taking their place, amid the fabulous displays of azaleas, camellias, rhododendrons and tree heathers.

The Surrey Hills at War

In 1875, a force of Volunteers was sent by train to Horsham to intercept a German invasion, but it arrived

▼ Labour of love – the wonderfully imaginative topiary garden at Feathercombe in Hambledon

too late and had to fall back on the promontory of Leith Hill. Caught in a pincer movement by the superior enemy forces, the Volunteers retreated through Coldharbour towards Dorking in a bid to hold the Dorking Gap, only to be routed at Denbies. The result was the defeat of Britain and the collapse of the empire. This is, of course, fiction; a story written by Colonel, later General, Sir George Chesney MP and printed in *Blackwood's Magazine* in May 1871. It was, however, based on sufficient truth to act as a warning to the Government of what might happen unless Britain looked to her home defences. It certainly had an effect.

Against a backdrop of recurrent threats of invasion, a ring of forts or mobilization centres was built on the downs escarpment as a defensive line to repel an attack from the sea and protect London. One of these forts was on Reigate Hill. The idea was to weaken the enemy advance by making the invaders fight on a long front. The forts were essentially centres for the storage of guns, small arms ammunition, tools and other equipment for the batteries and infantry defending a 70-mile stretch of downland. They were closed in 1906 when politics shifted: France became an ally and the new enemy was Germany.

▼ Illustration of the interior of Reigate Fort

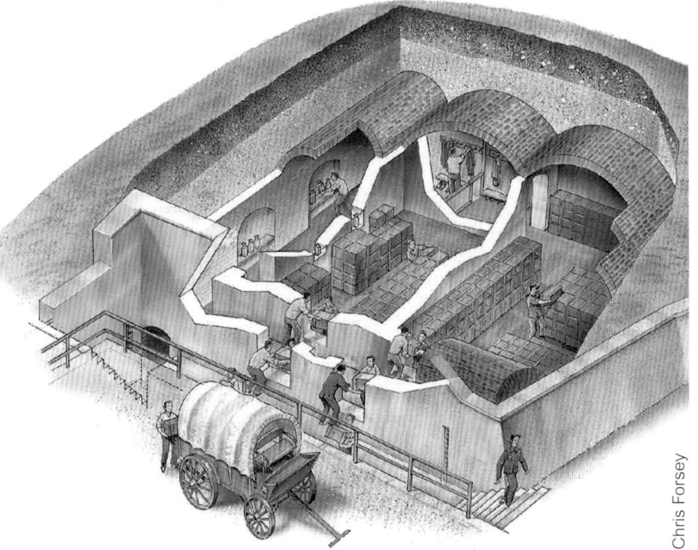

Chris Forsey

Reigate Fort was given a new lease of life during the Second World War when it was used for billeting Canadian forces. It was subsequently used as a scout camp before falling into disrepair. Now owned by the National Trust, the hilltop and fort have undergone extensive restoration and scrub clearance and visitors can find out about its history from interpretive material.

It was the threat of German invasion in the Second World War that had the biggest impact on the North Downs, however. Following the British retreat from Dunkirk, it was known that Hitler was contemplating an invasion of England. It might have been a bluff, to try and pressurize Britain into surrendering, or a genuine plan of attack. Sir Winston Churchill was not going to throw in the towel either way. He assigned General Sir Edmund Ironside to the task of creating Britain's home defences and his strategy was to build gun emplacements to hold up the invading forces. These defences included a network of concrete and brick 'pillbox' gun emplacements, anti-tank barriers, trenches and minefields using river crossings and hilltops. The North Downs was the GHQ Stop Line, and when Churchill gave his famous speech of defiance, declaiming 'we shall fight them on the hills; we shall never surrender'; the hills would undoubtedly have been the Surrey Hills standing between an invading force and the capital, London.

I interviewed one of the wartime officers responsible for making the concrete gun emplacements and anti-tank barriers that are still clearly visible on St Martha's, on the North Downs, in the Chantries, in the Tillingbourne, even in the middle of Guildford by the side of the London Road railway bridge. He told me how meticulous they all had to be, both in selecting locations for the pillboxes and in keeping them invisible from the air. They had to cover their tracks, walk round the edges of fields and avoid leaving any traces on the ground that would give away positions or indicate troop activity to the *Luftwaffe*. As archaeologists know, even minor crop markings and ancient buried building foundations are clearly visible from a few hundred feet up even if they are invisible at ground level, so the workforce had to be scrupulously careful. Everything had to be carefully camouflaged and recamouflaged to match the changing seasons, and enormous care was taken over security. Even natural features that could have guided bombers were camouflaged; for example Frensham Big and Little Ponds were both drained and all signposts removed.

The pillboxes were a well guarded secret but in true *Dad's Army* fashion, no one had thought to tell the builders the size of the guns that were to be shrouded inside. So when the guns arrived, they turned out to be too big to fit into them, and they had to go back to the drawing board. Being built to withstand enemy fire, however, the pillboxes are incredibly robust and have endured on the hillsides not so much as grim reminders of war but more as a testament to the dogged spirit of our fathers and grandfathers to fight their corner and defend their homes. The Surrey Hills would not have been a walkover. The Tillingbourne would also have put up a fight. Blocked by concrete tank traps, with dragon's teeth and barriers, it would have been a nasty ambush site.

The last battle before the storming of London was scheduled to take place at Shalford, with British and colonial forces fighting to the death to defend the Guildford Gap. The little village was thankfully spared its meeting with destiny. Only dim carving on a grey slab of stone in the wall by the Seahorse Pub gives a clue to the role that the village had been earmarked to play. The block is the remains of a huge anti-tank barrier across the main road which, combined with dragon's teeth and pillboxes, was designed to hold Hitler's army south of the downs. It is interesting that the architect of those barriers chose to settle in a house about 50 yards away from the Shalford stop line. He died a few years ago. The Surrey Defences Survey was set up in 1989 to try and record all the surviving defensive structures left in the county. There are thought to be around 2,000 different installations, many of them completely overgrown and forgotten.

Wartime in the Surrey Hills brought a massive increase in population. There were evacuees from London and troops stationed across the North Downs. Food was scarce, people were thrown back on their own resources, but for happy-go-lucky youngsters, it was a time of adventure. John Ellenger, who still lives in Gomshall, was just a boy when war broke out and he told me these tales of growing up in the 1940s.

> Late August 1939, a buff envelope arrived for my father. He had served in the RFC and the RAF in 1917–18 and had joined the RAF Class 'E' Reserve in 1938. This resulted in his call-up for active service, ten days before the Second World War broke out. I took the envelope to the Co-op store in Gomshall (now the vets), where he worked, and he promptly took off his white apron, came home and was off by train to RAF Farnborough before lunch that day. For me, the war had begun.
>
> My mother decided to go to work at the Co-op and when rationing came in, she would bring masses of coupons and 'points' cut from ration books, and these had to be sorted and counted – no mean task since many 'points' were about a quarter the size of a postage stamp!
>
> With the arrival of troops in the area, it was decided to build a YMCA canteen at Gomshall, just off Queen Street in New Road, where there are now three pairs of council houses. The YMCA comprised four large wooden huts, which provided refreshment and recreation rooms, and there was a film show most weekends to which we children would sometimes be invited – great fun! I used to chop firewood for the 'tortoise stoves' which heated the huts and make sure that the coke hods were kept full. It was there that I tasted my first doughnut, given to me as a small reward for my voluntary labours.
>
> On the roads, all signposts were removed and to further confuse the anticipated enemy, various mock structures were erected in open areas beside the roads, made of canvas on a wooden frame and painted to resemble buildings. I remember one of

these being in the form of a petrol filling station, about 150 yards short of Newlands Corner.

Schooldays during the war were quite exciting, with the arrival of many evacuees from London and Portsmouth, at least as many as the local population of children. It was an excellent opportunity for the 'townies' to learn country ways, and we 'yokels' probably had our wits sharpened by the streetwise from the great metropolis. We had no air raid shelter at Shere School, and during air raids we all had to go and sit on the floor of the main corridor. This could be a bit disappointing if there were some exciting dog fights in progress in the sky above, which naturally we wanted to watch.

I joined Guildford Royal Grammar School in September 1941, just before my eleventh birthday. We did have air raid shelters there, where we spent quite a bit of our time, and where we learned many bawdy songs, which no doubt kept our spirits up, as well as contributing to our general education! By 1943, I was able to join the Corps, formerly the school OTC (Officer Training Corps), but renamed the JTC (Junior Training Corps). For our first year in uniform, we were issued with First World War uniforms, including peak caps, tunics which buttoned up to the neck and, horror of horrors, knee-length breeches, which connected to the boots with Puttees – long strips of fabric which had to be wound round and round the leg, from the ankle to just below the knee, finishing off with a sort of tape tie. I well recall having great difficulty with these, but one of my uncles, who had served in the army in the First World War, was convalescing at our house while recuperating from phlebitis and he kindly assisted me from his sick bed. We were a bit embarrassed by these old-fashioned uniforms, and it was a great relief to be issued with battledress the following year.

I do not recall feeling particularly deprived of food and luxuries during the war. This was probably because everyone was in the same situation and it was a time of pulling together and making sacrifices where necessary. There never seemed to be much envy, or 'keeping up with the Joneses'. My father had always grown our own vegetables and for the first two and a half years of the war he was stationed at RAF Northolt, and managed to get home every other weekend, so with some assistance from me, we kept the garden going. We also kept about six to ten chickens, which provided plenty of eggs until a neighbour's ferret got into the henhouse and killed them all. I was paid one old penny per week for cleaning out the chickens and it was surprising how far you could make a penny go in those days!

As well as the local Home Guard, we had air raid wardens and official fire watchers, to be vigilant and available should enemy activity get too close. My own part in Adolf Hitler's downfall was to be recruited as a fire watcher's runner, which enabled me to operate a stirrup pump and wear a steel helmet (a bit on the large side….) we certainly were *prepared*!

The Army was encamped all around us and it seemed to give us a sense of security to see a sentry in a box at each end of the two drives up to Netley House. There were many huts and tents all along beside the A25 below Netley House and as I had a weekend paper round, I would generally take excess newspapers and sell them to the troops in these huts. They were always very pleased to have this service, even though the papers were very thin – often only about 8 pages, very tricky to fold and push through letter boxes.

As well as using the YMCA at Gomshall, the soldiers made up the majority of males at the Saturday night hop in Shere Village Hall. The band was the Tillingbourne Trio. Run by Mrs Harding, the church organist, on piano, plus a trumpeter and a drummer, their signature tune was 'That's a Plenty', and although they were nicknamed the 'Three in Agony', they made up for their small number by playing with great enthusiasm all manner of dance tunes, including quicksteps, foxtrots and waltzes. There was always the veleta, the Paul Jones, the ladies' excuse-me, and the odd Latin American tango or rumba. I remember the arrival of the jitterbug and was amazed at the energy displayed by some of our local youth.

One interesting event that we witnessed from Newlands Corner, on our way home from school on the Tillingbourne bus, was a massive fire accompanied by many explosions which seemed to cover a vast area of the woods towards Leith Hill: it turned out to be the result of a huge ammunition dump catching fire. Other events, such as enemy aircraft that had been shot down, were invariably items of great interest to us youngsters. The anti-aircraft guns along the top of the North Downs accounted for many of these, and we always tried to get to the scenes before guards were posted, in order to find a few souvenirs.

One important item to be broadcast daily was the Greenwich time signal, generally referred to as the 'six pips,' which people used as a reliable source for setting their timepieces. This signal actually came from the Royal Observatory, located just to the north of Leith Hill. Magnetic measuring equipment had been transferred there in the 1920s due to the inconvenient effects of the electrification of the railways which upset magnetic measurements at Greenwich. Hence, when the Blitz threatened the timekeeping equipment at Greenwich, it was decided to duplicate it all at the Leith Hill site, and from then on the six pips came from there, until the Observatory moved to Herstmonceux in the 1950s. I had the privilege of working at this establishment from 1947 to 1950, in the Electronics Laboratory.

John Ellenger was a good friend of Arthur Knapp, whose book, *If Only They Had Known,* is essential reading for local historians. He recalls Shere School growing vegetables to supply to the Royal Engineers camped at Netley Park. Digging for victory was taken very seriously. Wotton farmer Edward Matthews was in the Home Guard and also worked for the War Agricultural Committee, ensuring farmers produced enough food for the nation. Italian and German prisoners of war were billeted at the farm and worked on the land. Commercial flower growing in Shere was stopped by the war because of the need to concentrate on food production.

Arthur Knapp recalled the endless convoys of troops coming back from Dunkirk through Shere.

> We used to stand on the pavement outside our house at the top of Upper Street and cheer them as they went past. I remember … the troops taking over Netley House and Park. I think the first unit that moved in were the HAC (Honourable Artillery Company). They never stayed for long and were replaced by the RHA (Royal Horse Artillery), with their quads (armoured ammunition vehicles for towing guns and carrying crew and ammunition) and twenty-five pounder guns. I think both of these units were sent to North Africa where they were badly mauled. They used to practise their gun drill in our school playground.
>
> After the RHA's departure, the Royal Engineers moved into Netley with their bulldozers and heavy lorries and equipment, and the villages and its surroundings soon became an area of great activity as it prepared for war.
>
> A tank trap was dug all along the downs. From Newlands Corner it came down the fields and across Effingham Lane just above Medlands Farm, continuing across to London Lane. It went up the lane a little way and then along behind Netley House to Gomshall and Dorking. Coils of barbed wire were laid, almost encircling the village. Roadblocks were made for various points in the village, they were situated at the top of Middle Street and bottom of Upper Street and another one by the Village Hall. Another one was up the Effingham Road where the tank trap came across and others were at the top of Sandy Lane and at the top of Pathfields

Hill. Some of the large concrete rollers can still be seen in the undergrowth at the top of Pathfields Hill. Four huge concrete blocks were built across my Gran's garden between Rose Cottage and the Village Club. They were about five feet high and four feet square.

Later on, Canadian troops began to arrive in large numbers. They were stationed in the woods above Netley all the way along to Gomshall. The English-speaking ones were stationed at the Shere end and the French Canadians at the Gomshall end. They were also stationed in the woods at the top of Albury Park.

It was while the Canadian troops were there that the first tarmac road was laid along the top of the hill from Hollister Farm all the way along to the Gomshall end. I cannot remember when they left but I can remember going up the woods one evening to see them and they had disappeared. All that was left were their empty bunkers and dugouts where they lived for some time. I remember wandering about like a little boy lost, in and out of what had been their homes and thinking, 'We never said goodbye.'

Shortly after the Canadian troops had left, the whole area gradually became a massive arsenal in the build-up for D-Day ... We used to nose around to see what was in the small open-ended Nissen-type huts ... We got to know where everything was, from the very large shells down to small sten gun bullets, and if we didn't know what some things were we used to take them to the field below Gallows Gate and try and set them off.

Arthur Knapp's story of the VE Day bonfire would make any parent's hair stand on end. He and his friends had scrumped as much ammunition, flares, thunder-flashes, signal rockets and smoke bombs as they could carry from the stores on the downs and they let them off on the celebratory bonfire on Shere recreational grounds. It was a dangerous place to be that night but no one was hurt and the boys planned to use the rest of their loot for a VJ Day bonfire. The police got wind of what had happened, however, and the boys all went before the magistrates' court. That did not stop the second bonfire being embellished with the remaining ammunition however, and the boys were lucky to escape with a severe ticking off by the bench.

Anyone who had a big house during the war was expected to make space for either children or troops. Even the friary at Blackheath took twelve refugee children for a month in 1939 and in 1942 four friars were trained as stretcher-bearers for the village. Troops on manoeuvre on the heath were billeted in the guest wing, refectory, cloisters and chapter room. Staying in a friary was a bit of a shock to the non-Catholic soldiers, until they learned that six of the friars were ex-servicemen themselves. They showed a bit more respect than Cromwell's soldiers in the Civil War, who rudely stabled their horses in cathedral cloisters. The friars were chaplains to the troops on Abinger Common, and Catholic German prisoners of war housed at the Hallams on Blackheath in 1945–6 attended services at the friary.

The Canadian forces that massed on the North Downs and Blackheath were gathering in readiness for the D-Day landings in June 1944. Field Marshall Montgomery addressed the Canadian troops just before D-Day at a rally on Albury Heath and a cairn and plaque were erected by the Albury Trust next to the cricket pitch to commemorate the event. The evidence of their stay is still there around Hollister Farm and the woodlands by Francis Corner are crisscrossed by concrete roads. There are also old water tanks and the brick footings of military buildings. Many of the larger manor houses off the A246, such as Hatchlands, West Horsley Place and Clandon House, were commandeered for the officers and staff. Burrows Lea was taken over by the Canadians and formed part of an anti-aircraft battery. Searchlights were placed in the valley and gun emplacements were built in the woods.

The Canadians were also based at Tweedsmuir Camp between Elstead and Thursley. Much of the layout is still visible, as it is on Ministry of Defence land and the foundations of buildings and the concrete water tower have all been left.

A gruesome murder story is attached to this piece of wartime history. A nineteen-year-old girl called Joan Pearle Wolfe hung around the army camp, particularly the one on Hankley Common. There she met August Sangret, a Canadian Indian, who built a wigwam on the common where they would make love. When Joan was found murdered, detectives worked out that the curious circular holes in the front of her skull had been made by a blade with a most unusual parrot's beak blade. The finger was pointed at August and, despite protesting his innocence, he was hanged at Wandsworth Gaol in 1943.

A corps of Royal Canadian Engineers and the 9th Field Ambulance, Royal Canadian Medical Corps took over Merstham House, near Reigate and parts of Church Hill, and they were billeted in Nissen huts at Pendell Camp in Warwick Wold.

Because the Canadian Army was manoeuvring on Blackheath Common, locals and livestock had to be kept off. This marked the end of an era of grazing the heath and keeping scrub at bay. Goats were particularly popular among villagers at Blackheath. It was the grazing of the heath that had enabled the Victorian Volunteer Review to take place, but once the munching and browsing of tree seedlings stopped, birch and pine invaded the area.

Possibly the last person to keep goats on the heath was Monty Fox, who lived alone in a caravan in a grassy dell not far from Woodsmoke. He was an extraordinary man, who had lived for many years among the Romany and was an expert in their way of life. I kept a Jacob ram as a pet in the early 1980s and used to take him for walks on the heath, often passing by the glade where Monty's goats were grazing. Once he realized I had a sheep and not a dog, he became an instant friend. His mugs of tea made with goats' milk were interesting to say the least. I still have the sheep bell he gave me.

The birch scrub and conifers grew incredibly quickly during the 1950s and 1960s and no one seemed to take any action for years. The result was the loss of 40 per cent of the precious lowland heath since 1950. The value of this heathland habitat and the importance of managing it has fortunately now been recognized and all the landowners – National Trust, Waverley Borough Council, Shere Manor Estate and Albury Estate – work hard to re-create heathland without the animals to do it naturally. It is an uphill battle, using herbicide and volunteer muscle power. The issue of grazing has to be addressed, however, and tough decisions on cattle grids and access must be faced unless people give up and accept that trees will win.

The sixtieth anniversary of the ending of the war and the realization that the number of people with first-hand experience of life then was dwindling has inspired the National Trust and Surrey Hills AONB Partnership to preserve wartime structures and, where possible, create mini-museums. Six restored air-raid shelters on Limpsfield Common were reopened by the song-writer, presenter and local resident Richard Stilgoe in November 2006, in a poignant ceremony involving three generations.

Holding up a fragment of propeller salvaged from the wreck of a Hawker Hurricane that crashed in his fields at Godstone during the Battle of Britain, he explained the importance of triggers for memory. Only by remembering what had happened in the Second World War would it be possible to prevent it happening all over again, he said. The restored shelters, one equipped with pictures and information, would be a powerful trigger to the younger generations. His audience included pupils from Limpsfield Church of England Infant School, dressed as 1940s children and equipped with pretend gas-mask kits and a name label, villagers who had used the shelters during the war and members and supporters of the huge volunteer effort that cleared the site and opened up a stunning viewpoint. One of the shelters has been restored to its wartime condition to be used as an educational resource for local schools and the community. The other five have been adapted to encourage roosting bats.

Donald Leigh, who moved to Limpsfield with his family in 1939, was fascinated to see the shelters restored, as he remembered them as a small boy with the Battle of Britain raging overhead. 'We looked forward to going in the shelters,' he said, 'We took gas masks and tuck boxes.

The shelters now look just the way they were.' The shelters had originally been built for Limpsfield Church of England Infant School and its twenty-first-century pupils now go there to learn about their village during the Second World War.

In Guildford, it was the rediscovery of the dragon's teeth by the railway bridge in London Road that reawakened interest in the town's wartime defences, and I remember the unveiling of a memorial plaque by a senior army officer. A tiny, poignant ceremony. There were only three of us there. Guildford still has some fascinating wartime structures, including a shelter big enough to house 1,000 people below Foxenden Quarry. It had bunks, a toilet and medical facilities. For over half a century it was locked up but it is now opened to visitors once a year for Heritage Open Day.

Burrows Lea and Harry Edwards

When the war was over, Burrows Lea, a large late-Victorian mansion on the ridge above Shere that had been used by an anti-aircraft battery and was a bit the worse for wear, was put up for sale. Its previous owners had included Sir Anthony Clay, Lieutenant-General Sir Hubert de la Poer Gough and Jeremiah Colman, of Colman's mustard fame. It was bought by an extraordinary man, who became a legend in his own lifetime. Harry Edwards made an international name for himself as a healer. Born in London in 1893, he followed his father into the printing trade before serving with the Royal Sussex Regiment in Iraq during the First World War. It was there, while helping organize a rail link, that he first discovered his talent for healing. Iraqi workmen naturally turned to the young British officer for help when they were ill or injured, and although he had few resources and no professional medical knowledge, he had a marked success rate.

Harry had started off as a Church of England sceptic on spiritualism but by the time he came back to England after the war, he was conscious of his apparent healing powers and became a convert and eventually a medium. He intervened successfully in cases of terminal illness, and gradually healing began to compete for his time with his printing business. By the 1940s, healing had taken over as the most important part of his life and he needed more than just the front room of his London home to use as a healing sanctuary. Burrows Lea was perfect, with its large rooms and beautiful grounds.

As his fame spread, thousands of people wrote to him for help every week and he toured both in this country and abroad, giving healing demonstrations. Like practitioners of alternative therapies and homeopathy today, he never received professional recognition for his healing. He went to great lengths to try to convince both the Church and the medical establishment of its effectiveness but they remained dismissive. He provided evidence for the Archbishops' Commission on Divine Healing in 1953 to no effect, but this lack of establishment endorsement did not damage his reputation. The ailing public ignored the rebuff and continued to flock to his sanctuary.

Harry Edwards died in 1976 but the sanctuary continues, though now in a rather different vein. It has been revamped and relaunched as a wedding venue and conference centre, in addition to its role as healing sanctuary. Visitors can come for a weekend break, attend a retreat, hire rooms for meetings, stroll in the grounds or enjoy the excellent restaurant facilities. The healing room at its heart has an atmosphere a bit like a chapel, but contains symbols of many different religions. Harry Edwards's chair is there too, where it was when he was alive, and visitors are requested, in hushed tones, not to sit in it. His presence – his spirit – is very much revered here. This can make some people feel a bit uncomfortable, but for people worried about an illness or injury, Harry Edwards's reputation as a successful healer is undoubtedly the most important thing.

The Lions of Blackheath

Walking across Blackheath and Farley Green in the 1960s and 1970s a visitor would have heard a sound to strike a chill in the heart – the deep-throated urrggh urrrggghhh of a fully mature lion, sounding worryingly close. In fact it was the sound of two lions, named Napoleon and

Josephine, who lived for many years in a compound in the garden of Candleford on the edge of Blackheath, at the junction of several bridlepaths. Diana Boyd-Gibbons and her husband had been given them when they were just cubs. An attempt to resettle them in a safari park failed as they pined, so they returned to Blackheath where they lived for a long time, and they were buried at Candleford. Blackheath historian Brigadier Dick Hume recalled one occasion when a hot air balloon spotted a patch of grass that looked an ideal landing place. It turned out to be the lions' enclosure. Napoleon and Josephine were understandably terrified of the balloon and hid inside their house. 'The balloonists were hastily evacuated by the irate owner who berated them soundly for frightening her lions!' he said.

I have always called the area round Candleford and Woodsmoke 'the Lions' and a part of me still half expects to hear that throaty call as I ride past. I can hear it inside my head now.

Country Traditions

Rural communities have strong traditions. Many of the villages have choirs and amateur theatrical groups, and great communal bonfires on Guy Fawkes Night. Several of the latter have become enormous public events despite the strangling tentacles of health and safety legislation. Brockham, Holmbury, Cranleigh, Ripley and Chiddingfold bonfires are legendary, and people come from miles around to watch them.

Harold White ran the Chiddingfold bonfire for twenty-five years. It was such a major event that it was even filmed for television one year and such was the producer's enthusiasm for the dramatic that Mr White had a very narrow escape. The producer was absolutely adamant: Mr White was to climb a ladder to the top of the 40ft bonfire, wearing a white anorak so that he would show up clearly on camera, and recite the special bonfire prayer which would be broadcast to the nation.

What everyone forgot, in the fluster of television crews and last minute hitches, was that the prayer ends with the command to throw the processional torches onto the bonfire, to set it alight. And that the heap had been liberally doused with old sump oil specially saved by local garages. Mr White climbed up, the spotlight was shone upon him and he recited the prayer. Then to his horror, he saw the dozens of torches arcing through the air towards him. The ladder was slippery with oil but he shinned down it through the volley of torches to safety just as the flames took hold. The white anorak, however, was a write-off.

Over the years Mr White has had to search the heap for gas cylinders after anonymous threats, turn away motorcycle gangs and organize last minute rebuilds when it was lit prematurely by vandals.

The village green is a triangular sweep of grass – houses, pubs and church strung out in the distance around its edges, and in the middle, all year round, is the vast telltale roundel of grey ash. The event involves several hundred villagers, and on a good year 10,000 visitors. Profits are turned into vouchers for local pensioners to spend in the village shop.

When cynics jibe that Surrey is a county with no indigenous population, just a through-flow of people on the make, one can cite couples like the Whites. For thirty-three years Harold and his wife Margaret ran Chiddingfold Horticultural Society. He was in the Surrey Guild of Judges and Lecturers and a judge for the Royal Horticultural Society. He was the local historian, with a couple of books to his credit, and a Lieutenant-Colonel in the Territorial Army. He edited *Chiddingfold Parish and Village Magazine*, was a church warden and keeper of the church records dating back to 1562, and he ran the churchyard. This last duty is fascinating because Chiddingfold is one of the burial sites for the royalty of the travelling community. Kings, queens, princes and princesses are buried there and Mr White had to exercise great diplomacy when a family was denied the exact plot it wanted. 'They are very hierarchical,' he explained. 'They line up all the males down the path. The funeral procession will start at the south coast – huge cortèges with massive floral tributes that decorate the entire churchyard.'

Industrious Surrey

The Surrey Hills have been tapped for their natural resources ever since man first took up residence, and at times the area would have been far noisier and more polluted than it is today, especially the Tillingbourne valley with its profusion of mills. The use of wood as both building material and fuel, a wide variety of stone, clay for bricks, water for power and transport meant Surrey was a busy industrial place, though obviously not on the scale of the Midlands in the Industrial Revolution.

Quarrying

The North Downs were extensively quarried and mined, and the activity has in places given them the consistency of Emmental cheese. Apart from the famous swallow holes at Leatherhead, where the River Mole disappears below ground, Surrey has no large natural caves. Its halls and tunnels are instead a tribute to the ingenuity and recklessness of farmers, landowners and cottagers, who harvested the stone, chalk, gravel and sand. And they are incredibly extensive. In one quarry, there are 10 miles of tunnels snaking back and forth in a single mile of rock.

The north-west of Surrey was dug for gravel, and the pits are mostly restored as lakes and reservoirs. Coming in to land at Heathrow one has an incredible view of the extent of the old gravel workings, the interlocking lakes and pools glistening in the sun. In the Surrey Hills, the quarries and sandpits have proved to be an environmentalist's nightmare. Holes in the ground seemed a convenient solution to the twentieth century's problem

▼ The old mill at Godalming

of domestic and commercial waste. The sandpit at Albury is one of the largest rubbish tips, a great blot on the landscape as one looks north from the edge of Albury Heath, and a great producer of smelly methane gas if you live in the valley. The sandpits east of Farnham, the chalk pits at Betchworth and further east are all used for rubbish. Runfold, on the Pilgrim's Way outside Farnham, has been badly affected by the concentration of sand quarries on its doorstep. The tension between the need for stone and sand for building and the secondary industry to backfill the hole created continues, with the latest battle raging in Eashing near Godalming.

Near Puttenham, at the foot of the Hog's Back, is a 4-acre network of bricked-up sand excavations dating back to the sixteenth century that local tradition also connects with the smuggling trade, as they were known as Smugglers' Store-houses. Local farmhouses had similarly rangy cellars that would have been convenient for hiding smuggled goods, and Dorking's caves may have been used in a similar way.

Quarrying in Surrey probably dates back to Roman times; it was certainly well established by the Middle Ages. Local historians at Merstham point to the Roman numeral VII carved in the original entrance to one of the quarries, which was lined to form two continuous arches. Every stone in the smaller arch bore this numeral and it is thought that the seventh legion oversaw the quarrying here. A little further east along the downs, the hills produced Chaldon stone, which does not weather well but is light and ideal for decorative interiors and for carving, and so crops up across medieval London as pillars, capstones and vaulting in churches.

The quarries at Chaldon and Merstham produced stone for the Palace of Westminster in the thirteenth century, and in 1360 John and Philip Prophete were appointed wardens of both Merstham and Chaldon quarries with a remit to provide stone for Windsor Castle. It was a serious commission. They were given authority to press-gang men to work for them, and any who refused could be sent to prison. The quarries later produced stone for Westminster Abbey.

The Great Fire of London in 1666 created another surge in demand for more permanent building materials than the highly combustible wooden frames and wattle

▼ Quarrying on the North Downs

Malcolm Pendrill

and daub of the medieval and Tudor periods. Engineers also used Merstham and Chaldon stone to rebuild London Bridge both after the Great Fire and again in 1824.

Chalk and Lime

Chalk has many uses, from fertiliser to whitewash, and the Surrey Hills were a major resource. All along the downs are domestic chalk pits and lime kilns associated with farms. The kilns were used to burn the lime to sweeten the soil. When slaked with water it was also used for mortar or whitewash. Quarrying chalk and burning lime became big business in the eighteenth and nineteenth centuries. By 1860, Hall Brothers were using the Merstham stone quarry as a site to burn lime, until in 1864 their lease expired and negotiations failed. The quarry was used a few years later by Alfred Nobel for experiments using dynamite to blast stone, and in 1872 J.S. Peters took over the lime works and eventually Quarry Dean. He built a connecting railway line and a little steam engine known as *Gervase* hauled loads from the lime kilns to the new Merstham Station. This was just one of several industrial branch lines along the North Downs, which connected with the main rail network. There would have been self important 'Fat Controllers' at Betchworth Station and Merstham, strutting up and down sorting out the 'Thomas the Tank Engine' looka-likes on the lines from the quarry and the big trains on the main Reading–Tonbridge line.

The great white chalk scars on the downs overlooking Betchworth bear witness to hundreds of years of industry. The quarry which produced hearthstone and firestone as well as lime, was ⅓ mile wide and went down some 300ft, with further workings leading off the main hole. The Dorking Greystone Lime Works, set up in 1865 by William Findlay, was big business and it

▼ 'The Major', the little Betchworth Quarry freight train that hauled stone from the quarry to the main Tonbridge line, has been rescued and is in service for visitors at Amberley Working Museum in West Sussex

needed an extensive railway network within the quarry to bring basic and processed stone to the siding for loading onto the mainline freight trains. Several of the brightly painted standard-gauge trains are now on display at the Amberley Working Museum at Arundel. The quarry itself has been used as a rubbish dump and is now re-landscaped and green; just the chalk face remains as a reminder of Betchworth's industrial past. Quarrying at Merstham ceased in the 1950s and in 1961 the Croydon Corporation bought the lime pit there to use as a rubbish dump as well. The quarry's fate was sealed by the construction of the M23 and M25. The threat of the caverns collapsing meant that they had to be filled and sealed.

Oxted Greystone Lime Company was set up in 1884 when the London, Brighton and South Coast Railway opened. In 1959 it bought the Dorking company and later aquired Betchworth as well. Chalk was dug and burnt on the Oxted site until the Second World War and was again in full production in the 1960s, the kilns spewing smoke into the air as they burned imported chalk.

Brockham's Lime Works, adjoining Betchworth Quarry, cover a huge area of 110 acres. Surrey Wildlife Trust manages the lime works as an SSSI and the land around the quarry as a nature reserve, on behalf of Surrey County Council. The quarry itself is private. Several industries were carried on at the Brockham Lime Works before the site was abandoned in the 1930s – chalk was quarried by hand for lime, hearthstone was mined and clay was dug for brick-making. The hearthstone and firestone were used in the glass-making industry or for whitening steps and hearths in the home. Nature reclaimed the land with enthusiasm and many rare and interesting species have made their homes there. The old Pilgrims' Way passes batteries of old lime kilns and walkers can get a good flavour of a busy Surrey industry here, as the line of the railway, the buildings and even a ring of bricks and a metal grille, which covers the shaft of the hearthstone mine, can all still be seen.

There are only two genuine chalk mines in Surrey, a small one at West Humble, now colonized by bats and protected as a nature reserve, and the other near Racks Close beneath Guildford Castle, which has been sealed for many years but probably gave its name to Quarry Street.

Arch Mine, Godstone Main Series and Marden Mine at Godstone produced hearthstone and building stone, and there are still some 5 miles of accessible tunnel, although the mines are in rather poor condition and have been colonized by bats. Sand was also worked at Godstone. Surrey's subterranean secrets have been extensively researched by the Wealden Cave and Mine Society which was founded in 1967 to investigate and explore all manner of underground sites, not just natural phenomena. The society controls access to the mines and quarries on behalf of the landowners because they are dangerous. It has a strong interest in the preservation and recording of industrial history, so it appeals to both the adventurous pot-holer and the archaeologist and historian. Its members have been actively engaged in a comprehensive study of the firestone quarries of east Surrey, amassing an impressive library of research material in the process, including some wonderful personal reminiscences.

The mines were owned by local estates and involved just a few men, who worked incredibly hard by today's standards. Quarrying hearthstone at Godstone, two men would go down the open shaft, leaving ordinary household candles stuck in the wall to guide them and light the tunnel. The quarryman would drive chisels into the stone face and then hit it with a sledgehammer, releasing a torrent of stone which would then be loaded by his assistant onto a horse-drawn skip. The horses would make their way unaided along the tunnel, much as working forestry horses do hauling logs.

This type of research, using oral history, is particularly good because it throws up details that would otherwise be lost for ever, such as the leather and straw padded hats worn by the carthorses to protect their heads if they accidentally hit them on the roof of the tunnel. When not being quarried, the dark, dank tunnels were put to other uses. The men interviewed remembered French and Portuguese workers using Godstone Quarries for mushroom-growing in the 1920s.

The Reigate and Dorking Caves

The society's expertise is well recognized, and it has been entrusted with the management of the public face of subterranean Surrey – the Reigate caves. The one-way system round Reigate circles the soft sandstone mound on which the 2nd Earl of Surrey, William de Warenne, built his castle soon after 1088. It was surrounded by a dry moat, with timber buildings and defences on the mound, or motte. In the twelfth or thirteenth century, the timber structures were replaced by stone ones and the castle extended to include an outer bailey with a second moat. It eventually fell into ruin in the sixteenth century, although it made a convenient billet for troops of both sides in the Civil War. All the stone above ground has since been robbed for other buildings, leaving just the mysterious Baron's Cave, a professionally carved Gothic arched tunnel, believed to date from the eleventh century, leading from the castle keep right down through the mound to the moat. This tunnel is the subject of the rumour that the barons held a secret meeting there on their way to Runnymede to sign the Magna Carta, an event that would have involved a bizarre detour.

Steep, straight and sandy, with a side gallery large enough to harbour several hundred people, the tunnel is a mystery, and one can only guess at its purpose other than as a refuge in time of siege. What is certain, however, is that all the tunnels have a very long history as a tourist attraction, as well as a source of valuable silver sand for passing trade and domestic use. I would hate to think what the tunnels would be like if visitors had been handed paint sprays over the last 500 years to perform their art work – Banksy could have had a field day – but there is a lot of evidence to suggest that people were actively encouraged to carve their names or draw pictures in the soft sandstone. The walls are etched deep with overlaying initials, patterns, dates and names. Peter Burgess from the Wealden Cave and Mine Society pointed out one that was at least 12ft up the end wall of the refuge tunnel, dated 1644; he suggested that it had survived because it was so high up. Possible earlier graffiti lower down would have been rubbed out and carved over. There are some splendid faces and a horse's head

▼ The stone quarry near Godstone

Trevor Hadrell

that are over 100 years old. Baron's Cave is mentioned as an attraction in the early nineteenth century and surveys go back to the eighteenth century. Richard Barnes, who owned the mound in 1780, built a folly-style gateway on the top and a pyramid covering the top of the tunnel, and stagecoaches stopped at Reigate on their way from London, leaving passengers time to explore the caves. I Skinner, Brighton, 1783, was one visitor who left his mark.

The Wealden Cave and Mine Society restored the caves in the 1990s and open them to the public during the summer for tours. The original plan was to open just Baron's Cave but subterranean Reigate has a lot more to offer. The road tunnel, aptly named Tunnel Road, is another extraordinary man-made feature. It flies in the face of all sensitivity to history or aesthetics because it was driven straight through a Norman castle mound that is now a protected scheduled monument. But it is the oldest surviving road tunnel in the country, built in 1823 as a business venture, charging tolls to London traffic. And leading off on either side are extensive tunnels that are now also opened by the society for public visits.

A huge area beneath London Road and the Red Cross Inn was also a warren of sixteenth-century sand-pits and tunnels, some later used for winebars, cafés and storage. This undermining of the area made it very unsafe. On 19 May 1860, the *Illustrated London News* reported that Reigate reverberated to a loud report, which was thought at first to be an earthquake. It turned out that the roof of a large sand cave belonging to the premises of the Red Cross Inn had fallen in, taking with it five cottages and leaving ten others dangling. Remarkably, twenty-three people escaped unhurt, though a very sick old lady had to be rescued through a window. Not surprisingly, the remaining caves in this area were filled in and made safe when the EU raised the maximum permitted weight of lorries on British roads.

The Tunnel Road caves are quite different from the castle tunnels. To the west are old sand tunnels but on the east side the caverns were probably built as beer and wine vaults after the road was cut, as they are largely lined with brick. During the First World War, high explosives were stored in the sand tunnels to the west, and during the Second World War, the eastern tunnels were put to civic use, housing an air-raid wardens' report centre, a police post, a fire brigade post, and a first aid post. They were also used as huge air-raid shelters for local people and Londoners fleeing the Blitz. The Society has acquired a number of wartime artefacts associated with the tunnels' use, some from the disused Cold War bunker beneath the Town Hall, and the eastern tunnels now have the makings of an excellent museum. A lot of restoration has already been done, including the installation of electric lighting, but there is still a lot to do.

Dorking residents quarried sand from caves in the town centre over several hundred years and these impressive caverns are open to the public for guided tours as well. A discreet doorway by the War Memorial in South Street takes visitors through a series of galleries, used until recently as wine cellars, some of it smuggled. From the wine cellars a series of shafts lead down, deep under Rose Hill, to a mysterious seventeenth-century domed chamber with a bench around its edge. Suggestions for its purpose range from a gentleman's folly to a meeting place for religious dissenters, a witches coven, and a wine-tasting room.

Brick-making

The Romans introduced bricks as a building material to Surrey. Near the Roman branch road from Rowhook to the temple at Farley Green are the remains of a Roman brick kiln, indicating that the legions understood the value of the Cranleigh clay for the manufacture of bricks, tiles and pipes. Like other Roman technologies, such as chimneys, running water, hot baths and underfloor heating, bricks disappeared for over a thousand years. Once rediscovered, however, brick- and tile-making once again became a major industry in the Weald, because of the high quality of the clay.

The arrival of the railway in 1847 and increase in mining of the Brockham Hills brought new workers to the Reigate area. The building boom needed raw materials and the Brockham Brick Company was set up. The company's lease ran out in October 1910 and all its assets were put up for auction. The amount of machinery gives an idea of the scale of this industry. The list includes Whitaker & Co brickmaking machinery plus wire-cutting machines, grinding mills with elevators, a steam engine and machinery, a 20hp engine by Clayton & Shuttleworth with travelling wheels, a 6hp vertical engine by Garret & Son, shafting, driving wheels, pumps, brick presses, iron winding gear, railway track and wagons, a trade building, thirteen circular kilns, a 100ft high brick shaft, sheds, offices, barrows, trucks, tools and scrap.

Brick-making survived through the twentieth century at Smokejacks Brickworks at Ockley, Nutbourne Brickworks at Hambledon, Clockhouse Brickworks at Capel, works at South Holmwood, South Godstone, Manfield Park, Baynards and Smithbrook Kilns in Cranleigh. The industry has now collapsed, however, and these redundant sites are causing problems for their neighbours and for the planning authority, Surrey County Council. The fuller's earth pits in the Redhill/Nutfield area, the UK's main source of production, also closed in 1998 and were backfilled with rubbish.

Any new planning application for mineral workings in and around the AONB sparks passionate opposition. It was one thing for stone to be trundled to a siding and loaded to a freight train in the Victorian era; quite another to contemplate a steady stream of massive lorries on country lanes working twelve hours a day or more. It is no longer acceptable for Surrey to be an industrial county.

Iron-working

The scene on a sunny afternoon at Abinger Hammer is quintessentially English. In the background there is a village cricket match, whites dazzling against emerald grass, producing that unique sound of summer – the thwack of leather on willow followed by a pitter-patter of applause. In the foreground are a scattering of colourful picnic groups and in the Tillingbourne itself, children big and small, bare-legged, splashing, pond-dipping with nets and playing in the clear, fast-flowing water. The little Tillingbourne runs swiftly and peacefully for just over 10 miles along the valley between Dorking and Guildford, gurgling and sparkling, shallow enough for paddling, almost clean enough for drinking.

Do not be fooled. This stream, barely wide or substantial enough to be a river, has a long history as a very hard worker, a muscular power source for heavy industry that was both noisy and dirty. The scene at Abinger is deceptively peaceful, for the 'Hammer' in its name refers to one of the noisiest activities on the river – iron-working. A 3-acre hammer pond fed by the Tillingbourne produced enough pressure in the sixteenth century to work huge bellows and drive a deafening trip-hammer that hit an anvil thirty times a minute. The ear-splitting *clang* would have resounded down the valley, echoing up the North Downs, and an enormous amount of tree-felling would have been required to fuel the forges. John Evelyn, who was an expert on trees and a lover of nature, wrote in 1664 that it would be better to import iron from America, in order to preserve the English woodland.

The hammer pond became used in time for watercress beds irrigated by spring water instead. It was farmed by the Arminson family until EU regulations and foreign competition forced them to abandon almost all the beds, although Barry Arminson still grows enough to sell as a speciality at his Kingfisher farm shop. The Tillingbourne at Abinger is used to breed trout.

The famous clock jutting out over the A25 from its tower on the edge of a cottage, was set up as a memorial to the first Lord Ferrar of Abinger Hall, who died in 1899. Jack the Hammer strikes the hours on his anvil. The clock bears the legend 'For you at home I part the day, work and play twixt sleep and meals' on one side, and 'By me you know how fast to go' on the other. There is still a working forge there. The blacksmith, Howard Cooper, now retired, is a past Master of the Worshipful Company of Farriers and ran a large team of apprentices. Horses are still shod there from time to time.

Iron ore for smelting was found in the sands and clays of the Weald, and during the early Roman occupation and in Tudor and Stuart times, most of the country's iron was produced further south in the Fold country of Surrey and Sussex. There are Roman hammer ponds on the Wintershall Estate at Bramley, and clues to past activities in place names such as Furnace Copse near Godalming, Furnace Place at Haslemere, Hammer Hill and Hammer Bottom at Thursley.

Glass-making

Chiddingfold was known for its glass-making and Roman glass has been found there; some of it is now in Guildford Museum. In the thirteenth century Simon de Stokas granted land in Chiddingfold to Laurence the Glass-maker. The industry peaked during the sixteenth century under Elizabeth I when there were eleven glass-works around the village green. It was high-quality glass, and examples of it are found in St Stephen's Chapel in Westminster and St George's Chapel, Windsor. St Mary's Parish Church in Chiddingfold has a unique lancet window made out of an amazing 427 uncut pieces of local stained glass dating from 1226 to 1612. The glass-makers were predominantly Flemish. Alfold was also a busy glass-making centre and a slab of Sussex marble in St Nicholas's churchyard is reputed to be the burial site of a Frenchman, Jean Carre, who was one of the last French glass-makers in the Fold country and had been granted a licence to make glass using French techniques. He died in 1572.

Gunpowder

The Tillingbourne rises in springs high on Leith Hill, seeping down through the woods to the valley at the foot of the North Downs until it forms a recognizable stream at Wotton, incorporated by Evelyn into his Italianate landscape garden at Wotton House. The stream is shallow – there are still driveable fords in Shere – but with dams and weirs it is a powerful source of energy and its industrial history goes back to Saxon times and beyond. By 1086, the Domesday Book lists mills at Wotton, Abinger, Gomshall, two at Shere, Albury, Chilworth and three at Shalford. At its industrial peak the Tillingbourne powered an incredible thirty-one mills. Paper was produced at Chilworth, Albury and Postford Mills, and wire and nail manufacture, leather tanning, flax retting, iron working and brewing all contributed to the intensive industrial

▼ Reigate Windmill taken from the air

Malcolm Pendrill

occupation of the valley. Its greatest claim to industrial notoriety is for gunpowder, a particularly dirty and dangerous process.

England was perilously short of home-produced gunpowder until the reign of Elizabeth I, when the narrow escape from the Spanish Armada made her ministers anxious to increase production. George Evelyn and his son were licensed in 1589 to manufacture it. Their first mill was at Kingston, but when George retired his sons took the industry to Godstone and Wotton. According to historian Eric Parker, the East India Company set up powdermills on the outskirts of Windsor Park but they frightened the deer and were moved to Chilworth in 1626. When the royal monopoly on gunpowder contracts was abolished by the Long Parliament of 1641, it became a free for all. The Evelyns diversified into brass, wire-making, and fulling (the cleaning and controlled felting of woollen cloth). The major problem facing the gunpowder manufacturers – apart from the danger of the whole process – was getting the monarch of the day to pay for the goods. One owner, who had the splendid name of Sir Polycarpus Wharton, ended up in debtor's prison because of the poor cash flow. During the Civil War, however, Chilworth supplied Cromwell, not the king.

William Cobbett, with his love for orderly agriculture and a traditional pastoral way of life, thought the Tillingbourne valley was both beautiful and ruined. He was outraged at what man had done to it.

> This valley which seems to have been created by a bountiful providence, as one of the choicest retreats of man; which seems formed for a scene of innocence and happiness, has been, by ungrateful man, so perverted as to make it instrumental in effection two of the most damnable of purposes; in carrying into execution two of the most damnable inventions that ever sprang from the minds of man under the influence of the Devil! Namely, the making of gunpowder and of bank-notes!

In 1704 the Lower Works by Blacksmith Lane had been closed and converted into paper mills making bank notes and later the Upper Works at Postford were also used for paper. It was the Middle Works that continued

▼ These menacing ruins deep in the dank woodlands of the Gunpowder Estate at Chilworth are all that remains of a deadly industry that dominated the valley for hundreds of years

to make gunpowder. In 1885, a German-led consortium took over the Chilworth Gunpowder Mills to make a new type of powder called 'brown' or 'cocoa' powder, which was more suited to the large guns then being developed. A Prussian officer, Captain Otto Bouvier, was put in charge, with a team of German foremen, and the works were modernized with state-of-the-art German machinery. Ironically, the mills produced powder for the British forces in the First World War.

Gunpowder was a very dangerous business; a woman was beheaded as she sat outside her cottage door by one particularly powerful explosion and the body of one man was blown right over the paper mill in 1755. Another explosion in 1763 blew the tower off the Church of St Martha-on-the-Hill. The Percy Arms was regularly used as a morgue and for inquests, and the ghost of George Smithers, one of the victims, is said to haunt the pub still. Villagers lived in constant danger of explosions for centuries. The gunpowder workers eventually persuaded the company to build them new cottages over the hill in Blackheath, where they would be safe. There is no record of a village at Blackheath before 1810, and the few families who lived there in 1833 inhabited what are described as mud huts – single-storey cottages faced with flint and stones gathered from the heath. The neat rows of gunpowder workers' cottages built in the mid-nineteenth century were known as the Barracks and the men would walk down Sampleoak Lane, lit by a string of oil lamps, to work in the valley below.

I well remember old Mr Brett, a loyal Wonersh churchman and retired cobbler, who lived next to the village stores. White-haired and gnarled, he seemed to me as a child to belong to the Victorian age. He made the special boots worn by gunpowder workers, which had to use wooden pegs instead of metal nails to avoid sparks, but explosions occurred regularly despite all precautions. In 1901, one particularly violent explosion killed six men just after their breakfast break and blasted the two-storey Black Corning House to pieces. There was another serious accident in 1913. They were the last victims. By 1920 it was all over. Some of the buildings were made into houses and people lived there until the 1960s in a community known locally as 'Tin Town', but now the area is empty and quiet. One is more likely to find a string of llamas being taken for a walk than anything

▼ Elstead Mill, on the River Wey, where you can still see the waterwheel. Mills like this were at the hub of agricultural life

▲ The Guildford Crane at Millbrook and the restored barge and equipment at Dapdune Wharf are all that remain of Guildford's great river industry

connected with industry and sudden death. The soggy woodland, criss-crossed by ditches, watercourses and stream has almost, but not quite, reclaimed and obliterated all signs. Eerie outlines of ruined buildings emerge from the undergrowth, steps lead down to nothing, and there are empty windows and roofless rooms. All is silence, except for the gurgling of water and the odd bird call.

Other mills

The Tillingbourne's other mills kept going until steam power and then electricity made them commercially obsolete. The repeal of the corn laws put some corn mills out of business. But corn was not the only commodity using water power in the Tillingbourne valley. In the seventeenth century there were twenty mills, four in just the one small village of Gomshall, where fustian-weaving and leather-tanning were the key industries. The tannery, which had been started in Tudor times, finally closed in 1988. The last working grain mill, Botting's at Albury, only stopped milling animal feed in 1990. It was demolished to make way for a residential and office development in an idyllic position surrounded by woodland, the mill stream and lakes. There are plenty of other redundant mills still around. Gomshall Mill, now Blubecker's Restaurant, dates from the seventeenth century and Shalford Mill from the eighteenth. Both still contain some milling machinery and a waterwheel kept behind glass.

Water for Transport

It was not just the Tillingbourne that was busy. The River Wey was an important working waterway, carrying a wide variety of goods to the Thames and on to London. Only five horse-drawn boats still work the rivers and canals of England and Wales, and it is significant that one of those, the *Iona,* plies its trade on the River Wey. It attracts coachloads of people because the trip is free from twenty-first-century noise and diesel pollution. One can hear the birds and the water; one can almost hear the wildflowers growing. Jenny Roberts has run the Godalming Packetboat Company for more than twenty years, using a stretch of the Wey that is unusual in that it is wholly owned by the National Trust and incorporates both a natural river and a navigation or canal.

The Wey was only the second river to be made navigable in the whole of the UK, its canal sections built in the seventeenth century as a result of an Act of the Commonwealth Parliament, more than 100 years before the great era of canal building in the late eighteenth and early nineteenth centuries. The brainchild of Sir Richard

Weston of Sutton Place, it cost a fortune at £16,000, as over half the distance from Guildford to the Thames consists of artificial cuts, but it finally opened in 1651. It was successful, and made money after a rocky start and much talk of fraud and scams, and it was extended to Godalming in 1763. For a short period in the early nineteenth century, the Wey and Arun Canal linked the two rivers to complete the water highway from London to the South Coast, but it was already too late: the Guildford–Horsham railway opened in 1865 and took just three years to kill off the waterway. It was so final that in 1871 an Act of Abandonment had to be passed. Stretches of it remain carpeted in green algae, behind Birtley Green and crossing Run Common. It is being restored by enthusiasts but it is doubtful if it can ever be reunited with the Wey.

In its heyday, the Wey was teeming with life. Records for 1664 detail 14,000 barge-loads of timber using the navigation, as well as corn and other cargoes, and by 1839 trade had risen to a peak of 23,000 tons. The main cargoes were corn, flour, timber, coal and chalk, but barges also carried bark for tanning, rags for paper-making, barrel hoops and other ironwork, sugar and groceries, and until after the First World War, even gun-powder from the powdermills at Chilworth. The Wey managed to compete with the railways for freight traffic, and corn, coal and imported timber were still being hauled along the navigation well into the 1930s. The last commercial barge reached Guildford in 1958, although there was a brief revival in the 1980s.

The 20 miles of the Wey and Godalming Navigation are kept in condition by the National Trust and it is very hard work. There are fourteen weir keepers who live by the river and are on twenty-four-hour call, controlling the flow of water hour by hour to prevent flooding. After a spell of heavy rain in the winter they can be out adjusting the sluices ten times in a night, easing the water downstream and into the Thames. The fourteen locks are all manually operated by the people taking their boats through, and when the river is in spate the locks are literally locked for safety reasons.

Guildford river boats include the *Harry Stevens* and the *Alfred Leroy*, named after men with strong associations with the River Wey. Harry Stevens was the last private owner of the Wey Navigation and he donated it to the National Trust in 1964. Alfred Leroy was one of two brothers who in the early 1900s hired out rowing skiffs and punts from boat houses in Guildford and Farncombe, near Godalming.

The National Trust manages the river from an extra-ordinary oasis in the middle of Guildford, Dapdune

▼ The *Iona* horse-drawn barge at Godalming keeps alive a wonderful old tradition

Wharf, just behind the county cricket ground off Woodbridge Road. Definitely worth a visit, it is a small waterways museum and includes the *Reliance*, an original Wey barge in dry dock, plus a smithy, a stable, a gunpowder store and a barge-building shed.

Rural Crafts

If mineral extraction and water-powered milling are no longer part of Surrey's profile, some of the other traditional rural industries are making a comeback. Forestry management and the harvesting of different types of wood, from hazel wands to mature trees, are once again becoming financially viable. Until the banning of charcoal-burning for glass, brick and iron-working around 1600, the onslaught on the dense woodland of the Weald was as ruthless as the butchery of rainforests is today. Evelyn might have valued the trees saved, but in reality the monarch was more interested in allowing them to grow to maturity to harvest for ship building. Conifer plantations proliferated during the twentieth century, but until recently most woodland was neglected because it was unprofitable. Niche industries like Cooper & Sons' walking stick business of Witley, which coppiced ash as well as hazel around Chiddingfold, kept going until relatively recently, but the Hindhead broom squires stopped making besoms long ago.

Coppicing is coming back into favour, charcoal-burning is still practised and wood as fuel is enjoying a resurgence in the form of wood chip, wood pellet and dried logs for wood-burning stoves. Unlike in the sixteenth century, however, this harvesting of wood for fuel is not a mindless rape of the forests but is managed to create a sustainable source of energy that protects the environment. Cobbett, I am sure, would approve.

The Wealth of the Land

Surrey's coats of arms and logos abound in woolsacks and oak leaves. They are almost the county's trademarks. Guildford, Godalming and Farnham were all at one time wealthy wool towns. Godalming has names like

▼ Hops were a staple crop the length of the Hog's Back and Farnham still boasts a number of recognizable oast houses where the hops were dried.

Woolsack Way, Guildford has Racks Close, but Farnham bears witness to changes in fortune, changes in agricultural and trading patterns. When Surrey lost its monopoly of wool, landowners turned to corn and then hops. In the 1950s hops were grown all along the slopes of the Hog's Back. Agricultural records show 120 acres were still put to hops in 1950, but the days of conspicuous hop wealth have gone, though there is still a hop garden on the Hampton Estate at Puttenham, serving the Hog's Back Brewery. The historic importance of hops, however, lives on in Farnham's converted oast houses, the pub called the Hop Blossom and, most importantly, the Maltings arts and entertainment centre. Tony Poulsom, who farmed Manor Farm, Tongham, and now lets his farm buildings to the Hog's Back Brewery, believes hop-growing in Tongham ceased before 1900, driven out by cheap foreign imports and disease. The local hop was the Farnham Whitebine and it was particularly susceptible to mildew or rust. The fungus was resistant to copper sulphate, the only fungicide available at the time. The fuggles variety is more resistant to the mildew and that is the crop grown today.

▲ A few acres of hop garden at Puttenham, where the Hampton Estate grows fuggles hops for the Hog's Back Brewery at Tongham, are all that remain of a once thriving and valuable agricultural industry

▼ The hop harvest at Puttenham. When dried, the hops are packed into sacks called 'pockets' and sent off to the breweries

Architecture and Gardens

The Surrey edition of Nairn and Pevsner's *The Buildings of England* makes an interesting point: Surrey 'was so remote in the Middle Ages that it does not possess a large medieval parish church; yet today there is hardly anywhere in the county where one can feel free of London.'

Surrey's small, rural, medieval population may not have warranted large churches but there are numerous small ones that are absolutely delightful and I would take issue about the omnipresent influence of London today. The glory of the Surrey Hills is that, although close, London does not breathe down one's neck as one wanders around Coldharbour, Blackdown, Chiddingfold or Abinger. More insidious features of nineteenth- to early twenty-first-century life in Surrey are suburbanization and gentrification – bi-products of a wealthier population and the high cost of housing. It is evident in the horror of mud, the intolerance of cockerels, the PVC double-glazed windows, the block-paving drives and electronic gates, the professionally landscaped gardens and the paving of front gardens to provide off-road parking. The gentle decay, peeling paint, subtle blending of countryside, country garden and country path, simplicity – poverty even – that I remember in the 1950s and 1960s, have almost disappeared. Poverty still exists, but it is manifested in different ways.

The Domestic Buildings Research Group

Architecturally there is little in the Surrey Hills that pre-dates the Norman Conquest – St Mary's Church in Quarry Street, Guildford, windows in the Saxon church of St Michael at Thursley – but the county's medieval domestic buildings are more exciting. Surrey is now famous among medieval architecture historians for its distinctive smoke-bay houses, thanks to the work of the Domestic Buildings Research Group (DBRG), which was founded for the study and recording of traditional domestic architecture by the late Joan Harding, in 1970.

These house detectives know their Scissor Braces and their Dragon Ties. They are a mixture of professionals and self-taught amateurs who can read irregularities in a wall or a wood-wormy roof timber like a book. Joan Harding was full of enthusiasm and energy, and was fired by a passion for architectural history, and under her leadership the group got off to a racing start. The value of her work was recognized with an MBE in 1991 for services to the national heritage in Surrey.

The DBRG has now amassed detailed information on more than 4,000 buildings in Surrey, an extremely impressive county record unmatched in Britain. Their analysis and detailed recordings, plotting the distribution of surviving buildings, has thrown up interesting patterns, ripe for social and economic interpretation, such as the dearth of medieval buildings along Stane Street. There are only three in Ockley whereas the little medieval parish of Godalming has thirty and Shere twenty-five. The reason is unclear.

So far, the earliest DBRG-recorded domestic building is Forge Cottage in Dunsfold, dated at 1254, but Martin Higgins, the Historic Buildings Officer for Surrey County Council, who has been a volunteer researcher with the group since 1975, thinks there might be even older buildings yet to be investigated.

The DBRG offers a voluntary service. It is not a campaigning organization, and it does not force its way into

▶ Ornate patterns of half timbering are specific to small areas such as Godalming Church Street

people's houses demanding access to the loft, or insist that buildings be listed, or complain about modernization. It simply waits to be invited into buildings and then records them – and it does even that extremely discreetly. The descriptions, analysis, drawings and dating process are given free to the owner of the building and copies are deposited in the National Buildings Record of the Royal Commission on the Historical Monuments of England, at Swindon, and also in the Surrey Record Office at Woking. The individual reports are not published, and only serious researchers can access them.

Joan Harding, then a keen member of Surrey Archaeological Society, started the DBRG when she realized that no one was taking much interest in buildings, only on what lay under the soil. Its early members knew her through the Workers' Education Association (WEA) courses she ran and recruits included amateurs like Pam Bowley, whose encyclopaedic knowledge of the architecture and history of the Horsleys, acquired over thirty years, marks her out now as the doyenne of local historians. Martin Higgins was drawn into the group through his mother. 'She needed me to hold the other end of the tape measure,' he said. Together they would scramble round the roof timbers recording the style of construction and carpenters' marks.

The information amassed by the group enabled the late Peter Gray to write the authoritative manual: *Surrey Medieval Buildings, an Analysis and Inventory*. He identified 856 medieval buildings in the county, mostly in the southern half because prosperity spreading out from London enabled people in the north to demolish and rebuild.

The group has been able to use the data to interpret the effects of political events such as the introduction of the hearth tax in 1662 followed by the window tax in 1696. They discovered that the elaborate timber framing in the houses in The Street, Wonersh, in Great Tangley, in cottages by the railway line at Goose Green, in Gomshall and in the centre of Godalming was a short-lived fashion that occurred in a very small area only between 1570 and 1585. The more buildings are recorded, the more accurate the dating becomes and the DBRG has recently taken a giant step forward, with support from Surrey Archaeological Society, Surrey County Council and the

Heritage Lottery Fund, introducing dendrochronology. This compares the tree-ring pattern from a core sample of a medieval beam against a master chart. Some of the findings have been surprising. Some buildings have turned out to be older than expected and some younger. One cottage in Betchworth was dated at 1590 instead of 1620; its tree rings showed the timber had been felled in 1589, the year after the Spanish Armada.

Delving behind updated façades has revealed the driving force of fashion and one-upmanship. When glazing was introduced it took the wealthy by storm. Wooden-framed houses could take any amount of glass, and sometimes this frieze fenestration ran all around the front of a house in a continuous clerestorey. Vann is a good example. But there was a dilemma: brick was a more fashionable building material, but it could not accommodate all that glass – oh decisions, decisions. The window tax was the final straw.

The timbers for timber-framed houses were the original Ikea flat pack. They were sawn and prepared in the builder's yard, and each piece marked for easy construction later. Sometimes frames intended for houses were changed so they could be used as workshops or barns, so the detectives have to read the marks and smoke stains to understand what happened. One conundrum they are working on is the absence of medieval kitchens in Surrey. Where did people do their cooking? When timber buildings are taken down they leave few traces.

Great Tangley Manor

Pevsner may be disparaging about medieval Surrey architecture but there are some stunning buildings to be seen. Great Tangley Manor at Wonersh is the best of Surrey's half-timbered sixteenth-century houses, based around a medieval hall, complete with nineteenth-century moated grounds. Great Tangley deservedly enjoys Grade I listing; the site has been inhabited for more than 1,000 years

▼ The elaborate timber framing seen on Gomshall's Malthouse Cottages framing was a short-lived fashion

and is still superb. It started off as part of the Manor of Bramley, although it is not listed in the Domesday Book. In 1196, Bramley Manor was recorded as belonging to John, Count of Mortain, as Prince John was then. Tradition has it that he used Great Tangley as a royal hunting lodge and base for his forays into the Forest of Anderida. It was given a facelift with fancy timbering in 1582 when a first floor was inserted into the hall. There is a theory that a Catholic priest hole was also included during these alterations, as in January 2004, Wonersh History Society reported that a small room was discovered leading off a chimney. Other entrances might have existed behind panelling. The house is also believed to contain wood from the Armada fleet incorporated into the dining room and in the panelling. John Carrill, who owned the house in the late sixteenth century, certainly made a contribution to the English defences against the Armada.

The next major alteration to Great Tangley was during the flowering of the Arts and Crafts Movement that had such an impact on architecture in the Surrey Hills. The new owner in 1880 was Wickham Flower, who had connections with the movement, and he commissioned east and west extensions by the architect Philip Webb, who was working closely with William Morris. He also created the pleasure gardens and bridge across the moat. Webb was the architect of Coneyhurst, a fine brick and tile-hung house on the slopes of Pitch Hill at Ewhurst, built in 1886, probably around the same time as he was working at Great Tangley.

When all Webb's alterations were completed, the royal family, including King George V and Queen Mary, visited the manor and signed the window of the dining room with a diamond ring. Signatures of King George VI and Edward VIII can also be seen on the dressing room windows of the master suite. This is the kind of graffiti that is definitely socially acceptable, and it goes down well with the guests who hire part of the house for very exclusive weekend breaks and celebrations.

▼ Great Tangley Manor, Wonersh

Vann

It is interesting that John Childe, who was Mayor of Guildford three times during the second half of the seventeenth century, should have at different times owned both Great Tangley and another outstanding early Surrey building – Vann, at Hambledon. He also built Guildford House, one of the finest buildings in Guildford High Street. The name Vann goes back to the twelfth century and probably referred to boggy ground – a fen – and the house received the stately south end addition to the early sixteenth century building, constructed in brick vernacular Dutch style, during Childe's ownership. Vann predates Loseley with core dating putting it at 1542. It was leased in 1907 to W. D. Caroe; the family bought it in 1930 and still lives there.

Caroe was one of the great figures of the Arts and Crafts Movement and architect to the Ecclesiastical Commissioners. His Surrey commissions included the Church of St John the Baptist in West Byfleet. With supreme confidence, he doubled the size of Vann by incorporating its barn and hovel (animal house) and constructing outbuildings. He was a master of open-planning and spatial relationships and his eye for detail is still visible in the quality of joinery and decorative metalwork.

By 1948, however, when it passed to his son, Alban, also an architect, the place had become very run down. No one really wanted to live in such a rambling house, so it was divided into two, one half let and the other used as a weekend cottage. W. D.'s grandson Martin, who followed the family tradition as another cathedral architect, inherited it in 1969, and the house has since been steadily restored without any of the jarring notes of modernization that would have so upset W. D.'s friend and neighbour, Gertrude Jekyll. The continuum of family life has almost created a living museum of domestic history. There are bamboo carpet beaters and stone hot water bottles, and Elizabeth I would feel completely at home in the parlour. The house was chosen in 2006 for an episode of the quirky but popular BBC series, *The Curious House Guest*.

The sixteenth-century frame of the house was made of local oaks and it would originally have had a simple opening in the centre of the roof to let the smoke out. Chimneys were added later in the seventeenth century. Childe created a large extension to the south, making two fine rooms on the ground and the first floors, with a bedroom in the garret. As well as pouring love into the family home, the Caroes particularly adored the gardens. In 1911, they invited Jekyll to advise them on how to turn the valley below the little dammed stream into a woodland water garden. It was exactly the kind of project that Jekyll loved. Mary Caroe explained:

> The yew hedges were planted in 1909 and that part of the gardens is very much in the Jekyll style. We know she came to tea here to talk about the water garden and her notebook lists the 1,500 plants that came from her own nursery. My mother-in-law was a very good gardener and the whole family was bamboozled into helping. In the holidays they dug out the ponds and the smell was so bad they had to be fed outside. When Martin was fighting in Korea his letters home were always full of questions about the garden.
>
> We first opened it to the public in 1971 and raised £32 but with the recent Jekyll centenary and interest in her work, numbers shot up and over the years we have raised more than £84,000 for the National Garden Scheme.

This part of Surrey, often referred to as the Fold Country, is ideal for woodland gardens. Ramster, an extended Jacobean farmhouse with a great beamed and panelled Long Hall, at Chiddingfold, is famous for its 20 acres of flowering shrubs sheltered by oaks and larches with a lake and a bog garden, while Feathercombe, at Hambledon, is renowned for its azaleas and rhododendrons.

Loseley

If Vann is an example of a medieval yeoman's house that evolved over the centuries, Loseley demonstrates what can be achieved when you have pressing urgency to create a house fit for a queen to visit, and by lucky chance there is access to the dressed stone of a newly dissolved abbey. The result is a house that makes a grand and satisfying statement, but is also surprisingly cosy and 'liveable in'. The More-Molyneux family has always believed firmly in making it a home, using the state rooms for formal occasions like Christmas dinner and birthday parties. Nowadays the state rooms can be hired for functions, so the house is fully used.

Loseley was built quickly, between 1562 and 1568 at a cost of £1,640 19s 6d, (£1,640.97). All the original accounts have been preserved, showing how most of the stonework was rescued from the ruins of the Cistercian Waverley Abbey. The house today is little changed since Elizabeth I visited it with her enormous retinue. A north-west wing, incorporating a chapel, a 121ft picture gallery and a riding school, was built in the early seventeenth century, but was demolished in 1820, and there may have originally been an east wing and gatehouse.

The drawing room contains a masterpiece of stone carving – an ornate and intricately decorated floor-to-ceiling chimneypiece created from one enormous slab of chalk. It is an outstanding achievement. Period furniture and wonderful paintings, tapestries and hangings complement the architecture to give a Tudor feel. Would Queen Elizabeth I feel at home there today? Quite possibly. She would certainly appreciate the cleanliness and good husbandry of the estate as a whole, because she criticized the dirt after one of her visits in the sixteenth century.

Chilworth Manor

One of my favourite country houses is Chilworth Manor, nestling under St Martha's Hill. Originally a monastery, it was rebuilt as a house by Vincent Randyll, who ran the gunpowder works in the 1650s. He is probably responsible for the warm brick façade and pillared entrance, and the big Dutch gable in the Artisan Mannerist style. The owner with the biggest impact on the house, however, was the feisty Sarah, widow of the Duke of Marlborough, who moved there from Blenheim Palace in 1725, having bought the Chilworth estate for £30,000. She built a completely new wing to the north of Randyll's creation. It was more sophisticated than Randyll's house, a well-proportioned rectangular building dressed in red brick, decorated with stuccoes and Ionic pilasters. She also created the three-tiered Baroque walled garden, carved out of the side of the hill, which is still known as the Duchess's Garden. It was designed to display flowers and plants just at the time when exotica from foreign parts was beginning to capture the imagination of the aristocracy.

When she died in 1744 the duchess left the house to her grandson, the 2nd Earl Spencer, but he was forced to sell it to pay for Althorp and so the manor once more passed into the hands of gunpowder magnates, this time the Tinklers. Henry Drummond of Albury also owned it for a while in the nineteenth century. During the war it was used as a billet for the Canadian Army, and Sir Lionel and Lady Heald bought it in 1945 after their house in Regent's Park had been bombed. Air Commodore Sir Lionel Heald was Attorney General in Sir Winston Churchill's Cabinet from 1951 to 1954, and Lady Heald was a passionate gardener who for many years was chairman of the National Gardens Scheme. She opened the gardens of the manor for sixty years, raising thousands of pounds for charities. She also allowed it to be used as a film set. It featured in *The Novel Affair*, *Daniel Deronda*, *Foyle's War* and the *Just William* episode in which a herd of goats was let into the strawberry patch.

Model Farms

By the eighteenth century, visitors to the big country seats would not have been restricted to the state rooms and formal gardens. Agricultural reform was encouraging landowners to display their pioneering technology and their philanthropy, and Surrey has a number of model farmyards, solidly built in brick, attached to big houses, and sometimes even dairies and game larders that were specifically built for show. House guests would have been invited 'à la Marie Antoinette' to take tea in the dairy. There are model farm buildings at Hampton in Seale, at Home Farm, Albury, at Horsley Towers in East Horsley and at Sondes Place Farm in Dorking.

Norbury Park Farm at Mickleham has one of the best examples of a dairy/game larder that was obviously meant to be visited by guests from the big house. This pretty octagonal building, built around the turn of the nineteenth century, is lined with blue and white Minton tiles featuring pictures of a dairymaid and game birds, an outlay far in excess of any practical agricultural needs. Its visitors may have included Fanny Burney and the aristocratic French refugees. The model farm at Horsley Towers was designed by Lord Lovelace to be an educational facility for village children as well as a working farm.

The Arts and Crafts Movement

We know that the master mason who oversaw the building of Loseley in 1562 was a man called Mabbanke, but it is extremely unusual that his name should have been preserved – a testament to the meticulous record keeping of the More-Molyneux famiy. Mabbanke would have been both mason and architect, discussing his plans with Sir William More and overseeing his team of skilled workmen; however, the craftsmen of this period are normally anonymous. Even the brilliant men who designed and built the great medieval cathedrals are

▼ The late eighteenth-century buttery-cum-game larder at Norbury Park Farm, lined with beautiful painted Minton tiles

almost all nameless. As we move forward in time, names begin to crop up, and in the Regency, Victorian, and early twentieth-century periods there is a large number of professional architects stamping their identity on Surrey. The county's early classical phase is represented by the early eighteenth century Clandon Park, designed by the German-trained Venetian architect, Giacomo Leoni for Thomas Onslow, and the early nineteenth-century Polesden Lacey at Great Bookham, built in a Grecian style with Ionic columns by Thomas Cubitt.

The most exciting period in Surrey, however, came when the Arts and Crafts Movement began to influence everything from building materials to wallpaper design. Inspiration for the possibilities of creative design came from the Great Exhibition of 1851, with a swing away from factory production to a general appreciation of craftsmanship and a hankering for honest country ways. There is a lot of nostalgia for a lost rural paradise here.

Gertrude Jekyll was so conscious of the genuine country way of life disappearing in front of her that she collected information and photographs and recorded everything she saw, gathering it together in her authoritative book *Old West Surrey*. She recorded cottage life before the contemporary obsession with shopping and materialism had gathered its unstoppable momentum. The cottagers had few possessions, made their own quilts and rugs and lived close to nature. Their homes were damp and badly maintained and had little in the way of hygiene. Jekyll saw the picturesque natural harmony of both buildings and way of life but she was not blind to the need to improve their standard of living. She had the good sense to see that modernization could be achieved sensitively, providing local materials and local building traditions were used. So often they were not. Perhaps it is the English way to hanker after a disappearing rural idyll. Cobbett did it, Jekyll did it and I catch myself doing the same for a less wealthy, less acquisitional 1950s Surrey.

The railways kick-started Surrey's nineteenth-century middle class housing boom. Architect-designed homes were springing up throughout the countryside. Philip Webb, who did the alterations to Great Tangley Manor

▲ The Norbury dairymaid in painted Minton wall tiles in the game larder at Norbury Park Farm. She is the reproduced on the label of Norbury Blue cheese

was one giant of nineteenth-century architecture. Another was Richard Norman Shaw, whose early work was influenced by the tile-hung cottages of the Weald. Hopedene in Holmbury St Mary was one of his first houses in the Surrey Hills. Alderbrook, built in 1881 on the slopes of Winterfold, Burrows Cross on the ridge south of Shere in 1886 and The Hallams, Blackheath in 1894, are all substantial country homes set in impressive grounds. Shaw was extremely eminent – a Royal Academician from 1877 and one of the editors of a book exploring the role of the architect – *Architecture, a Profession or an Art* – a subject that was very topical within the Arts and Crafts Movement. Pevsner mentions nine of his Surrey commissions and comments on such a high number in just one county. Given his national importance, it is a real indicator of the wealth coming into Surrey.

Shaw was at his peak when Sir Edward Lutyens began his career as an architect and he had a huge influence on him. Tile-hanging and Tudor vied for his favour. Lutyens built Munstead Place and Chinthurst Hill in the early 1890s and then came the meeting of minds when he was commissioned to design Munstead Wood for Gertrude Jekyll. His country homes seem moulded to the Surrey Hills. They are neither jarring nor dramatic, but seem completely at ease, sprawling organically in their country settings. Jekyll's partnership with Lutyens was for many the perfect combination of house and garden designer. To have a Lutyens house with a Jekyll garden was to buy into the Edwardian rural idyll and her house, Munstead Wood, above Busbridge, designed by him with gardens by her, is still a Mecca for people seeking harmony of buildings and nature. Both had early connections with Surrey. Jekyll was brought up at Bramley Park and Lutyens at Wormley.

A good example of their collaboration is Little Tangley in Wonersh. Lutyens knew its owner, Cowley Lambert, through his father, and Lambert commissioned him to make alterations to the house, including a marvellous hall and oak staircase. Its subsequent owner, the Doulton porcelain heiress Mrs Hooper, commissioned Jekyll to lay out the gardens. It is likely that the three large terraces to the east were Lutyens/Jekyll creations. As an aside, it is fascinating that while most sprawling Surrey mansions were later taken over for the war effort in the 1940s, Little Tangley was taken over by dogs. Its owner was a prominent breeder and according to Wonersh History Society, was rumoured to have used the billiard room for her puppies.

But Lutyens had a career to carve out and he moved on, entering a period of international importance as architect for British imperialism. Munstead Woods and Little Tangley are a very far cry from Government House in Delhi.

Shaw also influenced another significant architect who was very creative in Surrey in the 1890s. Charles Voysey specialized in country homes with low roofs and a rustic Arts and Crafts design, in keeping with his belief in spiritual harmony. Greyfriars and Prior's Field at Puttenham, and Norney at Shackleford, are Voysey houses. He would have been at the heart of the argument over architecture as profession or art. He embraced the broader design opportunities of the Arts and Crafts Movement and designed wallpaper, fabric and furnishings as well as buildings. It was a period of great creativity and understanding of natural materials but it did not last. The clean verticals of the Georgian style were already gaining popularity and by the end of the First World War, Surrey was attracting not so much wealthy clients wanting individual country mansions, as developers eyeing up the possibility of mass producing pastiche country suburbs.

Farnham

Farnham town centre has almost seamlessly absorbed great changes in its business fortunes and architectural fashions. At the height of the wool trade it was a throbbing centre of industry, with warehouses, courtyards and stabling, and tiny lanes and traffic leading from the main streets down by the great town houses to the fields beyond. Corn, then hops, took over as the economic mainstay. The architecture adjusted to cope with these changing commodities, but with the decline of agriculture, the town was left with a huge number of redundant buildings, yards and alleys. Like redundant farm buildings now, they needed to be given a new lease of life.

That Farnham retains its unspoilt character today is largely due to the intervention of influential architects and townsmen with a sense of history. Harold Falkner, a Farnham-based architect steeped in the Arts and Craft Movement, who died in 1963, made the town his career project, aiming to make it even more beautiful. He was among the architects who worked with Gertrude Jekyll. What may appear ancient to a casual visitor, may actually be a piece of beautiful Faulkner imaginative illusion. He 'Georgianized' the town where it was deemed imperfect.

Less deceptive are the recent yard and mews conversions. They do not pretend to be hundreds of years old but they have, in the main, been designed to fit in absolutely beautifully with the old. Probably the key is the scale. This is domestic architecture: cottages, terraces, small shops and offices, a happy mix of individuality totally in keeping with the piecemeal development of the town over the centuries.

Lion and Lamb Yard, Borelli Yard and St George's Mews are causes for optimism. What were dark, dilapidated, redundant corners have become vibrant and very pretty little arcades and residential areas that invite exploration. The name Borelli is significant. This successful Farnham jeweller and town councillor practically ran Farnham with his friend Falkner. It was their partnership that kept post-war architectural horrors at bay.

The 2004 government *Report on Urban Renaissance in the South East* cites Farnham as 'a good example of how a concerned local community, working with conservation minded local authorities, can retain and enhance its heritage and special character while developing and diversify its centre, so as to keep it vital and viable. It boasts one of the longest established conservation societies – and one of the longest established building preservation trusts – in the country.'

It is telling that once Borelli and Falkner had relinquished the reins, the town made its first disastrous foray into large-scale redevelopment – the Woolmead.

The Lovelace Effect

England prides itself on producing eccentrics and the Victorian era had some good examples. The first Lord Lovelace left an enduring, completely eccentric legacy: a whole village, plus surrounding hamlets and a large tract of the North Downs stamped with his unique architectural signature. From his magnificent, idiosyncratic home, Horsley Towers, right down to humble estate workers'

▼ Horsley Towers, ornamental flint and brick extravaganza created by Lord Lovelace

cottages, a decorative harmony of flint and red brick sets them apart from buildings anywhere else in Surrey. The result is stunning but completely unreal.

His grand masterplan essentially involved an act of wholesale architectural vandalism, something more usually associated with councils in the twentieth century. Lovelace simply could not resist demolishing and disguising existing cottages on his estate and giving them his idealized flint-and-brick treatment. The cottages he destroyed would have dated from the fifteenth to the eighteenth centuries – all transformed to his whim. This makeover of some fifty buildings around East Horsley took thirty years, from 1846 to 1877.

Lady Ada Lovelace was the daughter of Lord Byron. She was a very remarkable woman, a brilliant scientist and mathematician at a time when high-born women were still expected to content themselves with child-bearing, embroidery and a little light social work – but then her mother had also been mathematically precocious. Ada practically invented computer programming through her pioneering work with Charles Babbage, helping him by translating Italian treatises and then working out applications. Her portrait is the watermark on Microsoft stationery and in 1998 the Lovelace medal was struck in her honour, awarded annually for contribution to British computer technology. The US Defence Department named its computer language Ada after her.

Lovelace married her when she was nineteen. It was a bitter blow when she died of cancer when she was just thirty-six. She was not an easy wife to cope with, having inherited the poet Byron's intelligence but also his roller-coaster personality. Lovelace created such a splendid bathroom for her that it is separately listed. When she died, he threw himself into his architectural project. The gatehouse to Horsley Towers on the corner with the A246 demonstrates perfectly his enthusiasm for a mock Gothic idyll. The main house, built by Sir Charles Barry, who designed the Houses of Parliament, had to endure constant creative tinkering by the earl until his death in 1883. Lovelace built the stuccoed clock tower, the great hall, more towers, a chapel and a maze of cloisters using painted bricks and flint to startling effect.

The cottages are scattered up the little lanes that snake their way across the North Downs between Horsley, Polesden Lacey and Dorking. But it is not just flint cottages that Lovelace dotted across his large woodland estate. He also built fifteen bridges – extraordinary single-span works of art deep inside his private forest. Each one of these horseshoe bridges was individually designed, uniquely decorated and meticulously crafted. Even a beautifully crafted little bridge cannot survive the intrusion of tree roots and extremes of weather for well over 100 years without suffering, however, and by the end of the twentieth century they were in a sad state. Several had disappeared completely and the survivors were losing the battle with the encroaching forest. There is a happy ending though. The ten capable of rescue are currently being equally meticulously restored.

Quite why Lovelace expended such love and attention on the bridges is a mystery. They would appear to have been made for his commercial timber business, but there were rumours that he was deformed and wanted to travel to and from Horsley without being seen by villagers on the main road. It is more plausible, however, that he decorated otherwise utilitarian structures to impress his house guests when he took them out on tours of the estate. It would certainly tie in with the fashion for visiting model farms and show-piece dairies.

Coming upon them suddenly in the woods, one gets a wonderfully gothic sense of romantic decay, which is helped by their names: Raven, Troy, Hermitage, East and West Briary, Stoney Dene, Robin Hood and Meadow Platt. The bridges owe their rescue to Peter Hattersley, who has dedicated a huge amount of time and effort to setting up an expensive restoration project. Initial attempts to generate interest failed, but when Mike Dodd joined the Horsley Countryside Preservation Society committee, with an interest in the bridges, and by happy coincidence the parish council's footpaths and bridleways committee decided to look at bridge repairs, things started moving. Professor Alan Crocker of Surrey

Archaeological Society was enthusiastic and Peter secured the support of Surrey County Council, Guildford Borough Council, the Surrey Hills AONB, Horsley Countryside Preservation Society and Forest Enterprise. The project is not just about bridge repair. It is also about opening up a lovely area of the North Downs to disabled access. The target for completion is 2010, the 150th anniversary of the building of the bridges. Peter said:

> The Lovelace Bridges Project was launched in March 2003 in the grand hall of Horsley Towers. I was able to announce a SITA grant of £13,000 to add to the £2,000 allocated from Surrey's Historic Buildings Fund and £1,000 from the county's local committee budget. Our first target was Stoney Dene, the most vulnerable of the crumbling bridges and the Lord Lieutenant Sarah Goad started the restoration by doing some ceremonial repointing of the flintwork.

Stoney Dene was renovated first. Des Hollier, chairman of the preservation society and former parish council chairman, was in charge of the flintwork and the arch now boasts smart new decorative brick detail and a stabilized structure. Troy Bridge required a complicated concrete saddle superstructure to mend its crack, and the knowledge and experience gained was applied to each bridge in turn. Volunteers put in hundreds of hours clearing the undergrowth invading the other bridges and each one has had a bronze interpretive plaque added.

An easy-access Village Link route has already been created, taking people from St Martin's Court in East Horsley up to Stoney Dene where they can join the Lovelace Trail. The project attracted two awards. Peter

▼ Stoney Dene, one of the little gems of bridges built by Lord Lovelace on the North Downs at East Horsley and now undergoing restoration

won the Mayor of Guildford's Award for Community Service and the Horsley Countryside Preservation Society won the Surrey Industrial History Group's 2007 Conservation Award. The project caught the local imagination and one man, reading about it, remembered he had taken home a tile, engraved with the date 1871, from one of the ruined bridges in 1955. He had kept it safe for fifty years and he sent it back for inclusion in the restoration. Other pieces of architectural detail and decoration have been found buried in leaves and soil, where they had fallen decades before.

Follies

There is something about a hilltop that makes people want to go higher still. The idea of a tower seems utterly irresistible. The Surrey Hills has several famous hilltop towers; on Leith Hill at Coldharbour, Box Hill at Mickleham and Chinthurst Hill, Wonersh. Turning dreams into reality however, needs eccentricity. Richard Hull from Bristol, who moved to Leith Hill in the mid-eighteenth century, had the extra incentive of getting the hill to a satisfying round figure of 1,000ft or just over, so that it qualified as a mountain. Early photographs show it with a completely bald top, but modern visitors get nowhere near the same 360° experience of standing on the top of the world because, despite recent National Trust clearance projects, views from some angles are still blocked by dense tree cover.

Hull built the folly around 1765 with the permission of the Lord of the Manor, in an accurate copy of a thirteenth-century Wealden tower. The top is the highest point in southern England, and apparently the next highest peak to the east is in the Ural Mountains in western Russia, where Europe meets Asia.

Hull was buried beneath the tower in 1772 and rumour has it that he was interred vertically, head down, as he believed that on the Day of Judgement the world would be turned on its head. In 1800, the equally eccentric Major Peter Labelliere of Box Hill was similarly buried upside down, 100ft deep. Hull's interpretation of Revelation, that the world would go topsy-turvy, and requests for burial upside down, were common in the eighteenth century.

Leith Hill tower was a tourist attraction from the start. Although it originally boasted two furnished rooms and was named Prospect House, it always welcomed visitors. The Latin inscription above the door says that Hull built it not only for his own pleasure but also for the enjoyment of others. Visitors were allowed to use a 'prospect glass', a small telescope, mounted on the roof to enjoy the panorama.

After Hull's death, the tower was vandalized and fell into ruin – there is nothing new in delinquency – and the tower was filled with rubble and concrete and the entrance bricked up in the early nineteenth century as a safety measure. The octagonal side tower was added in 1864 by the Evelyn family of Wotton so that visitors could still climb up and admire the views. In 1984 the National Trust opened up the tower again and cleared the rubble, uncovering Richard Hull's tomb. A café now shares the lower room with a history display. Hull would be pleased that his tower is still appreciated today. Nearly half a million visitors are believed to trek up through the woods to it every year.

It is quite possible that the little tower on Lodge Hill at Mickleham, built by Thomas Broadwood in the early nineteenth century, originally looked over to Leith Hill across the Mole Gap. Broadwood, a famous piano maker, built Juniper Hall in 1814 and the tower overlooks Lord Beaverbrook's mansion at Cherkley Court.

Chinthurst Hill, and its tower, is a landmark of my childhood. I was brought up in its shadow and ran wild in its woods, tobogganing down its slopes in winter. I loved the tussocky, fine-grassed summit with its little round tower, and I imagined all sorts of romantic stories about it. There is no romance there really, however, just a sad and surprisingly modern story. The great house on the hilltop was built by Lutyens for Emelia Guthrie, a descendant of Admiral Sir James Stirling, the first Governor of Perth, Australia, in the early 1890s. Stirling had strong connections with Stoke-next-Guildford and Emelia's grandmother lived at Stoke Park. Chinthurst Hill is a wonderful Lutyens creation, nestling comfortably into the hill with views to the south, but it has had a rapid succession of owners. Up for sale once again in 1937, it was bought by Kenneth Mackay, the 2nd Lord Inchcape, whose father had founded the P&O shipping line. He loved the grounds and built the tower, but tragically he died suddenly on the eve of a big party he had planned in order to celebrate its completion. One could still go inside when I was young but uninhabited follies are a magnet for vandals and it suffered over the years; it is now blocked up.

The tall, elegant, octagonal Booker's Tower next to the Mount Cemetery at the end of the Hog's Back overlooking Guildford, was built in 1839. It was commissioned by a former Mayor of Guildford, Charles Booker, in memory of his sons, who had died tragically, but in the end it was formally dedicated to the marriage of Queen Victoria and Prince Albert. It was reputedly used by a Victorian scientist for lighting experiments.

Chinthurst Hill is a Surrey County Council Open Space and Leith Hill is owned by the National Trust, but most follies are private, although visitors may be welcome. Hascombe's folly is a private project, but visitors can ask to go and see it. It is not a tower, but a henge, probably the first henge ever built in Surrey.

Priests alarmed at the thought of black magic and pagan rituals inside the stone circle initially tried to block its construction. Luckily common sense prevailed. Now mellowing in a sea of tall grass and wildflowers on a knoll overlooking the Weald, the circle actually exudes benign tranquillity. It is a space for contemplation; rites and ceremonies are forbidden. Called the Dragon Circle, it consists of nineteen pieces of Portland stone weighing an average of 7 tons each, set in alignment to the positions of the moon according to Celtic tradition. It was built by the stone circle specialist Ivan McBeth, with help from engineer Cliff Osenton and upwards of 150 helpers. Ropes, pulleys, windlasses, sleepers and rolling pins were all experimented with, as Hascombe's was the first of the new generation of henges to be set up by hand. The rest cheated with machinery.

Hascombe has other claims to fame. In 1877, Edward Lee Rowcliffe of Hall Place built a water fountain for the village in memory of his brother Henry. It consists of a spout channelling pure spring water into a stone trough and it is still in use 130 years later. The water is of exceptionally good quality and it has a widespread reputation; people come from miles around armed with containers which they fill at the spout and take home for the week. It is particularly busy at weekends and it has been known for queues to form and for people to have to wait an hour before they finally get to the trough. The water is regularly checked by the authorities. Occasionally microbes get in and a sign is put up warning people not to use it, but spring water quickly recovers and people just wait for the signs to come down and then it's back to the queue.

Hascombe was also important for national communications. The hill had been used for a beacon, but at the end of the eighteenth century, with the threat of invasion by Napoleon's forces, an Admiralty station was set up there to pass news between London and Portsmouth. It used a telegraph involving six shutters that could be arranged in sixty-three different ways to communicate complicated messages accurately across distances of about 12 miles. There were ten stations between London and Portsmouth and messages could be relayed in just fifteen minutes. Hascombe communicated north to Netley Heath at Shere and south to the station at Blackdown. There must have been far fewer trees in 1796 when the stations went live. The shutter system was replaced by semaphore but Hascombe was bypassed: the semaphore hut was placed on Pewley Hill at Guildford instead.

I am definitely not a modernist, and most twentieth-century attempts to ape traditional styles miss the mark, but one man's eccentric yearning for a smaller-scale rural idyll is worth looking at, as it is as unique to East Horsley as Lovelace's flint-mania. Heavily influenced by the Arts and Crafts Movement yet not in the Lutyens league, Frank Chown was responsible for the timber-and-thatch mock-traditional cottages that form the basis of the village's expensive suburban dormitory and climbs up into the downs at Sheepleas. He was able to follow his dream when the Lovelace Estate was broken up and sold off in lots in 1920. The estate had been bought the previous year by Tommy Sopwith the famous racing driver and founder of the Sopwith Aviation Company. He is credited with having saved Britain from German invasion in 1940 through his development of the Hurricane and his foresight in stockpiling it, and a picture of the Horsley Hawker still hangs in Horsley Towers. However, in 1919, his company went under and Sopwith had to sell up.

Frank Chown, an architect, bought large plots, starting off near the railway station, to develop as houses and shops for the new breed of London commuter. He sold on many small plots, on the strict condition that he would be the designer of the houses to be built there. He also included restrictions on housing density, as he wanted the development to be high quality – specifying a luxurious four houses to the acre – and he based his designs on the traditional local cottage style, before the Lovelace makeover. Chown houses are solid and well built, their oak beams and staircases giving them a Tudor feel, and the wrought-iron handrails, polished wood floors and oak window frames and doors speak of quality craftsmanship. Many have attractive thatched roofs. He built the estate of Pennymead and Woodland Drives and the popular village sports club that separates them. The original Nomad Theatre was the old Chown storage hut. Frank and his sons Kenneth and Donald started the theatre group, which was called the Nomads for a very sound reason: they would rehearse in a newly built Chown house, and when it was sold they would move on to the next one. The Nomads are still flourishing but they now have their own little theatre.

▼ Thatched roofs and high quality rustic design characterize these East Horsley houses built by local architect Frank Chown. He must have been a bit of a romantic at heart

Wildlife

The Surrey Puma

My Christmas present in the bitter winter of 1962 was a donkey called Topper and I was totally besotted with him. I would go to bed with the weather raging outside, worried sick that the Surrey puma was about to slink down from Chinthurst Hill, leap the fence and sink its fangs into his neck. 'Dear God, please don't let him get eaten' I fearfully intoned every night from under the bedclothes. Thankfully the puma never turned up and the donkey stayed with my family for another thirty-four years before eventually succumbing to old age. The 1960s was very much the decade of the puma, but surprisingly, sightings are still reported. Several have been recorded since the Millennium, so the idea of a big non-native feral cat stalking the countryside is an enduring one. Reporters working on the *Surrey Advertiser* would say to one another when news was thin, 'about time we had a sighting'. It was almost an expected annual event – like the first swallow arriving, or the first cuckoo in spring – the phone call from an excited member of the public to say they had definitely 'seen the Surrey puma.'

Sceptical, moi? .... Well ... I keep an open mind. The sightings have now spanned more than forty years and the colours recorded range from yellow to tawny to grey to black. One animal? Unlikely. Breeding secretly? I'm unconvinced. I am very conscious of all the other wildlife teeming naturally and mostly indigenously in our countryside that could be mistaken at a distance, in undergrowth, for a big cat. One of the best photographs of the 'puma', taken on Smithwood Common outside Cranleigh, looked suspiciously like a small deer, although large pug marks that were found in sand and wet mud are a puzzle. An analysis of sightings, and the sad trail of mutilated sheep corpses found in the 1980s, produce a variety of traits that don't really spell big cat, more likely big dog.

Whatever there is out there, like most Surrey folk who have grown up with the legends, I enjoy the mystery and the lack of proof either way. These animals – puma, lion, dog or feral cat – have been incredibly discreet and pretty well behaved. They have restricted themselves to killing a few sheep and one steer over nearly half a century. Verified dog attacks have resulted in many more deaths, and many more newborn lambs and afterbirths are snatched every year by hungry foxes.

The earliest recorded sighting of a possible feral feline beast was by William Cobbett in October 1825. His 'puma' was a grey animal the size of a medium-sized spaniel, which he watched during a visit to Waverley Abbey. There were then no more recorded incidents for over 100 years. But by 1959, sightings were being reported regularly in the area around the Surrey and Hampshire border. One man described it as a Labrador-sized animal that walked like a cat and was stalking some lambs in a field. A similar animal was reported near Heathy Park Reservoir on the North Downs at 7.45 a.m. on 16 July by Ernest Jellett, a water board worker. He said he saw a large cat that looked like a lion chasing a rabbit but it turned tail – a long thin one – when he shouted at it. The police took his description seriously and searched the area but all they found was a patch of flattened grass where a large animal might have lain down. Sightings of pug marks and animals continued at a variety of locations, from Munstead to Hascombe, Worplesdon to Frensham, Hindhead, Chiddingfold and Elstead. Farm dogs were said to cower indoors when the puma was abroad and in

1964, a vet pronounced that bite marks on a calf carcass were made by a non-native predator. Puma hair was said to have been found at Peaslake in 1984, and in 2000, George and Barbara Quelsh said they saw a puma cross Stoke Park near Spectrum Leisure Centre, in broad daylight at lunchtime, probably the most urban of all the sightings. In June 2003, a large, rabbit-coloured cat was seen twice around Holmbury St Mary, and in April 2004, villagers in Abinger Common also reported seeing a huge cat. Long may the sightings continue.

Deer

Anyone living in the Surrey Hills will be familiar with the depredations of deer in the garden, the sharp intake of breath when one leaps across the road in front of a car and the encounters with them in the bracken on the heaths. There are more deer in Surrey now than at any time in history. They are no longer claimed by the monarch, they have no natural predators and they breed very successfully. Like all wildlife, they have no respect for property boundaries and unless one installs 1.5m fencing, one cannot be entirely sure that ones flowers, vegetables or newly planted trees will be safe from their dawn nibbling. Depending on whether they wreck your flowers or leave your garden alone, they are either a disaster or a delight.

Where deer are a nuisance, they are difficult to control. Even expert stalkers find it difficult to get safe shots in this crowded county. Compared with the Scottish highlands, the heaths and moors of Surrey are on a very cramped, domestic scale. The venison on sale at farmers' markets is often wild rather than farmed, so some are culled, but Surrey deer are far from endangered, and they are more likely to be killed by a car or an out-of-control dog. It is ironic that because culling is so difficult it is hard to get new woodland established.

The wooded Surrey Hills are predominantly roe deer territory; the odd fallow deer is probably an escapee from a privately owned herd. Muntjak, little dog-sized deer that look decidedly foreign, are also rarely sighted. Roe deer weigh up to 55lb and a full-size buck will stand about 2ft 6in at the shoulder. In the summer they have a beautiful chestnut coat which dulls to greyish brown in the winter and a patch of white fur on their rump. Their antlers are short, with just three points. Roe are quite solitary, but the does will have their kids with them in summer and autumn and if you see one deer cross the road in front of you, be on your guard as there may be others following on behind. A doe can have up to three kids so one may see a family group.

Surrey has several privately owned herds of deer. The best known is the herd of white fallow deer at Hascombe, believed to have been introduced into Britain by the Normans.

Other Mammals

Considering the volume of traffic and the dense spider-web of roads, Surrey has a very healthy wildlife population, with badgers, foxes and squirrels flourishing right across the county. Road kill is a good indicator of abundant species: rabbits, foxes, badgers, squirrels, deer, owls, frogs and toads. One only sees the odd hedgehog these days, however.

The wildlife of the Surrey Hills is relatively well protected. If there is any hint of a hibernating bat, for example, entire housing projects grind to a halt. Wildlife is given field margins and hedgerows to nest in and rangers

G. Sweetnam, courtesy of Surrey Wildlife Trust

◀ Roe deer, which thrive in the woods of the Surrey Hills

patrol the commons and open spaces, creating habitats and building artificial homes for a variety of animals and birds. For some species, however, this emphasis on conservation has come almost too late. Surrey Wildlife Trust Countryside Services Ltd, which looks after a large area of the AONB, much of it designated SSSIs, is involved in several projects to help struggling species survive. David Williams, its mammals officer, is working at half a dozen sites, including the North Downs at Pewley Down, outside Guildford, where dormice are still to be found, making tempting artificial nest sites for them. He is also trying to create habitats for the endangered water vole – 'Ratty' in Kenneth Graham's *Wind in the Willows*. These attractive little animals are tasty morsels for the mink that have very successfully colonized Surrey's waterways.

The Wildlife Trust and the Wey Valley Project also hope that eventually the otter will return to Surrey. These elusive and shy mammals went into rapid decline throughout the UK from the 1950s to the 1970s, largely because of the use of organo-chlorines in sheepdip. The survivors clung on in remote areas of Wales and the south-west, and with the phasing out of the chemicals they have slowly begun to migrate north and east. There have also been a few managed releases in Hampshire. David Williams said he had seen signs of otters in Surrey but not the animals themselves. They had popped over the border, inspected the territory, left their calling cards and returned to Hampshire. Public sightings usually turn out to have been mink. The River Mole, whose lush banks provide cover, would be a good place for otters to settle, as it holds the UK record for the number of fish species living there; pike, roach, bream, chub, perch, dace, barbel, gudgeon, rainbow trout, minnow, stoneloach, three-spined stickleback as well as crayfish and even terrapin, can all be found there. These would easily support an otter population and the Wildlife Trust has put in artificial holts at Leatherhead, Horley, Norbury Park and Dorking to encourage them to stay.

SSSIs

On the lowland heaths one might come across adders in the summer but one would be incredibly lucky to find a sand lizard. There have been releases, but the lizards are very well camouflaged and rather shy.

This heathland is one of the types of Surrey landscape protected as an SSSI. Chalk grassland, oak, beech and ash woods, alder copses and water meadows are also habitats that have SSSI designation. The Wey Valley Meadows SSSI near Shalford is an exceptionally important example of ancient undisturbed grassland and the Lammas Lands in the centre of Godalming are traditional autumn grazed hay meadows. The aim is to preserve as wide a diversity of plants and animals as possible, such as odd little plants with wonderful names like the great dodder, a clinger with tiny white flowers, parasitic on the stinging nettle, which grows by the River Mole. The Devil's Punch Bowl is protected for its heather, bell heather, cross-leaved heath, dwarf gorse, grasses and native trees. Like the Hurtwood at Holmbury, a similar wood-and-heath Greensand upland, it is home to several varieties of woodpecker, nightjar, stonechat and woodlark. Thundry Meadows near Tilford is famous for its rare quaking mire.

Butterflies and Orchids

Box Hill is not only valued for its ancient box trees, but also for its butterflies and wildflowers. The chalk supports a small scattering of rare Man orchids, but numbers have been declining in recent years. The number of orchids always varies from year to year but they are generally in gradual decline and it is hoped that the introduction of grazing will control the tall grasses which choke delicate species and lead to a stabilization of the colonies. The Man orchid is rather spooky if seen close up, as the flower spikes appear to be hung all around with tiny naked people.

Grazing will probably be the saving of the musk orchid as well. The best colony of these petite orchids in the whole of the UK is here. The Friends of Box Hill are working to preserve them, and also a rare moth and a butterfly. Mystery surrounded the straw belle moth because no one knew the exact conditions needed for it to lay its eggs or which plants the caterpillars fed on, so the Friends are conducting research. The importance of knowing which plants support which species is highlighted by Britain's smallest butterfly, the small blue, which was actually believed to be extinct until sighted in 2002 on Box Hill. This tiny, almost dove-grey butterfly has declined throughout the country in recent years, partly because the plant on which the larvae feed, kidney vetch, has become scarce, confined to a small area covering just a few square yards of the hill. This really brings home the fragility of the ecosystem; both kidney vetch and small blue need nurturing together.

The old quarries are now havens for wildlife as when the men and horses and railway trucks departed, nature moved back in. Violets, eyebright, milkworts, cowslips, primroses and orchids attract a wealth of insects and butterflies like the silver spotted skipper, which has colonized Brockham Quarry. Rare juniper trees also grow there happily.

Deep in Chiddingfold Forest is Oaken Wood, a small wildlife haven managed by Forest Enterprise where butterflies like the pearl-bordered, small pearl-bordered and silver-washed fritillaries abound along with wood whites, purple emperors, brown hairstreaks and white admirals. Wonderful names for stunning butterflies

Alien Invaders

Which plants qualify as native to Surrey and which are alien invaders is a tough question. So much of our established flora was imported by the Romans, for example, in the first few centuries AD. Fat hen, stinging nettles, most of our vegetables and herbs, even fruit trees, were deliberately imported to improve the variety of the human diet. Potatoes and sugar came later. With the Age of Enlightenment and the great voyages of discovery came an interest in all kinds of plants and flowers from the New World and the Far East. The most famous of the plant hunters was Sir Joseph Banks, who made his first trip to collect plants from Labrador and Newfoundland in 1766 when he was just twenty-three. He moved plants from continent to continent with gay abandon, and bringing exotica back to English gardens from foreign parts became a hobby for the wealthy. The great Surrey landowners were there at the thick of the action. A Japanese garden was created at Gatton Park, with wysteria and bamboo, while at Painshill Park, the Hon. Charles Hamilton was keen on American species. Seeds from the New World were like gold dust and the plants transformed the muddy-coloured English autumn with a display of leaves in flaming reds, pinks and oranges. When the first plants changed into their vibrant autumn colours it took society by storm.

Philadelphian John Bartram, the first American-born plant collector, shipped his first boxes of seeds, collected from the wilds of eastern North America, to eager subscribers in London in 1748. The boxes were a 'lucky dip'. No one sowing the seeds knew what they would turn into. It was a great experiment, an adventure, and they generated enormous excitement. Hamilton bought a £5 box and the plants that grew were planted around his park. Over 250 years on, in 2005, the journey of these seeds from American wilds to English landscapes was recreated in the walled garden at Painshill. Some of the plants were sent over again from the same places where Bartram had gathered them. The process of importing plants is a lot more complicated than it was in Banks's day. For example the import of viburnums and kalmias (calico bush) is banned because they carry sudden oak death, which affects rhododendrons. Imports that are allowed have to be inspected by a Department of the Environment, Food and Rural Affairs (DEFRA) official on arrival and the plants have to be quarantined and inspected again when the buds burst.

Such caution is sensible. Had officials known that Himalayan balsam, Japanese knotweed, ragwort, giant hogweed and floating pennywort would cause such problems they would never have allowed them into the country. Himalayan balsam looks very pretty flopping over the banks of streams with its pink and white flowers, but since its introduction as an ornamental in the 1830s, it has colonized banks so successfully that native species have been crowded out and erosion can occur. It has an amazing capacity for projecting its seeds via small explosions. It's is fascinating watching them as they ping through the air with a staggering range of up to 5 yards.

Japanese knotweed is not a problem in Japan but it has become a nightmare here, with every kind of herbicide and flamethrower directed at it to little effect. It was much admired, with its attractive heart shaped leaves, when it was first brought to England in the 1820s, but its liking for Surrey's soil and climatic conditions has transformed it into an indestructible triffid that can prise its way nonchalantly through metalled surfaces, break up concrete structures and strangle native plants, leaving native wildlife without a suitable habitat. Giant hogweed is another splendid looking but now much hated Victorian ornamental that is running riot in the Surrey countryside. I know from personal experience just how unpleasant the juice inside the hollow stems can be. When I was a child I was allowed to graze my pony in an old walled vegetable garden where the hogweed had been planted as a statuesque conversation piece in the corner. That was fine when there was a team of gardeners tilling and weeding and confining it to its allotted patch. Years of neglect enabled the hogweed to march right across the garden and I needed to cut it back hard to enable the grass to grow. Completely ignorant and full of enthusiasm, I took a sickle to the stalks and suffered ... really suffered. The sap is evil. It becomes toxic when exposed to ultraviolet rays and cause the most awful blisters, a bit like mustard gas blisters. I had them all over my hands.

▼ Himalayan balsam, despite its pretty, elegant, pink and cream flowers, is a real thug of a plant, choking streambeds, dominating banks and spreading into enormous 5ft high clumps

With so many wealthy Victorians colonizing the Surrey Hills in the nineteenth century, it is not surprising that these foreign plants, escapees from their exotic and vegetable gardens, are to be found everywhere in the area. If you don't recognise the three plants just mentioned, you are certainly going to know ragwort and rhododendrons.

Ragwort has feathery bright green leaves and bright yellow flowers and is found everywhere on verges, railway embankments, unkempt fields and commons. It is fatal to horses and if caught up in hay bales is hard to detect. Rhododendrons are known by conservationists and wildlife rangers as the Surrey weed. It loves the Surrey Hills, growing with exuberance and speed all over the Hurtwood, Leith Hill, Hindhead and Pitch Hill. It is tough and drought-resistant, and breeds freely. Beautiful red, cream and pink garden hybrids might require nurturing, not the wild variety. Our relationship with these magnificent invaders is complex, however. While the purple wild ones are summarily removed, the rhododendron garden planted at Leith Hill Place by Charles Darwin's sister Caroline is open to the public and much admired. Around Hindhead, where the soil is both well drained and acidic, specialist gardens and nurseries were established in the nineteenth century to propagate exotic imports and they colonized the ground beyond the nurseries so readily that they are having to be grubbed up here as well in order to restore the heath. There are still specialist nurseries, however, in the sandy hills at Hydestile.

Birdlife

Birds are monitored these days in an unprecedented way so the fortunes of the various species are closely followed. Apart from the great national surveys of garden birds, a number of specific counts have been carried out on individual Surrey farms. The Royal Society for the Protection of Birds (RSPB) has charted the comeback of some of the rarer and more endangered species as a result of hedge-laying and field-margin management as well as the reduction in the use of chemicals. A Dorking farm produced nine red-list species – those that are endangered – as well as some on the amber list. The count found dunnocks, house sparrows, linnets, spotted flycatchers, yellow hammers, song thrushes, grey partridges, skylarks, sparrow hawks, kestrels, grey and spotted woodpeckers, owls willow warblers – it's quite an impressive list. These surveys are interesting because they show the impact farming practice has on wildlife.

RSPB bird surveys have given some of the best evidence of the value of these environmental improvement schemes. In 2002, after ten years of advice from FWAG, Barrowgreen Farm at Lingfield could boast a bird count of some sixty different species, including shy reed buntings, linnets, redpols, little egrets and tree creepers as well as three types of owl, sparrowhawks, hobbies and kestrels. No misty sentimentalist, farmer Robert Young, whose family has farmed the Oxted area since the 1400s, could rattle off the wonderfully descriptive names of the grasses and wildflowers growing in abundance in a thick fringe around his crops. Chewings and red fescues, cocksfoot, crested dog's tail and browntop bent. The expanding population of insects were keeping the aphids at bay and harnessing nature was making commercial sense.

At the opposite end of the AONB at Shackleford, another of Surrey's ancient farming dynasties, the Stovolds, have also embraced biodiversity and been rewarded with burgeoning wildlife. Angus told me:

> We major strongly in conservation and I joined the Farming and Wildlife Advisory Group in 1992. The farm had always been neat and tidy but it wasn't wildlife friendly. I am particularly keen on encouraging small birds so I started leaving hedges to grow tall and then coppicing them in sections so that birds always had somewhere to nest.
>
> The results were startling. Linnets, finches, thrushes, blackbirds, tits and sparrows came back en masse. It was fantastic. It really opened my eyes. My father had built a lake but it had no wildlife until we put a hedgerow leading down to it for the wildlife to follow – nothing likes crossing open ground. Now it has lots of pipistrelle bats, marsh warblers and snipe. We have sparrowhawks and golden plovers and lapwings, hundreds of skylarks, goldfinches and starlings, and we now leave a six metre margin around the arable fields to encourage invertebrates.

▼ Back-breaking, painfully slow, but evoking such nostalgia for a less aggressive, less urban and materialistic age

Courtesy of the Stovold family archive

Tourism and Public Access

The Surrey Hills AONB is the best place in the whole of the UK for public access. Nowhere else will you find such a web of footpaths and bridleways across such a varied landscape of farmland, woods and heaths. Occasionally one may have to follow a lane for a few hundred yards and do battle with Surrey's other claim to fame – the highest number of cars – but generally it is possible to ramble for hours simply crossing the odd road. Not only is the countryside here accessible to locals, it is within easy reach of Londoners too.

In the Victorian and Edwardian eras, Londoners came down in droves on day trips with their bicycles, and the newly opened railway lines brought more tourists. Things were fairly relaxed and *ad hoc* in those days but now tourism and public access are key considerations woven into all the policies affecting the AONB. The sheer numbers of people coming into the hills to enjoy the scenery and have a bit of exercise has created a need to manage the various user groups, in particular mountain-bikers and off-road drivers.

Mountain-biking

The area from Pitch Hill to Leith Hill is a mountain-biker's paradise and a drive through Peaslake at a weekend gives one an idea of the number of people involved. Some thirty years ago it was the horse-riders who were accused of wrecking paths and intimidating walkers. Now it is the cyclists' turn, but the Hurtwood Control, which manages their paradise, is taking a sensibly cooperative attitude, working with the biking groups to everyone's advantage. Its goal is for walkers, horse-riders and cyclists to co-exist happily without damaging the landscape, and it holds regular forums for them to meet and exchange information and ideas. They have an ally in Richard Kelly who runs Surrey Hills All-Terrain Mountain-Bike Tours, based in Holmbury St Mary, which is backed by the Surrey Hills AONB's Sustainable Development Fund. Holmbury's Iron Age hill fort is both hugely popular and vulnerable to erosion and damage, so Kelly helps the cyclists to use the trails responsibly so that the sport is environmentally sustainable. Self-regulation does not have to be restrictive and boring. The biking is still fun, laced with adrenalin rushes for those who want it: trails include the Pitch Hill Widowmaker and Blind Terror. Richard says:

> I grew up in the area and always enjoyed taking my bike up into the woods. It struck me that people were coming up and not able to find the right trails and they were putting pressure on the environment in the Hurtwood, creating some conflict with other users.
>
> The mountain-bikers needed educating so that they can be part of the solution rather than the problem. I am now qualified as a mountain-bike instructor and I do a lot of training courses for people and lead groups. We encourage people to leave their cars at home and be a bit greener and we pick them up from the railway station.
>
> We teach them how to brake properly and how to use the gears, teaching them to ride responsibly using the right techniques. Otherwise the bikes can damage the paths.

The Leith Hill Access Forum's policy includes carrying out surveys on behalf of the major landowners – the National Trust, the Surrey Wildlife Trust and the Forestry Commission – in line with the Hurtwood Control's research on mountain-biking. It wants to encourage similar responsible cycling, and has drawn up a code of conduct, working with the mountain-bike groups to improve trails and make them safer, both for them and for other users, on foot or on horseback. There is also the potential to develop both single-track and family bike routes so that all the different groups are catered for.

Nordic Walking

Rambling societies have a long pedigree as social and access pressure goups, and the large numbers of cars in a Surrey Hills car park usually means there is a group of organized walkers nearby. But there is a new activity on the rambling scene – Nordic walking.

Nordic walking in the Surrey Hills is run by Jodechi and Eliot Morton from Abinger, who teach the technique. This is not just rambling with a pair of long sticks. Originating in Finland, the sport was developed by cross-country skiers who needed a method of training when there was no snow. They found that using special poles to propel the body forward with more power was a good way to stay in shape and improve their balance and posture. It burns up to 40 per cent more calories than normal walking because it uses more muscles even than swimming. Yet it can be practised by people who are unfit as well as by serious athletes.

'I saw it on television and we decided to train to become instructors,' said Jodechi. 'We started teaching it and it has taken off. We cannot believe it. It's great fun. Nordic walking is so good for you. It exercises almost your entire body so you are getting a complete work-out with nature in the beautiful countryside. That is what gives people such a buzz.'

Llama Walking

Llama walking in the Surrey Hills is a bit different. You can burn as few calories as you like watching your llama browsing the hedgerow on an amble through the hills. These extraordinary animals have an almost hypnotic quality. Stress drains away and people find walking with a llama incredibly calming, a bizarre natural therapy. Julie and Colin Stoneley have been running Surrey Hills Llamas for six years now, and won the Guildford Visitor Attraction of the Year award. Surrey now boasts the largest number of camelids (the umbrella name for llamas, alpacas, vicuñas, guanacos, camels and dromedaries) in the country, as well as the largest number of horses. They are incredibly popular lawnmowers for people with paddocks and are increasingly being used on farms as guard animals for sheep and poultry as they are very protective and drive foxes away.

Until 2003, the Stoneleys were both on the career ladder – Colin with his own electronics business and Julie as a trainer for a big city law firm, travelling all round the world. It was a pressurised existence and the realization that it was also pointless because they never saw each other, marked a turning point in their lives. Out went the well-paid jobs and in came eight llamas. Since then they have taken over 12,000 people on walks in the Surrey Hills. Driving through Chilworth, I had often been intrigued by the little woolly group tethered to the fence of the Percy Arms pub placidly munching the trees. This is their favourite meeting point for walks through the Gunpowder Estate beneath St Martha's. They do picnic walks and birthday treats, overnight camping and corporate awaydays. The Incas called the llama 'silent brother' and the Stoneleys also take the llamas to old people's homes, special needs schools and hospices where they work their therapeutic magic.

Horse-riding and Walking

One of the nicest ways of enjoying the Surrey Hills countryside is from the back of a horse. One can see over the tops of hedges and wildlife is less likely to run away. Albury Equestrian Centre takes people for guided rides, and like llama walks, they often incorporate a light pub refreshment. The bridleways of Surrey are unparalleled anywhere in the country, and there are probably more horses in the county now than at any time since the First World War. The demand for paddocks and stabling has increased as the viability of farming has decreased and there is a tension between the competing demands of horses and agriculture. One feature of the Surrey Hills landscape that would undoubtedly surprise a time traveller from the 1950s would be the profusion of equine sand schools.

For walkers, there is a mass of information on the Surrey Hills, Surrey County Council and North Downs Way websites. Routes are becoming increasingly accessible for wheelchairs and buggies, for example there are fantastic accessible viewpoints at Holmbury Hill and the Punch Bowl. There is a choice of beautiful long-distance paths – the North Downs Way, the Greensand Way and the Downs Link, which follows the old Guildford–Horsham railway line and is therefore straight, firm and ideal also for cycling. Maps of walks are available throughout the area so selecting a route is easy.

Theatre and Music

Great houses like Loseley, Polesden Lacey, Wintershall and Hatchlands make magnificent venues for arts events. Loseley has hosted opera, theatre and open-air charity concerts, and Polesden Lacey, home to the National Trust, has its own open-air festival every July. This festival has its origins in 1949, when Betty Harrison of Bookham Community Association decided to stage a pageant of Merrie England in the grounds. It was a great success and years of Shakespeare productions paved the way for the present week-long Polesden Lacey Festival, which includes a variety of concerts and fireworks as well as the bard.

Hatchlands in East Clandon echoes to the sound of classical music played on instruments originally owned by some of the great composers. If you have ever wondered what Chopin expected his sonatas to sound like, or felt bored by the consistency of the concert hall grand, the answer is a visit to Hatchlands to see and hear the keyboard instruments collected by Alec Cobbe. The old Tudor house on the site was demolished by the naval hero Admiral Edward Boscawen in1756, and using prize money gleaned through skirmishes with the French, he commissioned the young architect Robert Adam to create an interior that became famed for its 'uncommonlie beautiful' ceilings and chimney pieces. In 1980, the empty eighteenth-century shell was donated to the National Trust. The challenge of finding sufficient items of interest to make such a big house worth opening to the public resulted in an extraordinary chain of coincidences.

The Trust asked Cobbe, a painter and picture restorer who had worked at a number of historic houses, to resuscitate Hatchlands as a living home and furnish it with his family's collections of musical instruments, furniture and pictures, many of them from his family house, Newbridge, in County Dublin. It was an inspired choice, for some 400 years ago, Mr Cobbe's first cousin fourteen generations back, the legendary Irish beauty Lady Elizabeth Fitzgerald, had lived at Hatchlands with her husband, Sir Anthony Browne, Master of the Horse under Henry VIII. The Irish associations lasted until the eighteenth century and the Cobbe picture collection includes many paintings associated with those early Irish owners of Hatchlands. It is hard to imagine the house empty now, but 'it was very drear,' Mr Cobbe told me, 'It looked like an old folk's home, so we cheered it up.'

The most exciting thing about the instruments is that many of them were owned by famous composers, and they can be heard today in concerts and on Mr Cobbe's guided musical tours. The collection includes, for example, the Broadwood piano used by Chopin for his final London concert before his death, a seventeenth-century virginal from Whitehall Palace tuned and played by Purcell and a fortepiano owned by J.C. Bach that Mr Cobbe believes was used by Mozart for the first performance of his A minor Sonata. He also has instruments associated with Mahler, Elgar, Haydn, Beethoven and Schubert.

What started as a hobby rapidly got out of hand and has now become the Cobbe Collection Trust. A recent acquisition was Bizet's composing piano, built in 1850 as a table with a drawer containing a seven octave keyboard for his teacher, the then famous French composer, Fremental Halévy. Bizet married his daughter and inherited the composing table.

At Hatchlands, however, one can not only hear Chopin as Chopin played it. One can also see the face that Shakespeare fell in love with. The portrait hung in the library shows long tresses of wavy chestnut hair, an elaborate earring, fine arching eyebrows, gentle eyes and a rosebud mouth. The subject had been thought to be female but research has now shown it to be the earliest extant portrait of Henry Wriothesley, 3rd Earl of Southampton, great grandson of Sir Anthony Browne, first owner of Hatchlands. He is the 'fair youth' for whom Shakespeare wrote most of his sonnets.

In performance terms, however, nothing compares with the Wintershall phenomenon. A cast of hundreds plays to an audience of thousands in the wonderful grounds of the twelfth-century manor house south east of Bramley. The Hutley family, who moved to Wintershall in the 1960s, are successful entrepreneurs with a powerful business ethic, and with children, grandchildren and a busy social life. So whatever happened to drive Ann Hutley, by then a grandmother, to risk the horrific violence in Yugoslavia by trekking back and forth to Medjugorje at the height of the war there? Or to inspire Peter Hutley, a man more used to the cut and thrust of property development to become a scriptwriter of Biblical plays?

The change that took place is extraordinary, especially as for many visitors to Wintershall, it holds out the possibility of a personal vision of the Virgin Mary. They come not just from Surrey, or even the UK, but from all over the world, drawn by the huge Oberammergau-style religious dramas performed there and also by the opportunity for meditation, prayer and Christian observance. This ecumenical Christian centre, the huge estate dotted with religious sculptures, has almost acquired the status of pilgrimage destination.

The Hutleys themselves have enjoyed audiences with the Pope and received the Templeton Award in a ceremony at St George's Chapel, Windsor. The why and how have been addressed in a disarmingly candid little book entitled *Beloved Grandchildren, A Personal Reflection*, written by Ann Hutley, the catalyst for the family's change of direction. Ann narrates her confused and painful progress from Anglican to Roman Catholic. The fact that Peter and several other members of the family converted to Catholicism and that every year the Nativity, Passion, Life of Christ and Acts of the Apostles productions contain large numbers of younger Hutleys, as well as huge casts of local people, is evidence of the strength of support for Wintershall's new life.

The productions have come a long way in terms of professionalism and quality of spectacle, and inevitably some of the spontaneity and risk-taking that made the early years so refreshing has been lost. The first nativity plays staged in the late 1980s took place in and around the straw-lined hilltop Holly Barn – even the entrance was a gothic arch of strawbales – and the audience moved in and out of the barn during the performance to be with the shepherds on the hill or with Mary by the manger. The barn has proper seating now and everything follows health and safety rules, but the wise men still arrive on horseback and there are still animals in Mary's stable. The play is hugely popular, and for thousands of families it is probably the high point of their Christmas.

With the success of the nativity for encouragement, the family embarked on first an Easter passion play and then, in 1999, the enormously ambitious Life of Christ, completely outdoor productions lasting three to five hours. The actor playing Christ in the Easter Passion had to endure hours naked on the cross in a freezing English spring, with stinging wind, rain and hail, but there are few finer theatrical moments than the scenes with the fishermen on the Wintershall lake in first the Passion and then the Life of Christ, when members of the cast distribute basketloads of bread to the audience. It is genuinely inspirational.

▼ The kings arrive on horseback at Holly Barn for the Wintershall Nativity

Useful Contacts

Campaign to Protect Rural England, Surrey Branch (CPRE)
Room 1, The Institute, 67 High Street, Leatherhead, Surrey, KT22 8AH
01372 362720
www.cpresurrey.org.uk

Domestic Buildings Research Group
Secretary: Mrs H. Jones, The Ridings, Lynx Hill, East Horsley, Surrey, KT24 5AX
01483 283917
www.dbrg.org.uk

Horsley Countryside Preservation Society
Mr A. and Mrs P. Bowley, Little Orchard, Silkmore Lane, West Horsley, Surrey, KT24 6JB
01483 283934
www.surreycommunity.info/hcps

Hurtwood Control Trust
St Mark's Church Yard, Peaslake, Guildford, Surrey, GU5 9RR
01306 730100
www.hurtwoodcontrol.co.uk

National Trust South East
Polesden Lacey, Dorking, Surrey, RH5 6BD
01372 453401
www.nationaltrust.org.uk

Ramblers
2nd Floor Camelford House, 87-90 Albert Embankment, London, SE1 7TW
020 7339 8500
www.ramblers.org.uk

Surrey Archaeological Society
Castle Arch, Guildford, Surrey, GU1 3SX
01483 532454
www.surreyarchaeology.org.uk

Surrey Hills AONB Office
Warren Farm Barns, Headley Lane, Mickleham, Dorking, Surrey, RH5 6DG
01372 220650
www.surreyhills.org

Surrey Hills Society
Warren Farm Barns, Headley Lane, Mickleham, Dorking, Surrey, RH5 6DG
01372 220647
www.surreyhills.org/surrey-hills-society.aspx

Surrey History Centre
130 Goldsworth Road, Woking, Surrey, GU21 6ND
01483 518737
www.shs.surreycc.gov.uk/surreyhistoryservice

Surrey Wildlife Trust
School Lane, Pirbright, Woking, Surrey, GU24 0JN
01483 795440
www.surreywildlifetrust.co.uk

Index